185 Wireless Secrets®

Unleash the Power of PDAs, Cell Phones, and Wireless Networks

185 Wireless Secrets®

Unleash the Power of PDAs
Cell Phones, and Wireless Networks

Jack McCullough

Wiley Publishing, Inc.

185 Wireless Secrets®
Unleash the Power of PDAs, Cell Phones,
and Wireless Networks

Published by
Wiley Publishing, Inc.
10475 Crosspoint Boulevard
Indianapolis, IN 46256
www.wiley.com

Copyright © 2004 by Wiley Publishing, Inc., Indianapolis, Indiana
Published simultaneously in Canada

Library of Congress Control Number: 2004103160

ISBN: 0-7645-6814-0

Manufactured in the United States of America

10 9 8 7 6 5 4 3 2 1

1B/SV/QT/QU/IN

WILEY

Credits

Acquisitions Editors
Katie Mohr
Katie Feltman

Development Editor
Sara Shlaer

Production Editor
Gabrielle Nabi

Technical Editor
Tom Brays

Copy Editors
Stefan Gruenwedel
Howard Jones

Editorial Manager
Mary Beth Wakefield

**Vice President and Executive
Group Publisher**
Richard Swadley

**Vice President and
Executive Publisher**
Bob Ipsen

Vice President and Publisher
Joseph B. Wikert

Executive Editorial Director
Mary Bednarek

Project Coordinator
Erin Smith

Graphics and Production Specialists
Melissa Auciello-Brogan
Beth Brooks
Lauren Goddard
Joyce Haughey
Jennifer Heleine
Rashell Smith

Quality Control Technicians
John Greenough
Susan Moritz
Angel Perez
Charles Spencer

Proofreading and Indexing
Publication Services

About the Author

Jack McCullough is founding consultant of Razorwire Information Security Consulting. His technical expertise includes wireless and wired networks, computer security, physical security, programming, cryptography, and technical curriculum development. Jack's background includes 10 years of experience in the IT field. He has held positions as IT director, operations manager, network administrator, programmer, and software trainer. A respected IT and security authority, he is frequently sought out for informational interviews by both broadcast and print media services.

Jack has authored books, magazine articles, and white papers on computer security, and launched www.rzrwire.com, the first computer security Web site serving the average person with limited technical knowledge. His written works have been translated into several languages.

Many universities have used his books and white papers in information security courses, as have the governments of Australia, the Peoples Republic of China, Japan, Brazil, and Taiwan. Jack continues to actively research information security, discover new ways to exploit the weaknesses in networked systems, and determine best practices that enable the average computer user to address these threats in an efficient manner.

When he isn't writing about or researching technology, Jack teaches karate and self-defense under the watchful eye of Sensei Floyd Burk at the Alpine Karate Academy in Alpine, California, and practices writing about himself in third person.

To Erik and Donovan, who can't even comprehend a world without computers.

Preface

Welcome to *185 Wireless Secrets*. Wireless is the hot, new buzzword for technologists; everything seems to be wireless, or it soon will be. The Internet promised to change our lives and revolutionize the way we work and play; now this is the promise of wireless. This book introduces you to this technology and helps you get the most out of it.

While there are many books that deal with specific wireless products, or wireless networking in general, this book takes a broader approach. It introduces you to the full range of wireless technology, from wireless networks to mobile wireless devices and some related technologies.

Rather than discussing specific products, or taking you step by step through configuring a particular device or application, my goal is to answer some common questions and give you a basic understanding of wireless networking, mobile technologies, and security issues surrounding both. I hope that once you have an understanding of the topics covered in this book, you'll pursue them further and continue learning about them. Using this book you'll learn some of the following things:

- How wireless networks and mobile technology works
- How to plan and set up a wireless network
- How to choose a mobile device and carrier
- How to get the most out of your PDA or cell phone
- How to secure your wireless network against intrusion

All this, and a lot more. By the end of this book you'll be ready to move on to more technical challenges, armed with a firm understanding of wireless technologies of all kinds.

Who Should Read This Book

If you're interested in wireless networking, mobile wireless, and related technologies, but you aren't sure where to start, then this book is for you. You don't need experience or technical skill to benefit from the secrets I've presented here, although a general knowledge of computing and familiarity with basic networking and Internet concepts is desirable.

This book is for the beginning or intermediate computer user who wants a better understanding of wireless technologies, how they relate to one another, and how to benefit from them.

How This Book Is Organized

This book has been organized into six parts, with each part including chapters that address a common topic or theme. You can read the chapters in order or skip ahead to a specific part that interests you. This book covers a lot of different wireless topics; everything from wireless networks to cell phones and home entertainment. If information included in a preceding chapter is relevant to what you're currently reading, I will refer you back there. Here's how the parts are organized:

- **Part I: Introduction to Wireless Networking and Internet Access—**
  This part is an introduction to the standards and technology of wireless
  networking and mobile wireless. It dispels some myths and answers
  some common questions about wireless. Start here if you aren't familiar with wireless jargon, standards, and technology.
- **Part II: Unwired at Home and in the Office—**Part II discusses planning
  and installing a wireless network, connecting to the Internet, and
  extending the range of a wireless network. If you're primarily interested in wireless networking and you're somewhat familiar with the
  technology and terminology, you can start with Part II.
- **Part III: Mobile Wireless—**This part deals with mobile wireless, including cell phones and personal digital assistants (Palms and Pocket PCs).
  You'll learn about choosing a device, getting connected, using e-mail
  and messaging, as well as some fun things you can do with a mobile
  device.
- **Part IV: Other Wireless Technologies—**Here I discuss other complementary wireless technologies, whether for entertainment or for home
  automation.
- **Part V: Safe and Secure Wireless Computing—**This part is an introduction to the threats to wireless networks, and how to deal with those
  threats. It addresses securing a wireless network, protecting data, and
  secure mobile computing.
- **Part VI: Appendixes**. Here you'll find useful resources for wireless networks, mobile devices, and manufacturers.
- **Glossary**. A glossary of wireless terms used in this book is included.

Each chapter contains secrets that distill important and often overlooked information into useful tips. Some of these "secrets" may be familiar to old hands at
wireless technology, but most readers will find them to contain valuable and
practical information. This book introduces a broad range of wireless technologies, but as you read you'll begin to see how they are interrelated and often complementary. The goal of this book is to get you started on the right foot so that
you can take advantage of current wireless technology and be prepared for the
next generation of wireless devices and services lurking just around the corner.

Special Features

Each chapter in this book opens with a list of the secrets presented in that chapter. Throughout this book you will encounter icons that draw your attention to
specific types of information. Here's what each of those icons mean:

---

note   Notes provide extra or important additional information about a subject.

---

on the   This icon directs you to related Web sites for further information about a
web   topic.

---

insider
insight
: Interesting background information or insight into a subject; tidbits that you probably won't find elsewhere.

caution
: If you see this, I'm pointing out something particularly dangerous or where you should take extra care and be particularly diligent.

cross
ref
: This icon refers you to another chapter in this book for information related to the topic you're currently reading.

Enjoy the book; I hope you get a lot out of it and that it encourages you to seek out more information about wireless and experiment with some of the technologies that we'll be discussing. If you have any feedback, good or bad, you can reach me through my Web site at www.rzrwire.com.

Acknowledgments

The chance to undertake a fun project like this doesn't come along every day, and it takes a lot of exceptional people to make it happen. First and foremost, a big thank you goes to my literary agent, David Fugate of Waterside Productions, arguably the best agent working for technical authors today. He continues to find challenging and interesting projects for me and always has his authors' best interests at heart. Strangely enough, considering he has had an enormous positive impact on my career, I've never met him in person. David, I owe you lunch.

Another big thank you goes to the extraordinary team at Wiley for all of the help and hard work they put into this book. I look forward to working with all of them again in the future.

First, I want to thank Katie Feltman (Katie 1.0) for sharing her vision for the book and hiring me to write it, and Katie Mohr (Katie 2.0) who refined that vision and got this project moving forward.

A special thanks to my development editor, Sara Shlaer, who expertly guided me through preparing this manuscript and put so much work into editing it—especially as the vision of the series changed and several chapters needed to be rethought. Also for her subtle and gentle prodding that ensured that I finished on time.

Thanks to Tom Brays, the technical editor, for his work and for making sure that while simplifying the subjects and translating them into plain English I didn't omit anything important. Finally, thanks to the layout and production team at Wiley for putting this book together and for interpreting my scribbles into actual art that the reader can understand.

Contents at a Glance

Contents

Part I

Introduction to Wireless Networking and Internet Access

Demystifying Wireless Networking

Chapter

1

♦ ♦

Secrets in This Chapter

♦ ♦

In just a few years the marketplace for wireless networking products has exploded, and it continues to grow at an incredible rate. At the same time, the market has consolidated, with fewer competing wireless technologies available. Unfortunately, these changes haven't made wireless networking any less confusing for the average consumer.

Once you know which standards are the key players in the wireless space, you can make an informed decision about the design (or extension) of your own network. Setting up a home or small office/home office (SOHO) wireless network isn't difficult. It requires less effort and cost than a wired local area network (LAN). If you have ever networked computers using Ethernet cable, a wireless network should be an easy upgrade for you. If you haven't worked with Ethernet before, don't worry, you're still in good shape. Read on.

Secret #1:   You Don't Need Much to Go Wireless

Wireless—the name says it all: Cut the cord. Wireless networking is cable-free, no-strings-attached networking. Most wireless networks send data through radio waves, broadcasting in all directions.

note	One or two proprietary products use infrared light to send data. Other than infrared links between laptops and PDAs, you will probably never encounter infrared products outside the specialized environments in which they are used, such as for industrial controllers.

If you have never had to run Ethernet cable, then you can rejoice in your good luck and go skipping into the future free of the emotional (and sometimes physical) scars that many of us carry from years of pulling cable through walls or under houses (see Figure 1-1). If, like me, you suffer from Post Traumatic Ethernet Disorder (PTED), then take heart; you have pulled your last Cat5 cable. From this point on your computers are going to be free and untethered, as in the WLAN in Figure 1-2.

Wireless networks operate in the unlicensed band of the radio spectrum, typically 2.4 GHz or 5 GHz.

You need three things to set up your first wireless network:

♦ At least two computers
♦ A wireless network interface adapter (one for each computer)
♦ A wireless access point (at least one)

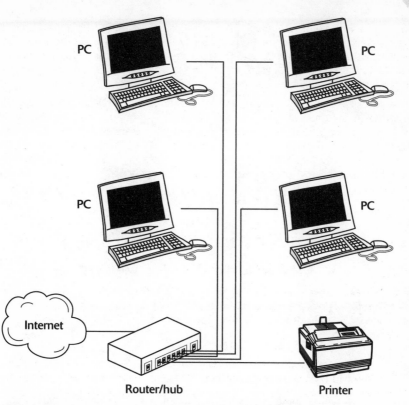

Figure 1-1: A typical home network using Ethernet cable.

Wireless Network Interface Adapters

Like the Ethernet card on a wired network, the wireless *network interface adapter* translates between your computer and the network. The network interface adapter is frequently called a *network interface card*, or NIC. Your computer and the network speak different languages, called *protocols*, and the NIC acts as an interpreter.

Wireless network interface cards come as PC cards, USB adapters, compact flash cards, or PCI/ISA cards. Each computer on your wireless network needs an adapter.

Wireless Access Points

A wireless *access point* (AP) connects wireless devices on your network to each other. Every wireless local area network (WLAN) needs at least one AP. An AP is usually the most expensive piece of hardware in a WLAN (other than the PCs, of course). Prices on wireless products have been coming down, with APs currently ranging in price from $80.00 for a bare-bones AP to over $300.00 for an AP with advanced features.

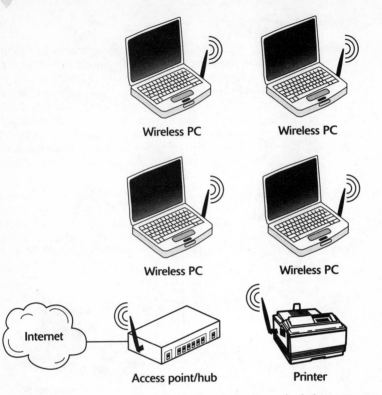

Figure 1-2: A typical home wireless network sharing a single Internet connection.

Secret #2:   Multifunction Access Ports

You can save money and improve performance by purchasing an AP that provides additional network services. Here are some of the features you should look for:

♦ **Print server**—Connects your printers directly to the WLAN and prints wirelessly without hooking your printer up to a PC

♦ **Dynamic host configuration protocol (DHCP) server**—Assigns addresses to each computer on the network

♦ **Network router**—Connects to your broadband Internet connection and routes traffic to and from your computers, allowing them all to share a single Internet connection

♦ **Network switch**—Connects PCs to the network using Ethernet cables and allows for faster communication between client PCs

You'll learn more about each of these features later in the book.

Why Go Wireless?

Besides the obvious advantage of not having to install or invest in Ethernet cables, a WLAN offers many advantages over a wired network. While the initial cost may be higher, in many instances it is cheaper to expand a WLAN than an Ethernet network. A WLAN is also easier to modify, and you can move computers anywhere in range of your WLAN's signal and remain connected. Sharing resources among users on a WLAN is just as easy as it would be on a wired LAN, only more flexible. You can easily share printers, files, and an Internet connection among many computers without running cables through walls, ceilings or under floors. With a WLAN you can remain connected but not attached. Try to do that with an Ethernet connection!

Wireless technology also can be used to expand an existing Ethernet network. Perhaps you already have a network but you would like the freedom to move around with a notebook or tablet computer. You can add an AP to the network and a wireless NIC to the notebook and be able to move around with your notebook while sharing resources and an Internet connection with PCs on your wired LAN (see Figure 1-3).

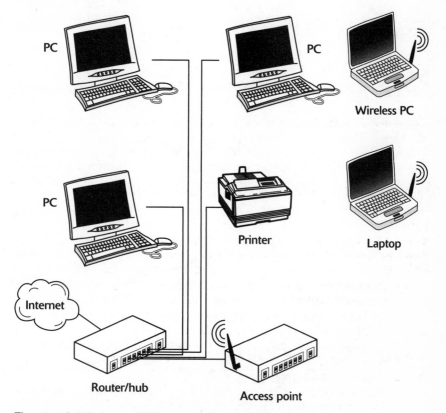

Figure 1-3: Wireless and Ethernet on the same network.

There are many myths about wireless networking, from health risks and security concerns to the expense of equipment and installation difficulty. Most are inaccurate, but some have a small kernel of truth in them. The following secrets combat some of the most common myths used as arguments against going wireless.

Secret #3:   Is Wireless Networking Expensive?

Setting up a WLAN costs a little more than a wired network, but expensive is a relative term. While the initial cost for wireless equipment is more, the time invested in installing is far less. In addition, being mobile instead of tethered to an Ethernet cable makes up for a lot of the cost.

Over the next year, high quality equipment based on older wireless standards will drop in price significantly as newer equipment hits store shelves. Already some multifunction APs have dropped in price by almost 40 percent. There are already opportunities to acquire some excellent equipment on the cheap, if you do your research and shop around. The benefits of mobility, flexibility, and aesthetics alone make scrapping your Ethernet cables and going wireless worth the small price difference.

Secret #4:   Are Wireless Networks Insecure?

Wireless networks broadcast data in every direction. It is possible for a hacker with a wireless NIC and a laptop to receive the signal from your WLAN and gain access. Don't panic; we can prevent this. With my background in security, I spend a lot of time looking for insecure networks and systems. I am the last person to defend products with weak or poorly designed security. That said, while WLANs do have some security issues, they are no more severe than those present in wired LANs.

Security firms, antivirus makers, and firewall vendors all like to exaggerate the threat from hackers, viruses, worms, and now terrorists. The threat is real to some extent, but hardly as grave as people in the industry make it sound. Good security is mostly good planning and common sense. You can sufficiently secure any network, and I will show you how to do just that in Chapter 15.

Secret #5:   Are Wireless Networks Dangerous?

People are becoming more concerned about the health risk associated with radio frequency (RF) devices. The scientific jury is still out on this question, but for the time being the general consensus seems to be that there is no health risk associated with low power devices used in WLANs.

Radio waves are a form of radiation. When most of us hear that word we tend to panic, but it helps to understand the difference between different types of radiation and distinguish between what is potentially harmful and what is considered safe. We are surrounded by radio frequency radiation (RFR) at work and at home. Microwave ovens, cordless phones, computers, fax machines, and cell phones all emit some form of RFR.

What raises concern with wireless network devices is that they operate at high frequency (2.4 GHz and above), and at higher frequencies radio waves have shorter wavelengths. Shorter wavelengths (microwaves) have a greater potential for harming living tissues than longer wavelengths.

The difference in the danger level is the power output of the devices. The Federal Communications Commission and other regulatory bodies have set strict limits on RFR emissions. In the U.S., current FCC regulations set the output for 802.11x devices at 1 watt.

Most available 802.11x devices have a power output of less than 100 milliwatts (1 milliwatt is equal to 1 thousandth of a watt); the majority produce around 30 milliwatts. This is far below the safety limit set by the FCC, and considerably lower than the power produced by a microwave oven. A microwave oven can emit up to 1100 watts, not milliwatts, 1100 times higher than the safety level imposed on 802.11x devices. Although a microwave oven is shielded, even a small leak is far more dangerous than components on a WLAN. Even the handset for a 2.4 GHz cordless phone emits around 5 watts of power. The base stations of many phones emit over 25 watts.

As long as you use unmodified, FCC-approved equipment, you should not be concerned. I say unmodified because there are many modifications that you can make to WLAN equipment, especially antennas, that can increase the range of a network and the power emitted, increasing the associated risk.

cross
ref   I discuss extending the range of a WLAN in Chapter 6.

Secret #6:   Is Wireless Difficult to Set Up?

A wireless network is no more difficult to set up than an Ethernet network. In fact, in most cases, it's simpler to do. The initial rollout of the network is far easier than Ethernet because you don't have to run cables to every component. The hardest part is deciding where to locate the AP. Configuring the AP and the wireless NICs is simple; the newest devices are extremely user friendly.

The most common sources of frustration in setting up a WLAN are issues with interference or performance degradation. You can avoid these problems through careful planning, and I will show you how to do that in Chapter 3.

Secret #7:   Is Wireless Slow Compared to Ethernet?

It's true: a wireless network will have less capacity than a 100 Mbps Ethernet LAN. However, unless you regularly move huge files around on your WLAN, or back up large disks, you aren't going to notice a difference. Your Internet connection won't be any slower, and gaming, file sharing, and printing won't be either. Depending upon how many users are on your WLAN, you should never notice a speed difference.

If you do move very large files (meaning 100+MB) around your network on a regular basis, you will notice a difference. The trade-off for the freedom and flexibility that a WLAN offers is relatively minor. WLANs are getting faster, and with the newer 802.11g standard equipment now available, the speed difference is becoming even less noticeable.

Navigating the Maze of Standards

Okay, I know, now that you're convinced that wireless is really better, you're ready to run out to your computer superstore, hand over your credit card, and start plugging things in. But before you can get to the "how to do it" part, you need a little more of the "how does it work" stuff. This section helps you understand the layers and standards of networking technology so you'll be a more informed consumer when you hit the Giant Store of Computer Stuff.

Standards are the key to the interoperability of networking products. It would be impossible for equipment from different manufacturers to communicate were it not for accepted industry standards. Standards define the protocols that networked devices use to talk to one another. Although standards are essential, the number of wireless standards and protocols is enough to baffle even the most technically-savvy consumer.

The standards that are of most concern to the average SOHO wireless networker are the 802.11x physical layer standards, particularly 802.11b, 802.11a, and 802.11g.

Secret #8:   Where Do the Standards Come From?

Two organizations are responsible for setting and certifying the wireless standards. The Institute of Electrical and Electronics Engineers (sometimes called Eye-triple-E) is an international, nonprofit, technical professional organization. The Wi-Fi (wireless fidelity) alliance is a membership organization founded in 1999 that certifies product compliance to the IEEE 802.11x wireless standards. Over two hundred companies are members of this non-profit organization. While the IEEE exists to define and promote standards among engineers, the Wi-Fi Alliance exists to promote these same standards to the public through product testing, certification, and the use of the consumer-friendly term "Wi-Fi" in place of 802.11x standard numbers.

The IEEE produces standards through consensus-based working groups. When the IEEE approves and publishes a standard, industries use it as a blueprint for developing compatible products, processes, or solutions.

Because of IEEE standards, we have the ability to choose between different vendors for WLAN equipment, or even good old Ethernet equipment (IEEE 802.3x standard). The alternative would be multiple incompatible standards and proprietary technologies. In short, because of IEEE standards, you can shop around for great deals, mix and match equipment (to some extent), and be sure that your IEEE 802.11x WLAN will operate.

The Wi-Fi alliance promotes the use of wireless technology worldwide by encouraging manufacturers to comply with the 802.11x standards when designing their networking products. The Wi-Fi Alliance also promotes 802.11x technology to home, SOHO, and enterprise consumers, has networking products independently tested to ensure that they are compliant with the 802.11x standard, and tests interoperability between certified products.

If a network component carries the Wi-Fi certified logo, it operates with other Wi-Fi certified products that operate in the same frequency range. This gives consumers a choice when shopping for WLAN products, enabling you to mix components from different manufacturers when building your WLAN.

> **on the web** For more information about Wi-Fi, visit the Wi-Fi Alliance Web site at www.wi-fi.org.

Standards address different aspects of wireless networking. Some refer to frequency and encryption while others address quality of service or are extensions of previously existing standards. Standards define each of the three layers of a WLAN network model: infrastructure, Media Access Control, and physical, as shown in Figure 1-4.

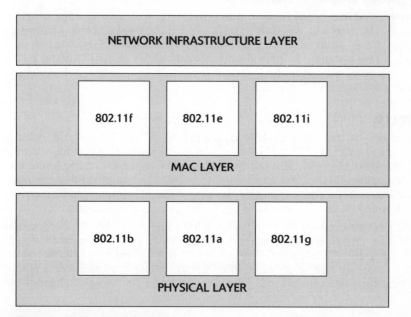

NETWORK INFRASTRUCTURE LAYER

| 802.11f | 802.11e | 802.11i |

MAC LAYER

| 802.11b | 802.11a | 802.11g |

PHYSICAL LAYER

Figure 1-4: The WLAN layers.

note Throughout the rest of the book, I refer to the standard 802.11 protocols as 802.11x, except where I am speaking about a specific standard (for example, 802.11b), and I use the term *Wi-Fi* in reference to the standards 802.11b, 802.11a, and 802.11g.

Performance and Interoperability

For WLAN devices to operate on the same network, they must use compatible standards and operate on the same frequency. Even though they are both Wi-Fi standards, 802.11b (2.4 GHz) products do not communicate with 802.11a (5 GHz) devices. They don't broadcast on or listen to the same frequency channel.

When designing your WLAN, be sure to purchase devices that operate on the same frequency and that adhere to the same standard. Some incompatible standards that share the same frequency with 802.11x devices can interfere with data transfer on a Wi-Fi network.

insider insight Although 802.11x devices operate only with compatible devices that use the same frequency band (such as 2.4 GHz), certified products that can operate in both the 2.4 GHz and 5 GHz frequencies have recently reached the market. This means that a dual band AP can communicate with an 802.11b or 802.11a NIC. If you have existing WLAN equipment, purchasing a dual band AP would enable you to upgrade to a faster 802.11a (more expensive) network in stages, while still being able to use your older (and much cheaper) 802.11b hardware. In the future, these dual band devices are likely to dominate because of the extended functionality they offer.

Physical Layer Standards

You only need to concern yourself with physical layer standards when deciding on a standard to use for your WLAN. The 802.11 specifications currently describe three physical layer standards for WLANs: 802.11b, 802.11a, and 802.11g. These standards have risen to dominate the market. Adding to the confusion, IEEE did not approve these standards in alphabetical order: 802.11b predates 802.11a.

802.11b

Also known by the consumer-friendly name "Wi-Fi" (Wi-Fi now also includes 802.11a and 802.11g), 802.11b came on the scene in 1999, competing with the rival standard HomeRF. 802.11b has since risen to dominate the home and SOHO market. The result is an abundance of 802.11b-compliant devices available to consumers. This means that the cost of 802.11b equipment is relatively inexpensive.

802.11b devices operate in the unregulated 2.4 GHz radio band, which means that unlike a ham radio, consumers do not need a license to operate the equipment. Although 802.11b allows for operation of 11 channels within the spectrum, devices usually utilize three to limit interference between access points. The maximum link rate is 11 Mbps, but heavy traffic on the same channel can significantly reduce maximum throughput. The data rate also decreases the farther you get from an access point (AP).

---

insider insight

Marketing departments often use the terms *data rate* and *throughput* interchangeably when promoting the speed of a networking device, or use data rate as if it were the actual speed when it really represents the *capacity*. This has led to a lot of confusion, even among IT professionals, so you're in good company if this has left you scratching your head.

Data rate refers to the number of bytes of data transferred in a specified unit of time. For example, an 802.11x device operating at 11 Mbps (millions of bits per second), has the capacity to deliver 11 Mbps of data. The data rate is not the true measure of speed on a WLAN, or any network for that matter.

What really measures speed and performance is the throughput of a connection. You can calculate throughput by determining the amount of information sent over time. Many factors affect throughput, including number of users on a WLAN, interference, and latency of connections (*latency* is the amount of time it takes for data to travel between devices).

Throughput is always less than data rate, without exception. Often, actual throughput is less than half the data rate; therefore, users on an 11 Mbps WLAN may have an actual throughput of 6 Mbps or less. Being able to distinguish between these two terms will aid you when designing your WLAN, and will help you make smart buying decisions.

802.11b also shares the 2.4 GHz band with other consumer electronic devices, including cordless phones and microwave ovens. When operating, these devices may interfere with 802.11b WLAN functions.

---

cross ref

I discuss radio frequency (RF) interference issues and ways of dealing with them in Chapter 4.

802.11a

Another Wi-Fi standard, 802.11a, operates in the 5 GHz radio band, which is free from interference from other household electronic devices (for the time being). It has a maximum throughput rate of 54 Mbps—almost five times faster than 802.11b. Unfortunately, 802.11a can only achieve this speed at a short distance from an access point; less than 30 feet is a good approximation. If you need to cover a wide area with Wi-Fi access, 802.11a may not be the best choice unless you are willing to invest in multiple access points.

Because it operates on a different frequency, 802.11a is not backward compatible with 802.11b, and upgrading requires you to purchase new equipment. Dual band equipment is available; these devices can operate on both 802.11b and 802.11a networks.

802.11g

This is the newest addition to the 802.11x physical layer standards. 802.11g is an extension to 802.11b and provides the throughput of 802.11a, but operates in the same 2.4 GHz band as 802.11b. 802.11g is backward-compatible with 802.11b and devices for both standards can coexist on the same WLAN. However, for full throughput speed on a computer using 802.11g cards, you must have an 802.11g access point. An 802.11g access point can communicate with slower 802.11b cards, enabling you to continue to use them and upgrade as you see fit. 802.11g is susceptible to the same interference issues as 802.11b because it operates in the same 2.4 GHz band.

> **insider insight** Because it offers the same speed advantages and is backward-compatible with 802.11b, you may think that 802.11g is a good alternative to 802.11a. In some cases it is, especially in a small WLAN in a home or SOHO environment, but when system capacity is important, 802.11a has the advantage. 802.11a has more channels available and can support more traffic. In a busy network environment 802.11a is a better choice, and ensures that you will be able to run mission-critical applications.

Secret #9:   Standards on the Horizon

Apart from the "big three" 802.11 protocols, users and installers of Wi-Fi really don't need to worry about many other protocols (except for Bluetooth, which can prove useful in many products that connect with your WLAN, such as personal digital assistants or smart phones). I present just a few of the more interesting standards here in brief to give you an idea of the scope of standardization and the direction that wireless may be heading. You'll find mention of still more standards throughout the Glossary of this book.

802.11i

Experts have exposed weaknesses in the current Wired Equivalent Privacy (WEP) algorithm implemented in current WLANs. 802.11i is a new security supplement to the 802.11 MAC standard. 802.11i will address security holes in the 802.11a, b, and g protocols and improve encryption, key management, distribution, and user authentication. This standard is worth remembering, because these improvements to security may be available as firmware and later hardware upgrades for your existing Wi-Fi network.

> **cross ref** WLAN networks do have some problems regarding security. I examine threats and the appropriate steps to take to secure your WLAN in Chapter 17.

802.11n

IEEE has recognized the 802.11n working group, which has begun investigating the next-generation wireless standard in the 802.11x wireless standards family. 802.11n is still approximately three years away, but reportedly will provide over 100 Mbps throughput. That is 100 Mbps of actual throughput, not a data rate. For example, the data rate for 802.11g is 54 Mbps, but the actual throughput is typically half of that.

Bluetooth and 802.15.1

Bluetooth is a wireless personal area networking (WPAN) technology developed by the Bluetooth Special Interest Group (founded by Nokia, Ericsson, IBM, Intel, and Toshiba). Its goal is to enable users to connect many different computing and telecommunications devices easily and simply, without the cables. It operates in the unlicensed 2.4 GHz band of the radio spectrum. Developers named Bluetooth for the Danish King Harald Blatand (Bluetooth) who unified Denmark and Norway in the tenth century. Like King Bluetooth, the Bluetooth standard means to *unify*—in this case, the telecom and computing industries.

Bluetooth does not compete directly with 802.11x standards; its range is too short and its throughput speed too slow (1 Mbps) to fill 802.11x's shoes. Bluetooth devices can coexist peacefully and in some cases interoperate with a Wi-Fi network. Bluetooth is a complementary standard to 802.11x.

Whereas Wi-Fi technology replaces Ethernet cables and connects computers in a WLAN, Bluetooth connects peripherals without all those annoying cables. Keyboards, optical mice, printers, digital cameras, and PDAs that employ Bluetooth are already available. All of these devices can communicate and operate without user intervention. The devices know how to connect and do it by themselves.

Bluetooth devices connect to create small ad hoc networks called *piconets* (see Figure 1-5). In a piconet, the device that initiates connection becomes the master. Depending on the connection (data, voice, or data and voice) each master in a piconet can manage up to seven slave devices.

If a Bluetooth device listens for other Bluetooth devices broadcasting and doesn't hear anything, it configures itself as a router (master) and broadcasts an "I'm here" signal telling other devices how to connect. If another device comes into range, a PDA for example, and it hears the master device's "I'm here" broadcast, it connects to the master and identifies itself. As other devices come into range they identify themselves to the master and share information about their capabilities and services. If a device with an active Internet connection were to join a piconet, the other devices might take advantage of this capability and check (or send) e-mail.

A Bluetooth device can be a member of multiple piconets at one time, but can only be a master in one. When piconets share one or more devices, they become a *scatternet* (see Figure 1-6). A maximum of ten fully loaded piconets can be part of a scatternet at any one time.

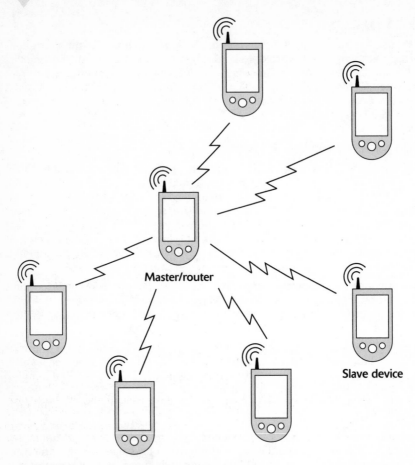

Figure 1-5: A typical Bluetooth piconet.

These devices can connect and disconnect without the user having to lift a finger, or even knowing that it has occurred. You won't have to worry about your PDA talking to every strange Bluetooth device it meets; Bluetooth is safe and devices employ a number of security layers, including an authentification process called *pairing*, and adequate encryption.

The IEEE licensed a portion of the Bluetooth specification when creating the 802.15.1 standard, creating a standard that is fully compatible with the existing Bluetooth spec giving Bluetooth greater support in the WPAN market. As the Bluetooth SIG further develops the standard, the IEEE will likely incorporate these changes into the 802.15.1 family of standards.

---

on the
web

The Bluetooth Web site provides information about Bluetooth-capable products. For more information, visit www.bluetooth.com.

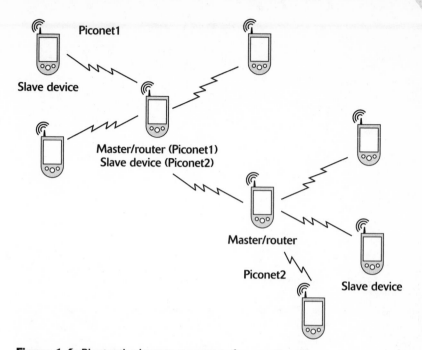

Figure 1-6: Bluetooth piconets connect to form scatternets.

Now that you have a good grasp of the key wireless networking standards, you can make informed decisions when you are planning your WLAN and purchasing equipment. However, wireless networking is only half of the wireless story. In the next chapter, I introduce *mobile* wireless standards pertaining to cellular communications.

Demystifying Mobile Technology

◆ ◆

Secrets in This Chapter

◆ ◆

The population today is more mobile than ever. Regardless of where they are, people want to stay connected. Whether for personal contact or business communication, more people than ever own cell phones, pagers, and *personal digital assistants* (PDAs). However, the market is changing, and the capabilities of the networks and services vary significantly. Even a passing knowledge of the different standards, services, and wireless generations gives you an edge when it comes to determining what sort of mobile technology meets your needs, and which carrier can best provide it.

Secret #10: Wireless Services Are on the Rise

Today, mobile wireless services go beyond the omnipresent cell phone. Now mobile carriers regularly offer data, fax, Web-browsing, messaging, and even multimedia services. Mobile devices enable us to remain productive, no matter where we are. Whether you favor a fully functional notebook computer, a PDA, or a digital phone, there is a device available right now that meets your needs and can help you stay connected, informed, and even entertained.

In the last few years, the cost of mobile communications has plummeted, and as newer and faster technology arrives, the cost-to-performance ratio of these services is only going to continue to move in your favor. Right now we are on the verge of the next generation in wireless technology. Networks are set to increase in speed and value with newer, more reliable services and applications already beginning to arrive on the market.

For a glimpse of the future, we need only look to Japan, a nation of technophiles like no other in the world. Already more Japanese access the Internet via their mobile phones than through desktop PCs. They have pioneered the use of mobile phones for everything from shopping to dating. Japanese carriers have already introduced location-aware handsets that can combine with an Internet dating service to notify subscribers when they are within 100 feet of a potential love interest. Both parties, once notified, can use their phones to view profiles and instant message one another before deciding to meet.

As advanced networks appear in the U.S., we will have access to similar services and applications. Already carriers are offering features like messaging, photo messaging, and Web browsing as part of standard service packages. As enhanced services arrive, it will be harder to resist being connected; in fact you may have to just to stay competitive.

Secret #11: How Mobile Wireless Works

Millions of people own cell phones, alphanumeric pagers, and other wireless devices, but few people have even the slightest clue how they actually work. While cell phones may mimic normal telephones in appearance and basic function, they aren't telephones at all—they are two-way radios. Every cell phone is a low-power, high-frequency *transceiver* (transmitter-receiver). When you use your handset, it is transmitting over the public radio spectrum in all directions. Because they look like telephones, we expect the same privacy and quality of service that we get from the *plain-old-telephone-service* (POTS). Before we investigate how cell phone networks operate, it's best to have an understanding of how POTS networks work. While an in-depth and technically-exact description of any phone network is beyond the scope of this book, the following simplified explanations should suffice for our purposes.

When you place a call on a POTS phone, the phone converts your voice to an electrical signal and transmits it over wires to your local telephone exchange. The exchange routes the call to its final destination over the phone company's network (see Figure 2-1). For the most part, the call never leaves the network, except perhaps in cases where you call a cell phone from a landline, or when your phone company routes a long distance call through a satellite.

Mobile phones are commonly called *cell phones* because of the basic design of the network that they operate within. In a mobile network, a number of transceiver sites are arranged so that their signals or coverage areas overlap. A *cell* is the name given to the coverage area of a particular transceiver site, or *cell tower* (see Figure 2-2).

The cell towers in a particular area link together through a central *mobile telephone switching office* (MTSO). Each MTSO authenticates and routes calls between transceivers in its service area, and handles billing. The software that handles calls at an MTSO is incredibly sophisticated. The MTSO also connects to the conventional telephone network and routes calls between cell phones and POTS phones (see Figure 2-3).

While the technology differs from carrier to carrier, the same general thing happens when you place a call with your mobile phone. When you turn your phone on, it notifies the network and authenticates itself. Authentication usually consists of the phone transmitting several pieces of information to identify itself and your account. One of these pieces of information is the *electronic serial number* (ESN). Manufacturers encode the ESN on a chip within the phone. The other piece of information is the *mobile identification number* (MIN). The MIN is your cell phone's area code and phone number. Depending on the carrier and the underlying network, there may be more codes used to authenticate your phone or establish calls.

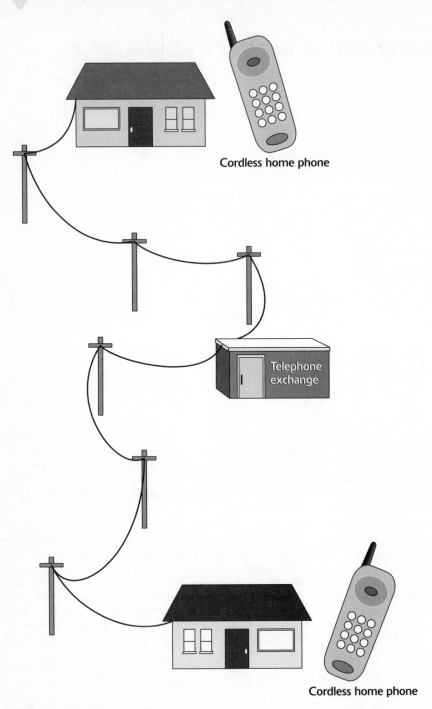

Figure 2-1: POTS network.

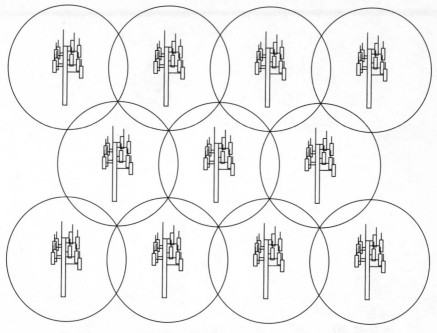

Towers arranged so that coverage areas form cells that overlap

Figure 2-2: Cellular coverage areas.

When your phone transmits this data, the closest cell tower receives it and routes it to the MTSO. Once the MTSO verifies your phone, it then accepts calls and routes them accordingly. If you have called a POTS number, your MTSO routes that call to the conventional phone network and routes the return voice signal back to your cell phone through the tower handling your call, where it is sent to you as a radio signal. If you have called another mobile phone, then the MTSO routes the call to the transceiver handling that phone, and then back to you.

While you are connected to the mobile network, the MTSO tracks your signal strength. The MTSO assigns your phone to whichever transceiver receives the strongest signal from your handset. As you move away from one transceiver your signal grows weaker, while at the same time, as you get closer to a new transceiver it receives a stronger signal from you. The MTSO then assigns the next transceiver to handle your call, where you must authenticate again, and switch to the new transceiver's frequency. This hand-off between cells occurs without you even noticing it and with no interruption in your call (see Figure 2-4).

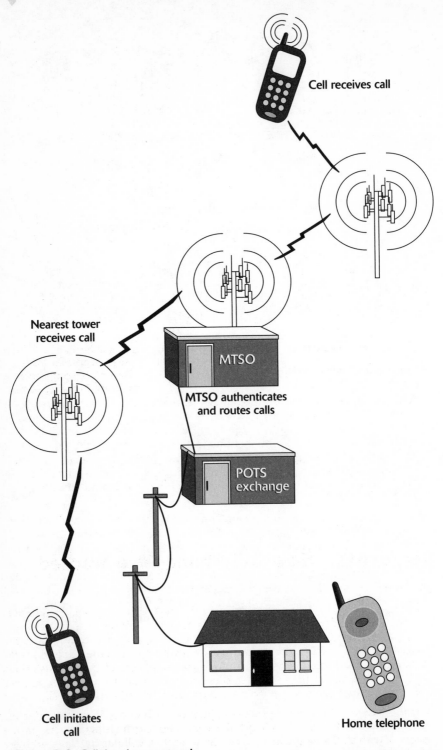

Figure 2-3: Cellular phone network.

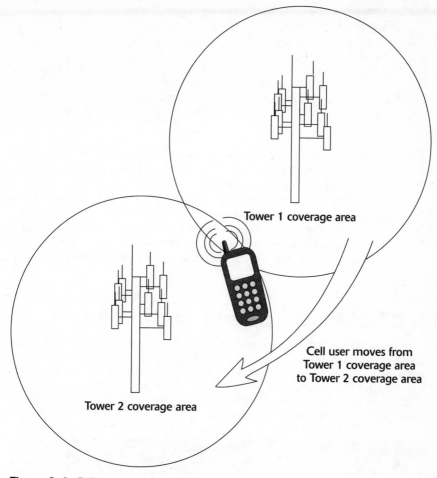

Tower 1 coverage area

Cell user moves from
Tower 1 coverage area
to Tower 2 coverage area

Tower 2 coverage area

Figure 2-4: Cellular network switching.

Secret #12: How Cell Phones Are Tracked

Each time your phone authenticates at a cell tower, this information is stored at the MTSO for billing purposes. From this record it is possible to place a cell user in a general area, because a tower may have a range of a couple of miles. Mobile carriers usually only release this data with a court order. In San Diego, prosecutors used this method to track the whereabouts of David Westerfield and to convict him of the murder of seven-year-old Danielle van Dam. His cell records revealed his movements in the days after Danielle disappeared.

Another way to track cellular users is through technology that calculates the time difference in arrival of a cellular signal among multiple towers, or the angle of arrival. These techniques can help locate a cellular customer within a much smaller area than by using MTSO records alone. This technology is used to locate people calling the 911 service from mobile phones, but it could just as easily be used in a criminal prosecution.

The most precise way to pinpoint the location of a mobile phone is through the use of the *global positioning system (GPS)*. GPS satellites orbit the Earth and transmit coded signals at regular intervals. A GPS-enabled device calculates the difference in arrival time of three or more signals and calculates its location to within a few feet. As more handsets come equipped with GPS, the potential to accurately track mobile phone users will become more and more of a reality.

note   Pagers may be receivers (one-way paging), or like cell phones, transceivers (two-way messaging and e-mail pagers). A pager network is arranged in a similar manner to a cell network. Instead of cell towers, paging networks use smaller *remote terminal units* (RTU). An RTU has a much weaker signal, so there are more of them in a given coverage area. RTUs are small and can be mounted on existing telephone poles or buildings. With the competition from low-cost mobile phone services, pager networks are in decline. *Personal communication service* (PCS) phones duplicate many of the functions of a pager.

Mobile Standards and Technology

When you read about mobile communication, you're bound to encounter talk of wireless *generations*. These refer to the different eras of cellular technology and networks as the industry evolved. Presently, cellular companies are moving into the third generation with enhanced services and features, but 2.5G, or *two-and-a-half-generation* technology, is still the most prevalent. This section describes the different generations of wireless, illustrated in Figure 2-5.

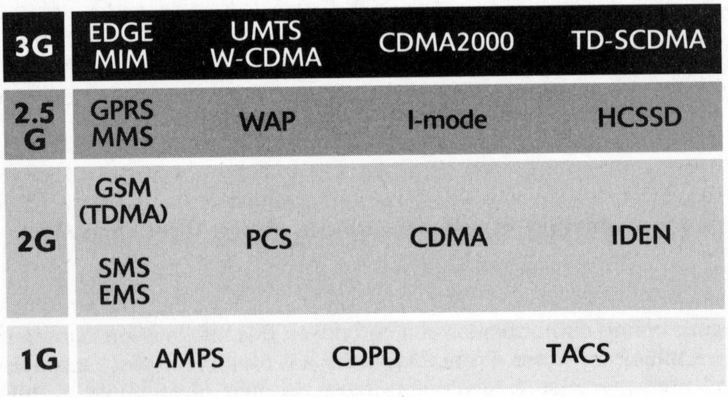

3G	EDGE MIM	UMTS W-CDMA	CDMA2000	TD-SCDMA
2.5 G	GPRS MMS	WAP	I-mode	HCSSD
2G	GSM (TDMA) SMS EMS	PCS	CDMA	IDEN
1G		AMPS	CDPD	TACS

Figure 2-5: Wireless generations in the U.S. and Europe.

First-Generation Technology

The analog mobile phone networks originally rolled out in the 1980s are *first-generation* (1G) networks. You may remember the original analog handsets, about the size of a brick with two-foot-long telescoping antennas. 1G networks carry voice traffic only, and data transmission. Analog handsets convert sound waves from voice to an analogous electrical signal (hence the term analog) and broadcast the signal in the clear, with no encryption. Because analog networks broadcast calls in the clear, 1G networks are not secure and it is possible to intercept calls with a radio frequency scanner.

note
The following case illustrates the vulnerability of 1G networks. In Florida, on December 21, 1996, a couple using a police scanner was able to eavesdrop on and tape a call broadcast on a 1G network. This call was between then House Speaker Newt Gingrich (R), Representative Bill Paxon (R-N.Y.), House Majority Leader Dick Armey (R-Texas), Gingrich's Chief of Staff Dan Meyer, Ed Gillespie (Communications Director for the Republican National Committee), and attorney Ed Bethune. They were orchestrating a GOP counterattack to the charges that Speaker Gingrich was facing from the House Ethics Committee. This phone conversation was in violation of an agreement that Speaker Gingrich had with the Ethics Committee. The couple supplied the tape to an unidentified Democratic member of Congress, who likewise supplied it to the New York Times. Because of the interception of this call, Speaker Gingrich suffered a lot of political damage, and the press had a field day with the story.

1G technology is obsolete and been replaced by newer networks in most locations. There are some 1G networks still in operation in remote parts of the country, and in some places overseas. While traveling, you may actually connect through these networks, even with newer digital phones; however, advanced features such as messaging and data are usually unavailable while roaming in analog mode.

insider insight
All mobile phones have a unique set of identifiers that are used to authenticate them on a network and route calls. *Cloning* is illegally copying one cell phone's identifiers onto another phone, allowing the user of a cloned phone to make calls on a victim's account without paying. When 1G (analog) systems were common, fraud from cloning was a real problem.

Analog phones broadcasted their identifiers in the clear with no encryption. Criminals could use modified scanners to capture cell phone data, and then copy it onto illegal, cloned phones. Criminals often collected thousands of numbers in a single day, and the revenue lost to fraud was substantial.

The use of digital PCS has reduced the incidence of cloning, but it hasn't been eliminated. Digital phones don't broadcast in the clear; they use digital encoding or encryption to secure all voice and data transmitted. However, when PCS phones roam between networks, or are using an analog cell tower (in analog roam) it's possible to capture the identifiers and use them to clone a phone.

Criminals can clone some phones with just the area code, phone number and the system ID. The system ID is unique to a specific carrier, in a particular geographic area. It is unlikely that you will ever be a victim of this form of fraud, but knowing about it will increase your awareness and allow you to stay alert to the possibility.

1G networks presented a range of technologies, including the following systems and services:

◆ **Advanced mobile phone service**—*Advanced mobile phone service* (AMPS) is a 1G technology originally tested in the late 1970s, and later became a commercial service in the early 1980s. AMPS used a technology called *frequency division multiple access* (FDMA) that divided the 800 MHz radio band used by AMPS into 30 kHz channels. Each call on an AMPS network required a dedicated channel. Increasing capacity on an AMPS network required adding channels. AMPS was the primary mobile phone service in North America prior to the arrival of *second-generation* (2G) networks.

◆ **Cellular digital packet data**—*Cellular digital packet data* (CDPD) is a technology developed as an add-on to 1G cellular networks. CDPD allows a 1G analog network to handle digital packet data, although at only 19 Kbps. CDPD modems are available for notebook computers and PDAs. CDPD service is available from several different wireless carriers in the U.S.

◆ **Total access communication system**—*Total access communication system* (TACS) is an analog 1G network that was developed in Europe in the late 1970s. TACS is modeled after AMPS, and like the U.S. network used FDMA. In the U.K., a version of TACS called ETACS (*extended TACS*) was widely used.

Second-Generation Technology

2G networks started to appear in the early 1990s. 2G systems use digital encoding to transmit voice over a wireless network. 2G networks offer superior call quality and better security. Although 2G systems primarily support voice traffic, many 2G networks provide low-speed, circuit-switched data service as well. Other 2G systems, such as *global system for mobile communications* (GSM), support limited text messaging. The following list presents some of the 2G technologies:

◆ **Global system for mobile communications**—GSM is a digital mobile phone system based upon *time division multiple access* (TDMA) technology (more on TDMA later). First deployed commercially in Europe in the early 1990s, GSM has since become the de facto standard. It is widely used in mobile phone networks worldwide and by some carriers in the U.S.

In addition to digital voice, GSM was the first of the 2G systems to provide limited text messaging through the *short messaging service* (SMS). GSM phones contain a card called a *subscriber identity module* (SIM) that contains the user's account information. GSM phones are very user-friendly and make upgrading to a new phone easy. Users can switch cell phones simply by removing the SIM from one cell phone and installing it into a new one, transferring all of their account data and activating the new phone simultaneously. The use of a SIM also makes GSM systems less susceptible to fraud than older analog cell phones.

Another advantage of having a GSM phone is that if you travel overseas, particularly to Europe, you still may be able to use your phone. Having cell phone access abroad depends on whether your carrier has agreements in place with foreign carriers.

European and Japanese consumers already enjoy more media-rich wireless services than U.S. consumers do. Europe chose to adopt GSM as a standard early on, and, as a result, Europeans have a more integrated mobile infrastructure than we do in the U.S. This has led to faster adoption of the network by developers, giving Europeans access to more content and applications. In Japan, NTT DoCoMo's I-mode standard has produced similar results.

The U.S. chose to let the market decide, and so far that hasn't happened. The U.S. market is split among standards and platforms, and developers haven't been quick to invest in developing content and applications for the fragmented U.S. market. U.S. consumers experience the result in the confusing array of standards, incompatible devices, and lack of content and applications (compared with European and Japanese consumers).

♦ **Short messaging service**—First introduced in GSM networks, SMS is now available on most digital mobile phone networks. SMS enables users to send short text messages, usually fewer than 160 characters, to one another via their mobile phones. SMS delivers messages via the handset's control channel, which is separate from the voice channel; thus, you can receive a message while conducting a voice conversation. Messages are stored at a message center, then forwarded when the addressee's phone is on and connected to the network. This allows you to retrieve messages even after your phone has been turned off, or you have been outside your coverage area. This differs from earlier paging technology, where messages were sent real-time and lost if the pager was not available to receive the page.

♦ **Enhanced messaging service**—*Enhanced messaging service* (EMS) is an extension that expands the capabilities of SMS. EMS allows users to send and receive formatted text, ring tones, sound effects, animations, and icons. Many networks support EMS, including GSM and *code division multiple access* (CDMA). EMS is backward-compatible with SMS in that if users send an EMS message to an SMS phone it is displayed as SMS, with no advanced features.

♦ **Time division multiple access**—TDMA is a digital encoding technology that divides an allotted radio channel into time slots, with each time slot handling one call (see Figure 2-6). TDMA more than tripled the call capacity over earlier analog systems. There are several technologies in the TDMA family; these include GSM, *general packet radio service* (GPRS), and *integrated digital enhanced network* (iDEN). All of these use different frequencies and channel sizes.

♦ **Code division multiple access**—CDMA transmits multiple digital signals in the same channel. This means that multiple calls can take place simultaneously on the same channel. Qualcomm developed CDMA, and Qualcomm digital handsets remain the chief users of this 2G technology. CDMA has better quality, is more efficient and is less costly to implement than other technologies. It is also far more secure, with calls being harder to detect or jam. The military has adopted CDMA for some applications because of this increased security.

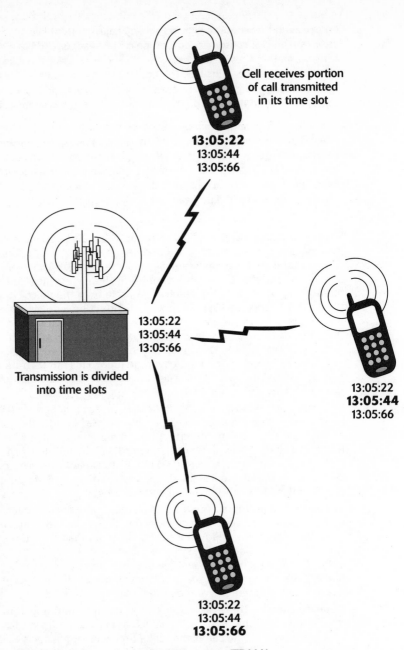

Cell receives portion
of call transmitted
in its time slot

13:05:22
13:05:44
13:05:66

Transmission is divided
into time slots

13:05:22
13:05:44
13:05:66

13:05:22
13:05:44
13:05:66

13:05:22
13:05:44
13:05:66

Figure 2-6: Time division multiple access (TDMA).

Allowing multiple calls to take place on the same channel may seem
to defy logic, but it is actually easy to understand (see Figure 2-7).
Imagine every CDMA phone on a channel is speaking a different language. Even though all of these conversations are taking place at the

same time, your phone hears another phone speaking its language and ignores all the rest. Each phone recognizes the digital transmission tagged with its identity code and ignores the rest, allowing multiple phones to share the channel.

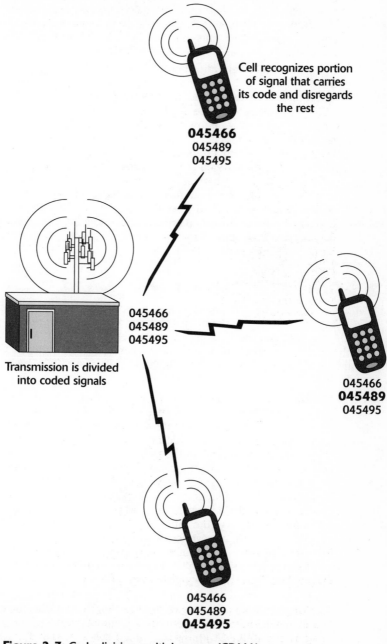

Cell recognizes portion of signal that carries its code and disregards the rest

045466
045489
045495

045466
045489
045495

Transmission is divided into coded signals

045466
045489
045495

045466
045489
045495

Figure 2-7: Code division multiple access (CDMA).

◆ **Personal communications services**—Can you hear me now? In 1994, the U.S. government began auctioning off commercial licenses in the 1.8–2 GHz range. PCS is the name given to digital cellular services offered in this range by the *Federal Communications Commission* (FCC). However, advertisers often use PCS to describe digital services regardless of the frequency. PCS devices typically provide voice, data, and paging services. PCS is a generic term to describe digital services offered by several carriers; it is not a standard unto itself. PCS carriers use different standards including GSM and CDMA.

◆ **Integrated digital enhanced network**—iDEN is a technology developed by Motorola. iDEN enables a single phone to support voice, data, SMS, and digital push-to-talk radio. iDEN uses a proprietary version of TDMA and operates in the 800 MHz and 1.5 GHz bands. When used as two-way radios, or walkie-talkies, iDEN phones don't have to be within range of one another because the radio feature uses the cellular network. While within their coverage area, iDEN users can have a radio conversation even if they are on opposite ends of the country. You might ask what the difference is between making a phone call with an iDEN phone or using it as a radio. Good question. The big difference is that as a radio you connect instantly, usually under a second, and up to twenty-five users can conference at once. Push-to-talk is usually cheaper than placing a cell call and offers the same level of security. Nextel has the largest iDEN network in the U.S.

2.5-Generation Technology

2.5-generation (2.5G or 2G+) networks are an interim step toward *third-generation* (3G) networks. 2.5G networks integrate technology that extends 2G networks to include packet-switched data service. Packet-switched data service is faster than the circuit-switched data service offered on some 2G networks. GPRS is an example of a 2.5G technology. The following list discusses 2.5G technologies in detail:

◆ **General packet radio service**—GPRS provides packet-switched data service to GSM networks. Because it uses packet switching like the Internet, GPRS makes many Internet applications available via a mobile device. Using GPRS, carriers can provide services such as Web browsing, games, e-mail, or file transfers at speeds up to 40 Kbps (much higher speed is theoretically possible, but unlikely due to the nature of cellular networks). To move data on a GSM network, GPRS uses the same time slots used for voice with each time slot carrying data packets. This allows for efficient use of radio resources, because several users can send packets over the same channel, unlike a circuit-switched connection that requires a dedicated line. GPRS allows for *always on* Internet connections, with many carriers only charging for the amount of data transferred, not the length of time actually connected.

◆ **Multimedia messaging service**—*Multimedia messaging service* (MMS) is an enhanced service for cell phones that provides for transmission of multimedia messages between mobile phones, and uses the *wireless application protocol* (WAP). Multimedia messages can consist of pictures, audio, video, and formatted text. MMS users send messages through an intermediary server, or *MMS center* (MMSC), rather than sending them in real-time. The MMSC receives messages and holds them until the receiving phone retrieves them. This is also known as *store-and-forward*.

A popular application of MMS is photo messaging, which enables users to take a picture with their phone and send it to another user, accompanied by a voice message or text (see Figure 2-8). Often, if a photo message is sent to a user with a phone that doesn't support the feature, the recipient receives an Internet address where he can view the picture.

MMS supports e-mail addressing and allowing users to send MMS messages to an e-mail address rather than a phone. MMS is usually backward-compatible with earlier messaging services, such as SMS and EMS, with users of those services receiving a modified message rather than a full MMS message.

Figure 2-8: An MMS-compatible photo-messaging phone from Sprint PCS.

- ◆ **Wireless application protocol**—WAP is a standard that enables users of mobile devices to access the Internet and view data on mobile devices such as phones. Comparable to HTTP on the World Wide Web, WAP is secure and most mobile networks and *operating systems* (OSs) support it.

  WAP was specifically developed for handheld wireless devices and uses very little of a device's resources to operate. WAP uses the *wireless markup language* (WML) but supports both the *extensible markup language* (XML), and HTML. For page scripting, WAP uses WMLScript, which is efficient and developed with mobile devices in mind. The latest version of WAP integrates the features of *I-mode*.

- ◆ **I-mode**—Developed by NTT DoCoMo of Japan, I-mode is a proprietary service that allows browsing of Internet pages on mobile phones, as well as e-mail, games, and chat services. Unlike WAP, which uses WML, I-mode uses cHTML, a subset of HTML. The I-mode service is one of the largest Internet service providers in Japan, with more users accessing the Internet from their phones than from desktop PCs. The latest version of the I-mode service uses an early version of the 3G technology, known as *wideband code division multiple access* (W-CDMA). Because of this, I-mode users enjoy speeds of up to 384 Kbps.

◆ **High-speed circuit-switched data**—Like GPRS, *high-speed circuit-switched data* (HSCSD) is another extension of GSM networks, designed to add data transfer capabilities. HSCSD uses circuit switching, and unlike GPRS, it requires a dedicated time-slot for data transfer. HSCSD devices simultaneously use up to four time-slots, unlike GPRS, which can allow different users to send packets in the same time-slot. Because it requires the dedicated use of multiple time-slots, HSCSD does not use radio resources as efficiently as GPRS. However, the use of multiple, dedicated time-slots has greater quality of service than GPRS. At increased data speeds, this increase in quality of service makes HSCSD a better choice than GPRS for delivery of live video. Because HSCSD uses a dedicated connection, it isn't ideal for *always on* Internet service, as users would have to maintain a connection and as a result would be charged more.

Third-Generation Technology

Third-generation technology (3G) will bring enhanced services to mobile users worldwide. The general improvements in 3G over previous networks will be in bandwidth and speed. 3G networks will deliver real-time multimedia and high-speed data, as well as enhanced voice services and Internet connectivity. Speeds may reach 2 Mbps depending on the application (mobile or fixed wireless). As defined by the *International Telecommunications Union* (ITU), 3G networks will provide data service at speeds no less than 144 Kbps.

Existing services like MMS will benefit from the broadband connectivity that 3G networks will provide. Users can expect better video, gaming, and messaging as well as real-time delivery of multimedia and video conferencing.

◆ **Enhanced Data Rates for Global Evolution**—EDGE is an enhancement to GSM networks that increases data rate up to 384 Kbps while using the same frequencies. Using EDGE, mobile customers will be able to simultaneously use different services, such as Web browsing and making a phone call. EDGE will use a version of GPRS known as *Enhanced GPRS* (E-GPRS), a version of GPRS that will run on an EDGE network and take advantage of the greater speed. While not quite as fast as *Universal Mobile Telecommunications System* (UMTS), EDGE will allow carriers to upgrade to 3G without obtaining a UMTS license because it uses existing GSM frequencies, possibly meaning reduced prices for consumers.

◆ **Universal Mobile Telecommunications System**—UMTS is the European implementation of 3G developed by Nortel Networks. UMTS will expand the speed of GSM networks by replacing TDMA with W-CDMA. UMTS will operate in the 2 GHz band and offer speeds up to 2 Mbps. UMTS is also known as *European WCDMA* (E-WCDMA).

◆ **Wideband code division multiple access**—W-CDMA is a 3G technology that supports speeds up to 2 Mbps for the delivery of voice and data. W-CDMA will increase the transfer rate on GSM networks by replacing TDMA, which is currently used. Like CDMA, W-CDMA enables different users to share the same channel by encoding the signal from different phones individually. W-CDMA supports many data services, including packet-switched and circuit-switched solutions. W-CDMA will be dominant in Europe as part of the UMTS 3G standard.

♦ **Time division-synchronous code division multiple access**—Just when you thought the acronyms couldn't possible get any longer, along comes *time division-synchronous code division multiple access* (TD-SCDMA). The *China Academy of Telecommunications Technology* (CATT), Datang, and Siemens are developing this 3G technology jointly. TD-SCDMA combines the efficient use of the radio spectrum of CDMA with TDMA's ability to deliver data asymmetrically. TD-SCDMA will also support speed up to 2 Mbps, and promises to be competitive with other 3G technologies. TD-SCDMA will probably be the standard within China.

♦ **CDMA2000**—Yet another 3G technology based on CDMA, CDMA2000 was the first 3G technology to be used commercially (in late 2000, hence the name). There are several versions or evolutions of CDMA2000, supporting speeds up to 307 Kbps or 2 Mbps (for data only). A number of CDMA-based networks already use CDMA2000.

♦ **Mobile instant messaging**—*Mobile instant messaging* (MIM) is instant messaging or chat moved onto a mobile platform. Like traditional chat programs, users can have an alias, manage contacts, and know when their *buddies* are online. MIM takes place in real-time, and users can interact as if they were using AOL Instant Messenger or MSN Messenger, for example.

---

insider
insight

3G networks are just starting to appear, but already there is buzz about *fourth-generation* (4G) technology. It's still a long way off, but be prepared to start hearing about it more often. Already there is a lot of heated discussion as to what 4G should be. Some say it should be an end-to-end *Internet protocol* (IP) network similar to Wi-Fi; others say that multimedia services will be the driving applications.

4G will provide on-demand broadband capability, with greater quality of service. Originally slated for 2010 release, some carriers are predicting 2006. The move toward 4G isn't just being supported by cellular carriers; wireless ISP's are driving development of the new technology as a solution for fixed wireless Internet services.

While you should be wary of much of the hype about 4G, some of the promises for speed and quality of service are likely to be realized. However, what remains to be seen is if 4G will make the U.S. market less fragmented and more attractive to developers.

Debunking Mobile Wireless Myths

Just like Wi-Fi, mobile wireless has its own share of myths, and some even have a slight basis in fact. Here are some of the most common mobile myths, and some background regarding each of them.

Secret #13: Are Mobile Phones Safe from Computer Viruses?

Hah! The only reason cell phones haven't been hit by as many viruses as desktop PCs is because not many virus writers have started targeting them yet. In 2001, a mobile phone virus surfaced on Japan's NTT DoCoMo I-mode service, took over basic functions of handsets, and caused them to dial 110, Japan's equivalent of 911. Like many PC viruses, this virus spread via e-mail. Hackers also are beginning to target cell phones and PDAs connected to networks with malicious code in an attempt to gain access to those networks. This trend is likely to increase in 2004 and beyond.

In early 2003, some cell phone users in the U.S. and Europe received malicious code embedded in what appeared to be a spam message. The message deleted the address books on the phones and disabled SMS. While malicious code and viruses are still extremely rare, they will become more common now that phones are becoming ubiquitous and feature-rich.

Virus writers tend to target systems where they can do the most damage and get the most bang for their buck. This is why more viruses attack Microsoft PCs than Apple's Macintosh. Because Microsoft controls more than 90 percent of the market, it is a better target. Now that phones can download executable code, and a few brands are controlling a major portion of the market, we will begin to see more viruses targeting mobile phones.

Secret #14: Can You Protect Your Mobile Device from Viruses?

Two of the most vulnerable operating systems for handhelds are the Palm OS and Microsoft Pocket PC. The reason they are vulnerable is that they have significant market share, run executable code, and are being integrated into new smart phones. This makes them attractive and likely future targets for creators of malicious software.

Now is the time to consider protecting your handheld against viruses and worms. Look for antivirus software that you can update easily and that comes from a reputable company. Symantec and F-Secure have both released software for handhelds, and other vendors are sure to follow. Antivirus software costs around $40, works well, and helps prevent malicious code from spreading to your network via your PDA.

on the web   **For more information about Symantec's PDA antivirus products, visit** www.symantecstore.com. **For more information about F-Secure's PDA antivirus products, visit** www.f-secure.com.

Secret #15: Do Mobile Phones Cause Car Accidents?

The jury is still out on this. While some studies, as well as common sense, suggest a connection between cell phone use and car accidents, accurate data is hard to gather because police seldom collect this information in accident reports. Studies and surveys often use self-reporting by drivers as a method of data collection. The problem here is obvious. Would you voluntarily report that you were using a cell phone at the time of an accident?

Some researchers are attempting to reduce this misclassification of data by cross-referencing phone bills and accident reports. By looking at the call times on phone bills and comparing them to accident reports, it is possible to establish a causal relationship between cell phones and auto accidents. Still, this method isn't perfect either, because it assumes that time data is accurate on both the bill and the accident report.

A 2001 survey conducted by the *National Highway Transportation Safety Administration* (NHTSA) indicates that at any given time, three percent of drivers are using cell phones (not hands-free types), which means roughly 500,000 people are driving and talking at any time during the week. While the NHTSA maintains that there appears to be an increased risk of being in an auto accident while talking on a cell phone, the magnitude of the problem cannot be estimated due to a lack of data. Many states are considering laws against cell phone use (handsets, not hands-free) by drivers, and New York has already passed legislation to that effect.

The NHTSA is still sorting the data out. In the meantime, we can all use a little common sense. Don't talk on your cell phone while driving unless you have a hands-free headset, and never send e-mail, check e-mail, or surf the Internet while driving (two percent of all drivers admit to doing this).

---

insider insight

Using a hands-free headset while driving is a smart move. Even better is using a wireless headset. Several headsets are available that use Bluetooth networking technology to connect to your mobile phone. Using one of these headsets, you can place and answer calls without even taking your phone out of your purse or briefcase.

The headsets work best with phones that support voice dial and voice command. Bluetooth headsets will connect up to 30 feet away from your phone, and operate with both Bluetooth-enabled and non-Bluetooth phones (with an adapter). For added security, choose a headset that supports encryption.

Secret #16: Do Mobile Phones Cause Brain Cancer?

In Chapter 1, I discussed some of the health concerns related to Wi-Fi technology. Many people have similar concerns about perceived health risks related to mobile handsets. There have been reports, largely based on anecdotal evidence, that link the use of mobile handsets with brain cancer, but research has not established a definitive causal relationship between the two.

The problem with anecdotal evidence is that it fails to establish a causal relationship between cell phones and cancer; it merely states that Group A uses cell phones, and has a slightly higher incidence of cancer than Group B, which doesn't use cell phones. For all we know, Group A also smokes three packs of cigarettes a day and works at a chemical plant.

The big misunderstanding here involves the difference between ionizing and non-ionizing radiation. Mobile phones produce low-energy, non-ionizing radiation. Ionizing radiation is radiation that is very high frequency (above a million MHz for X-rays) and high energy, which enables it to break chemical bonds such as those found in human cells. Ionizing radiation can damage DNA molecules, causing cell death or even cancer.

Cell phones are low power and operate at a much lower frequency than sources of ionizing radiation, such as X-rays. The non-ionizing radiation produced by mobile handsets cannot break chemical bonds. At very high levels of exposure, higher energy non-ionizing radiation can cause warming of tissues, much like a microwave, but handsets do not have that much power.

If you are concerned about possible health risks, limit your exposure, use a hands-free earpiece, and continue to monitor the research.

---

insider
insight

With the worries about cell phone–related health risks, it was inevitable that a few products would appear that would claim to mitigate some or all of them. The supposed health risk that creates the most concern, and headlines, is a proposed link between cell phones and brain cancer. One product that claims to mitigate this threat is a cell phone radiation shield.

These shields usually consist of an oval sticker that fits over the earpiece of your phone. Manufacturers claim that these bits of plastic, sometimes metal mesh, block harmful radiation. Even if the non-ionizing radiation from a cell phone were dangerous, placing a sticker over the speaker on your phone wouldn't protect you. Sound waves emanate from the speaker, not radiation. In general, radiation emanates from the phone in all directions so these stickers do nothing to block RF radiation.

Some manufacturers sell cell phone cases made of material that they claim blocks RF radiation. I remain skeptical that they can even block the RF waves, not to mention they usually have a clear plastic window over the keypad that will definitely allow radio waves to penetrate. If radiation shield cases really did work, you wouldn't be able to use your phone, because it wouldn't be able to send or receive a signal. So obviously, plenty of RF is escaping, not to mention what comes out of the antenna (which isn't shielded).

If you are genuinely worried about using your cell phone, don't waste your money on these products. Buy a headset and keep your phone away from your head. It's safer while driving, too.

Secret #17:   Do Mobile Phones Interfere with Aircraft Instruments?

Most airlines still restrict the use of *personal electronic devices* (PEDs), including phones and PDAs, on board commercial aircraft while in flight. If you ask why, you'll most likely be told that these devices can interfere with the aircraft's instrumentation and navigational equipment. What they will not tell you is that there is no scientific evidence to support this claim.

Reports of interference from PEDs are difficult to substantiate, and in many cases researchers attempting to duplicate the interference have been unable to do so. The FCC bans the use of cell phones on aircraft (including balloons) because it claims that calls from aircraft have the potential to interfere with cellular communications on the ground. This is also speculation.

The most likely reason for the airlines to support a ban on the use of cell phones is that they compete with air phones provided by the airlines, which are very expensive to use. If cellular signals were such a danger to commercial aviation, then turning off handsets would do little to protect airline passengers, because even at 30,000 feet the signal from a cell tower is stronger than the signal from a handset. Aircraft would be dropping out of the sky every time they flew over one of the thousands of towers in the U.S.

Pilots have blamed everything from pacemakers to electric razors for interfering with their instruments. Last time I checked, Grandpa could still get on a plane, pacemaker and all. This is a myth that has resulted in some ridiculous rules, but until these rules are repealed, you had better refrain from using your phone in flight, if only to avoid jail time.

Part II

Unwired at Home and in the Office

Planning
Your WLAN

Chapter
3

◆ ◆

Secrets in This Chapter

◆ ◆

The coolest thing about a home or SOHO wireless network is its flexibility. A Wi-Fi network is easier to expand and modify than an Ethernet network. Like wired networks, a home WLAN facilitates sharing between your computers. With a home network you can share files, printers, scanners, and a single Internet connection. However, unlike an Ethernet network, you also can add wireless consumer electronics, like stereo and video components, cameras, and even home control devices.

With your WLAN, you can play multiplayer games between PCs in your house, and if you have a broadband Internet connection, you can play against opponents over the Internet as well. You can connect all of the major game consoles to a WLAN by adding a wireless game adapter.

To get the best performance from your WLAN, and to have trouble-free installation and connectivity, you need to take the time to carefully plan your network before you begin. Oh sure, you can just buy some gear, plug it in and start connecting computers in an ad hoc fashion, but you will invariably run into interference and security problems. You also will end up spending a lot more money than you need to.

In this chapter we look at what you need to consider when planning your home Wi-Fi network. You'll plan the physical layout of your network and decide which hardware and software will best fit your needs. Regardless of what the final application for your network is, this chapter gets you ready before you make that first trip to the store.

Secret #18: Choosing Connectivity

The first thing you need to consider is whether wireless fits your needs, or if you should go with a wired alternative. I know, funny thing for a wireless book to even suggest, but Ethernet is worth considering for some applications. If you are planning to network just two or three computers and they are all in the same room, Ethernet may be the answer for you. In addition, if security is your main concern you may want to forego wireless altogether.

> **cross ref** I discuss the security concerns particular to WLANs and ways of securing your wireless network in Chapter 15.

Wireless is not the solution for every home network. You may be perfectly happy to hook up a few Ethernet cables and start networking. Perhaps you've purchased a house with Ethernet pre-installed in the walls (lucky you); why should you bother with wireless when the builders have done the hard part of Ethernet for you? Maybe you shouldn't. Ethernet isn't a dead end technology; it has plenty of uses and still has some advantages of its own. Some reasons to consider Ethernet are:

- Ethernet is cheaper than Wi-Fi. With Ethernet cables and equipment, you can network your computers for half the price, sometimes even less, than with Wi-Fi equipment. (That is, if you do all the wiring yourself and don't have to repair the holes you make in your walls.)
- Ethernet can be much faster than current Wi-Fi offerings.
- Obstacles like walls and ceilings do not affect Ethernet.
- Ethernet performance doesn't degrade over distance the same way Wi-Fi does.
- Ethernet is more secure than Wi-Fi.

That makes Ethernet sound good doesn't it? Well, no technology is perfect and Ethernet has its drawbacks too. Some of the reasons to consider a Wi-Fi solution are:

- Wi-Fi networks are flexible. Unlike an Ethernet network, you don't have to connect everything with a cable, so you can relocate computers and equipment with minimum hassle.
- Wi-Fi networks enable you to be mobile. If you have a laptop or PDA with a Wi-Fi connection, you can move throughout your house and remain connected as long as you can still receive the Wi-Fi signal. That's right, you can sit on the couch and watch Oprah while you sort through your e-mail.
- Wi-Fi networks are easy to expand. Unlike Ethernet, you can easily add equipment or expand your network without having to run additional network cables.
- Wi-Fi is easy to install. You don't have to run Ethernet cables through walls, attics, and crawl spaces. You don't have to deal with spiders, drywall dust, or accidental holes in walls and ceilings.

In reality, no single solution is right for every situation. Each system has its strong points, and in many cases a combination of wired and Wi-Fi may be the best way for you to go. This may be the case if you're expanding an existing Ethernet network, or if you want certain computers wired for additional security.

Secret #19: How Many Devices Will You Include?

The next factor to consider in designing your WLAN is to determine how many devices you want to connect wirelessly. You may want to connect everything right off the bat, or start out with a few devices and expand as your budget allows. Or you may be adding a few wireless elements to an existing Ethernet network. Almost every computing device can connect wirelessly: some models are Wi-Fi-ready right out of the box, others require the addition of a wireless adapter or network interface card (NIC). You can use the chart in Figure 3-1 as a guideline for creating your own checklist. This will help you when it comes time to shop for equipment.

How many computers do you have? Do you want all of these on the network? You can share resources and files between every PC on your WLAN, and each PC can have access to shared devices. Networked PCs also can share the same Internet connection. The number of PCs on your network and their location affect the amount of Wi-Fi hardware you need to purchase.

Device	Wi-Fi-Ready	Needs Card	Standard
Laptop	X		802.11g
PC		X	
PDA	X		802.11b

Figure 3-1: Device checklist.

> **note**
>
> Some handy network terms for you to know are *server, workstation,* and *client.* A server is a computer on a network that provides services to other computers on the network. Most home networks do not have, or need, servers because other PCs and network devices (routers, hubs, and so on) provide the services that a server would normally host.
>
> A PC on the network is a workstation, or client computer. Other network-aware devices, including game consoles, cameras, PDAs, and printers also are clients. The term client automatically implies that a PC or device is connected to a network.

How many printers do you have, and which of them is available on the network? You can make each networked printer available to all the PCs on the WLAN, which is cost effective as well as convenient. You can attach a printer to a specific computer or share it via a Wi-Fi print server. (If you have a high volume of print jobs, consider using a print server; otherwise the computer sharing the printer may slow down while other PCs are using its printer.)

If you have any wireless-ready, or wireless-capable entertainment devices, decide if you will include them on your network. Some home entertainment devices are Wi-Fi-ready, and others can connect after the addition of a wireless adapter. An example of this is a game console. You can connect all of the major game consoles (Xbox, PlayStation, and GameCube) to a WLAN with an adapter. There also are stereo and video components that can connect wirelessly to enable sharing of video and audio files.

If you have a PDA, you may be able to connect to your WLAN to synchronize your files, send e-mail, print, and surf the Web. Some PDAs are Wi-Fi-ready, while others require the addition of a card or adapter. Others may have Bluetooth connectivity built in, requiring you to purchase an adapter to wirelessly connect them to a PC. Research your options and the required hardware for connecting with your PDA.

If you have a broadband Internet connection, how will you share it? There are wireless routers available that you can use to share a cable or DSL connection, or you may have to connect a Wi-Fi access point to an Ethernet port on your existing router (see Figure 3-2).

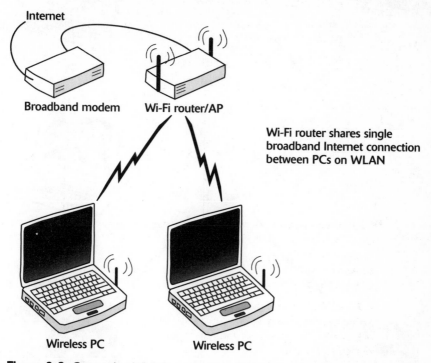

Figure 3-2: Connecting Wi-Fi to a broadband Internet connection.

Secret #20: Integrating Wireless with Ethernet

Perhaps you have a laptop that you want connected wirelessly, or maybe you don't want to run an Ethernet cable to connect your kid's Xbox for Internet gaming. If you have an existing Ethernet network you can easily add wireless connectivity for a few devices (see Figure 3-3). You also may want certain devices connected via Ethernet cable for the added security.

Many wireless access points have Ethernet ports that enable you to connect them to an existing wired network. You also can use these Ethernet ports when you initially configure an access point (AP), which is handy in case you make a mistake while configuring the AP and lose wireless connectivity.

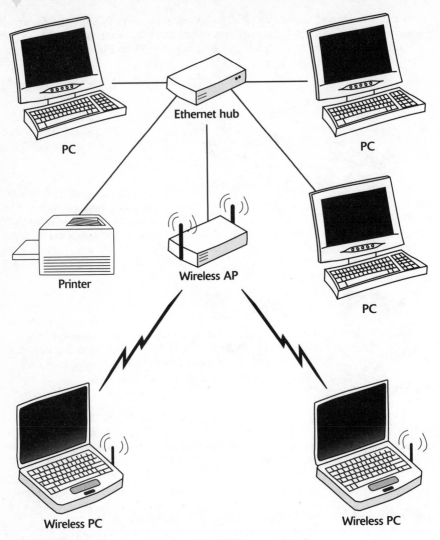

Figure 3-3: Integrating a WLAN with an Ethernet network.

Secret #21: Choosing a Standard

Careful planning in choosing which Wi-Fi standard your WLAN will be based on will help you avoid headaches and wasted money.

802.11b has been on the market the longest, and that means that there's a lot of 802.11b-compliant hardware on the market. Now that 802.11g and 802.11a have arrived on the scene, the prices on 802.11b hardware have fallen considerably. If you shop for 802.11b equipment, you are bound to find many bargains.

cross
ref   Refer to Chapter 1 for a review of the various standards.

In most WLANs, the likely throughput offered by 802.11b (6–7 Mbps) is plenty, so this may be the best way for you to go. If you feel that you need more speed in the future, you can get an 802.11g AP now and upgrade the wireless NICs to 802.11g in the future.

802.11g access points are backward-compatible with most 802.11b NICs, meaning that 802.11b devices work with an 802.11g AP, but only at their normal speed, not at the higher speed offered by the 802.11g standard. This enables you to purchase a faster AP and to upgrade cards to take advantage of the higher speed as you can afford it. However, the performance of some 802.11g APs suffers in a mixed 802.11b/g WLAN. If you take this route, your 802.11g equipment may not operate at full throughput when it shares an AP with 802.11b devices.

note   Some older 802.11b hardware may not interoperate with 802.11g hardware. Older 802.11b devices may not be upgradeable, or able to support new security standards (such as 802.11i or Wi-Fi Protected Access). Consider this if you decide to purchase older equipment and save money, or if you are combining components of an older network with new ones.

802.11g hardware is newer and costs more than devices based on 802.11b, but it supports higher throughput (typically not over 21 Mbps), and is more likely to support future firmware upgrades for security and performance. 802.11g operates in the same 2.4 GHz frequency range, so it is susceptible to the same interference as 802.11b devices.

802.11a has similar (or higher) throughput to 802.11g devices, but it is not compatible with either 802.11b or 802.11g equipment. 802.11a operates in the 5 GHz range and isn't as susceptible to the same interference as 802.11b or 802.11g devices. 802.11a works better than 802.11g in environments where there is a lot of network traffic; if your network is going to see heavy use by many users then you will see better performance with 802.11a compliant equipment.

However, the effective range of 802.11a tends to be less than 802.11b or 802.11g, so you may see performance drop unless you're close to the AP. This may require you to invest in more than one AP to provide coverage for your entire house or office.

cross   For more information about extending the range of your WLAN with multi-
ref   ple access points, see Chapter 6.

Secret #22: Planning for a Successful Network Layout

By carefully planning the physical layout of your WLAN, you will get the best performance and spend the least amount of money on equipment. Start with a rough sketch of the floor plan of your home or office where you are going to install your network (see Figure 3-4) and determine the area you want your WLAN to cover. Many manufacturers give an estimate for the range of the wireless signal, often over 300 ft. In reality, the effective range is shorter than that, often less than half as far in some environments.

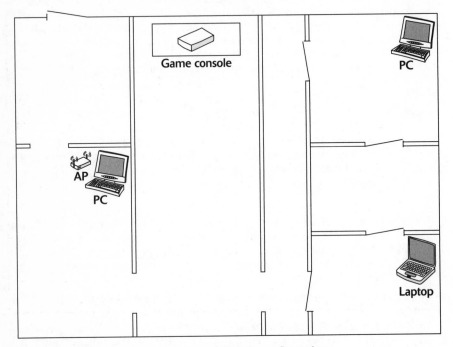

Figure 3-4: Planning coverage of your WLAN on a floor plan.

Many things can hamper or block the radio signal from an AP. These include construction materials, furniture, and in the case of a signal between buildings, naturally occurring objects such as trees and the topography of the surrounding area (see Figure 3-5). Some materials that weaken or block radio signals include

◆ Solid concrete walls, floors, and ceilings. Most homes are frame constructed, but some homes built on concrete pads may have concrete load-bearing walls in them that support the floors above. Contractors build many commercial buildings with concrete or concrete block.

◆ Stucco exterior walls. The metal mesh used as a base for many stucco exteriors can block or reduce the power of a radio signal. This works to your advantage when you are trying to keep the signal from extending outdoors too far, but if you want coverage by your pool you'll have to plan accordingly.

◆ Heavy furniture. Heavy bookcases or steel lockers and shelving can impede signal strength.

◆ Ducting for heating and air conditioning can weaken the signal.

◆ Heavy stone or brick fireplaces, particularly those built between rooms on an interior wall, can block radio signals.

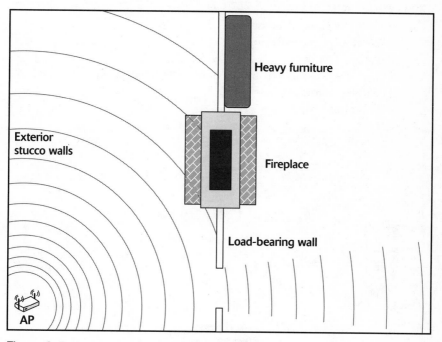

Figure 3-5: Construction materials affect coverage.

Position APs and client computers so that the environment poses as few obstacles as possible. Open thresholds between rooms and hollow interior walls allow the network signal to pass with minimum interference. Mounting an AP as high as possible also extends its signal a little further and prevents furniture and large appliances from blocking the signal.

If you are planning to cover more than one floor in a multi-level house and you notice a significant drop in signal strength on different floors, you may want to consider a new antenna for your AP, if that is an option with your model (see Secret #26, Selecting Antennas).

Secret #23: Planning Around Interference

Besides materials and objects that physically interfere with radio signals, there are sources of radio frequency (RF) signals that operate on the 2.4 GHz band and can interfere with the signal of your WLAN. This is because the 2.4 GHz band is "unlicensed" and manufacturers are free to develop wireless products that operate in this range (see Figure 3-6). Whether this interference is intermittent or regular, it can degrade performance to a point where you wonder why you even bothered to install Wi-Fi. Some sources of RF interference include:

- Cordless phones and headsets
- Wireless stereo speakers
- Walkie-talkies
- Wireless cameras (security or home monitoring type)
- Wireless intercom units
- Microwave ovens

Wireless cameras

Cordless phones

Walkie talkies

Wireless speakers

Microwave

Wireless intercom

Figure 3-6: Sources of RF interference in the home.

The easiest way to deal with this sort of interference is to avoid buying consumer electronics that share the same frequency with your WLAN. Manufacturers shield microwave ovens to prevent most signal leakage but the signal can even leak through the power cord at significant strength to cause problems. This should not pose a significant problem as long as you can plan to use the microwave around important network tasks (such as downloading large files). You also can position your APs to reduce the likelihood of the microwave causing problems

If you have a 2.4 GHz cordless phone, you may notice significant degradation in network performance whenever someone is talking on the phone. The typical cordless handset puts out over five times as much power as a wireless NIC. The same goes for wireless stereo speakers, walkie-talkies, and other devices; they all tend to put out significantly more power than Wi-Fi products.

If you already own a number of these devices, other than replacing all of them, your options are limited. If you haven't invested in your Wi-Fi gear yet, you can invest in 802.11a devices that operate in the 5 GHz frequency band. Electronic devices operating at 2.4 GHz won't interfere with 802.11a Wi-Fi gear.

Of course, even if you eliminate these sources of interference from your home, you may still run into occasional problems. If you live in an apartment, condominium, or townhouse, your neighbors may have one or more of these devices. The RF interference travels through walls and could be strong enough to cause problems. In this case, the best solution is a combination of diplomacy and experimenting with the positions of your clients and APs to minimize the disruption.

Selecting Hardware

After you've determined what you are going to network, which standard you are going to use, and where everything will be located, you can get down to the task of choosing the actual hardware that you will install to make your wireless dream a reality.

Secret #24: Selecting an Access Point

The central piece of hardware in your WLAN is the access point (AP). It sends and receives signals between clients on the network. The AP provides a central point of connectivity for all of the wireless clients and can interface with an Ethernet network or broadband Internet connection. In addition to providing connectivity to wireless NICs, the AP can provide other network services, usually supplied by a server or router in a large network. Some of the additional services that an AP may include are

   ◆ **Dynamic Host Configuration Protocol (DHCP) services**—DHCP automatically assigns Internet Protocol (IP) addresses to client computers as they connect to the WLAN. DHCP eliminates the need for you to manually configure each computer with a permanent IP address.

◆ **Router services**—Typically, an Internet Service Provider assigns a customer a single IP address. A router enables several users on the network to share a single broadband Internet connection. If your ISP uses a proprietary modem/router, you do not need this functionality in an AP.

◆ **Print server**—Some APs can act as a print server, and have one or more places to connect printers (both serial and USB ports), so that you can share the printers on the network. This is a nice option, but you also can get standalone wireless print servers that may cost less and won't degrade performance of your AP.

Look for an access point that is Wi-Fi compliant in the standard that you have chosen, and that is compatible with your operating system. Many APs also can operate in one or more modes: normal, client, bridging, and repeater (see Figure 3-7). Look for one that can operate in all of these; it will give you flexibility if you decide to extend or modify your WLAN in the future. The definition of each of these modes follows:

◆ **Normal mode**—The access point operates as a normal AP.

◆ **Client mode**—The AP operates as a network client (like an NIC) and does not communicate with NICs, just other APs.

◆ **Bridge mode**—The AP communicates directly with another AP capable of point-to-point bridging. Usually both APs must be the same model or from the same manufacturer. This is useful for extending a WLAN between buildings.

◆ **Repeater mode**—The AP repeats the signal from another access point, extending its range.

---

insider
insight
It is possible to create an ad hoc network between two or more wireless clients without using an AP, but the performance will be poor. Ad hoc connections are really only useful for connecting a couple of clients (like PDAs or laptops) for a quick file transfer.

There are dual-mode APs available that support both the 802.11a (5 GHz) and 802.11g (2.4 GHz) standards. These APs cost somewhat more than single mode devices, but give you greater flexibility when upgrading your network in the future.

Secret #25:   Choosing Wireless NICs and Adapters

For each client to be able to connect to and communicate on your WLAN, it has to have a wireless NIC or wireless interface adapter. Depending on the device you want to connect, adapters are either internal or external (see Figure 3-8).

◆ **USB wireless adapters**—attach to the USB port on any device and allow it to connect to the WLAN

◆ **PCI adapter cards**—connect via a PCI slot in your PC

◆ **PCMCIA card adapters**—fit into a PCMCIA slot on a laptop

◆ **Compact Flash (CF) card adapters**—fit in the CF slot on PDAs and similar devices

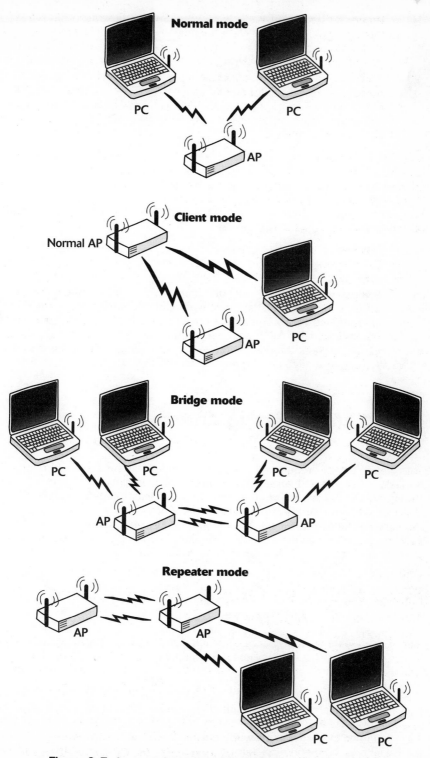

Figure 3-7: Access point modes of operation.

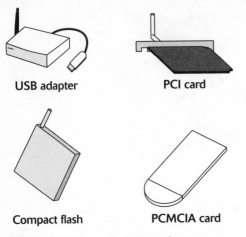

USB adapter   PCI card

Compact flash   PCMCIA card

Figure 3-8: Types of wireless adapters.

There are adapters available for just about every computer, printer, game console, and even some audiovisual equipment. When you're shopping for an adapter, make sure that it is compatible with your operating system, the device it's intended for, and your AP. It's good practice to select adapters produced by the manufacturer of your AP: it's more likely that they will interoperate without trouble. You can check the documentation for the device or visit the manufacturer's Web site to see which adapters are recommended.

Secret #26: Selecting Antennas

All wireless devices require an antenna of some sort to function. Although APs and adapters come with antennas, you may wish to install a third-party antenna to improve signal reception, or extend the broadcast range of a device. This isn't possible with all Wi-Fi devices, and even those devices that do allow for antenna upgrades often have proprietary connectors. Indoor Wi-Fi antennas range in price from $20 to over $100, depending on the type of antenna and its function. Antennas are either directional or omnidirectional (see Figure 3-9).

Directional antennas broadcast and receive in a single direction and are used for precise point-to-point transmission. This is useful when extending a network between buildings or in other design applications where having a signal broadcast in a single direction or tight beam is desirable.

Omnidirectional antennas broadcast the radio signal in all directions at once. This is useful for providing coverage indoors to specific rooms or floors of a building. Most APs and adapters come with omnidirectional antennas.

If you decide that you need to upgrade your antennas on either your cards or AP, you need to review the manufacturer's instructions and purchase a compatible antenna and connector. Many antennas require a *pigtail* connector. A pigtail is a length of cable with a connector on each end. For example, one end may have a connector to attach to a wireless NIC, and the other the appropriate connector for an indoor omnidirectional antenna.

Ceiling mount

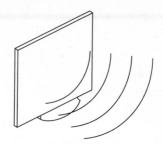

Flat panel

Omnidirectional

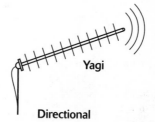

Yagi

Directional

Figure 3-9: Types of antennas.

On the Internet you can find plans for "home-brew" antennas made of everything from floppy disks to potato chip cans. Making an antenna and attaching it to a device is not for the faint of heart or the technical neophyte. If you decide to try this, you may damage your device and void your warranty.

> **cross ref**   I discuss antennas, connectors, and how they work in greater detail in Chapter 6.

> **on the web**   If you're interested in making your own antennas, consider visiting the following sites for more information.
>
> www.netscum.com/~clapp/wireless.html
>
> www.geocities.com/lincomatic/homebrewant.html
>
> www.turnpoint.net/wireless/cantennahowto.html

Secret #27: Choosing Cable/DSL Routers

To efficiently share an Internet connection between several computers, you need to have a router. As I mentioned earlier in this chapter, a router allows several computers to share a single IP address assigned by your ISP. If you have a broadband Internet connection, chances are that you received a modem or modem/router combo when you signed up. If you have a router, then you don't need an access point with this functionality.

If you don't have a router, you can use a wireless AP/router to share the Internet connection with wireless clients. Attach the AP to your modem with an Ethernet cable and configure the AP according to the manufacturer's instructions and you're ready to go (see Figure 3-10).

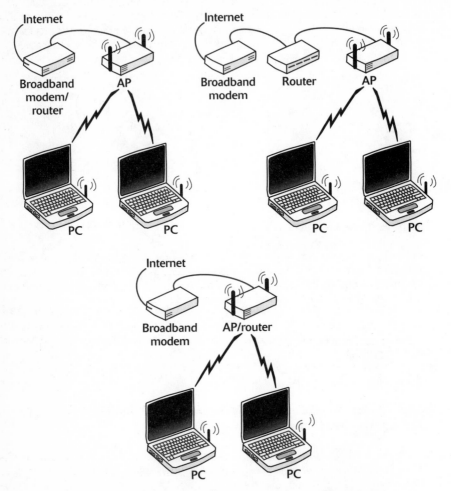

Figure 3-10: Possible configurations for sharing an Internet connection.

Secret #28: Selecting Wireless Print Servers

A wireless print server is an efficient way to share a printer among several wireless clients (see Figure 3-11). Although you can use an adapter to make each printer available on your WLAN, this can slow users down if there are a lot of clients using the same printer. A wireless print server can perform many of the same tasks that a PC acting as a print server previously did. Some Wi-Fi print servers have serial ports available for older printers that don't support Ethernet or USB connections (like my HP LaserJet 4L).

Wireless print servers range in price from $99 to $270, depending on the Wi-Fi standard, the features available, and the number of printers that can be connected to it at any one time. You also can use a PC as a print server, but if you don't have an extra PC, a wireless print server is more economical than purchasing a PC specifically for this task. If you decide to connect printers to a workstation and share them with other WLAN users, be aware that the workstation's performance may degrade while it is being used as a print server.

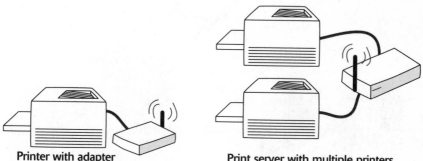

Printer with adapter   **Print server with multiple printers**

Figure 3-11: Wireless print servers.

Choosing Software

To set up a WLAN doesn't require much in the way of software. Any configuration software is included with your hardware. Windows XP also configures many Windows compatible NICs. However, in a pinch you can use software as a substitute for some hardware routers and access points.

Secret #29: Using a PC as a Software Access Point

A software access point (SAP) is a computer with a wireless NIC running software that enables it to function like an AP (see Figure 3-12). Software access points can be sophisticated and may duplicate many of the features of a hardware AP. A PC acting as an SAP may suffer performance degradation if there is a lot of network traffic, because more of the CPU's resources are required to handle the duties of the AP.

The PC used as an SAP must remain running and available or network clients will be unable to connect. If you are sharing an Internet connection, the computer acting as the SAP may have to run connection-sharing software (see the following section, "Secret #30: Sharing an Internet Connection via Software") to enable clients to connect to the Internet if the computer also is directly connected to the Internet. For best performance, a hardware AP is a better selection, but if you can't afford one or need a quick substitute, an SAP is a possibility. Even then, the PC running ICS software and sharing the Internet connection should be dedicated to that purpose for best performance.

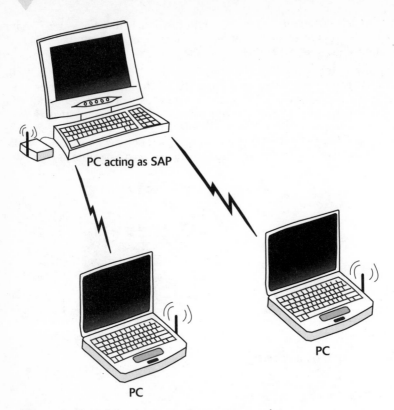

Figure 3-12: A PC acting as a software access point.

Secret #30: Sharing an Internet Connection via Software

To share an Internet connection, you can use connection-sharing software in place of a hardware router (see Figure 3-13). The software performs the same job as a router and enables multiple users to share a single Internet connection. The sophistication of connection-sharing software varies. Some solutions are very configurable, with many options. Others are simple with little opportunity for customization (or security).

Windows comes with basic Internet Connection Sharing (ICS) built in. ICS works, but isn't as efficient as many third-party software solutions. If you must use software to share your Internet connection, look into one of the many third-party solutions such as Sygate, Wingate, or WinProxy. Sharing an Internet connection via software requires that the computer sharing the connection is always on. If it crashes or if you turn it off, all of the clients lose their connection to the Internet.

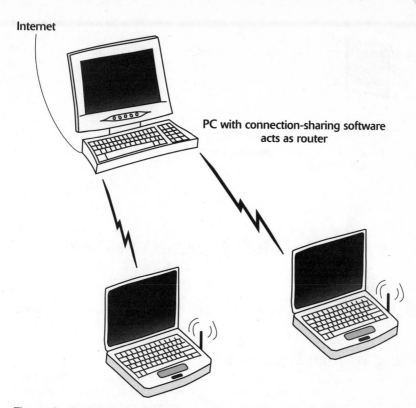

Internet

PC with connection-sharing software
acts as router

Figure 3-13: Sharing an Internet connection through connection-sharing software.

Secret #31: Protecting Your PCs with Personal Firewalls

A firewall protects your network from unauthorized trespassers. Many routers have firewall functions built in to check traffic leaving or entering the network, but you also should run a personal firewall on each client computer on the WLAN. Personal firewall software usually costs around $40 and it is often bundled with antivirus software.

A personal firewall is an application that runs on your computer and protects it against unauthorized access. Like a hardware firewall, it's configurable to allow or disallow different types of traffic to enter and leave your PC. Personal firewalls monitor *ports*, which are numbered software addresses that your computer uses for different networking tasks. For example, a Web server communicates through port 80, an e-mail server through port 25. Many of these ports aren't needed by your PC, and a good personal firewall closes or blocks unused or unneeded ports to prevent an intruder from accessing your computer through one of them.

A personal firewall also can monitor activity on your PC and alert you when an application attempts to reach the Internet or your WLAN. This is important because some worms and Trojan horse software attempt to use your computer to infect other computers, or to "phone home" to a cracker so that he can get into your computer. Personal firewalls are an effective way to protect individual computers on your WLAN.

note   I discuss firewalls in more detail in Chapter 15 and setting up a hardware firewall in Chapter 4. Appendix C includes a variety of vendors for personal firewall software.

Secret #32: Avoiding Common Mistakes

Keep in mind some of the following mistakes that people commonly make when designing a WLAN and you will save yourself the headache of repeating their errors.

Failing to Plan for Capacity

When you design your WLAN you can't just plan for coverage, you have to plan for capacity as well. If your WLAN is going to have a lot of traffic, you may want to consider multiple access points. Although many APs targeted toward home and SOHO networks can handle many simultaneous clients, the bandwidth available for each client shrinks as more clients join the network.

If your network is going to include wireless entertainment devices, such as media servers, set top boxes, and games consoles, you may see significant slowing of your network at peak usage. Consider adding additional APs to increase capacity where needed.

Neglecting to Make a Site Plan

Taking the time to make a site plan helps you avoid nasty surprises when you install your network. Failing to take the layout of a home or office and construction materials into consideration leads to "dead zones" where clients won't receive a signal, or where the signal is too weak for clients to connect.

Failing to Identify Potential Sources of RF Interference

Think ahead and plan around sources of interference. Identifying these sources in advance prevents problems from occurring during installation. This also helps you plan your budget accordingly should you have to replace devices that might interfere with your network (like cordless phones).

Ignoring Compatibility Issues

Do your research and make sure that all of the devices on your network are compatible, and support the same standard. Look for the Wi-Fi certification logo on WLAN products (see Chapter 1) to be sure that they will interoperate. Wi-Fi certified products are tested and proven compatible with other certified products for the same standard (i.e. 802.11a, 802.11b, 802.11g)

Do not mix and match standards unless you have an AP that supports multiple standards, such as a dual band 802.11a/802.11g device. Even then, be aware that some dual band devices suffer performance degradation when used in a multi-standard WLAN.

Putting It All Together

◆ ◆

Secrets in This Chapter

◆ ◆

Y ou've carefully planned your WLAN, researched all of your options, and now you've purchased the best equipment for your network. I'm sure you're ready to plug it all in and start surfing without wires. However, there are a few things you have to consider before you throw everything together and call it a WLAN.

The most important reference you have during this exercise is the documentation supplied by the manufacturer. This can be a little unsettling, considering how poorly-written most manufacturer-supplied documentation is. Too often, you may find that your biggest questions aren't answered or even acknowledged.

That's where this chapter comes into play. Because I can't take you step by step through the installation of every possible combination of hardware, I'll let your manual take care of the details and I'll address steps and concerns common to most installations.

> **note**
>
> I am assuming that you will set up your network in "Infrastructure mode" rather than "Ad Hoc mode." Infrastructure mode uses an access point to connect clients on the WLAN, while Ad Hoc mode does not. Infrastructure is efficient, supports a greater number of clients, and allows for easy sharing of services.
>
> I do not recommend Ad Hoc mode unless you are only networking a couple of computers in close proximity to one another. Ad Hoc mode is simple to set up and the documentation that came with your adapter will probably suffice to get you up and running.

Secret #33: Locating and Installing an AP

When you were planning your WLAN, you took the time to survey your home or office and choose the most effective location for your access point (AP). Because speed and efficiency of the connection drop off with distance and construction materials in your home reduce this even further, you need to make sure that your access point is located where you will get the most efficient coverage.

Mount your access point as high up on a wall as possible or on top of a high cabinet or shelf. This increases the distance that the radio signal from the access point can travel and improves reception for clients. However, if you are mounting your AP upon a wall, make sure that you can swivel the antenna to a vertical position. This is important because the antenna is the part of the AP that broadcasts the radio signal. Its position affects signal strength, range, and quality.

The signal from an omnidirectional antenna that comes with an AP, or one than is added afterward, tends to spread horizontally, and the signal geometry reduces on the vertical axis. This means you will reduce the signal strength if you mount your AP on a wall and leave the antenna in its original position (see Figure 4-1). If your AP has internal or fixed position antennas, mount it so that it remains in a level horizontal position, as if it were sitting on a shelf.

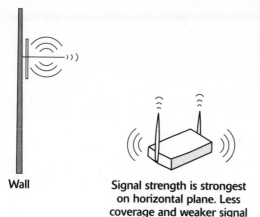

Wall   Signal strength is strongest
on horizontal plane. Less
coverage and weaker signal
vertically.

Figure 4-1: Antenna position and signal strength.

Of course, if you replace the antenna on your access point with a new antenna you can mount the antenna on a wall or ceiling instead of mounting the entire access point. However, this depends on the type of antenna that you selected and the maximum cable length between the access point and the antenna allowed by your equipment's manufacturer. Antennas are connected to an AP with a coaxial antenna cable, and the longer the cable, the less power will reach the antenna. This can reduce radio signal strength, preventing you from getting the best performance from the antenna. For more information about installing antennas and antenna cables see "Secret #36: Installing Antennas," later in this chapter.

Avoid mounting an AP flush against a wall or any other solid object. The wall or object will reflect the signal back onto the AP's antenna and create interference. Most Wi-Fi device manufacturers recommend that you leave at least 6 to 8 inches clear around an AP or antenna to avoid this problem.

If you are using multiple access points to cover a large house or office space, position the access points so that their signal propagation overlaps at the edges. This ensures that clients receive a good strong signal throughout the WLAN. This is especially important if you will be roaming, or moving through the WLAN space, such as with a Wi-Fi enabled PDA or a laptop.

You don't need to worry about choosing a location close to an electrical outlet for your access point. Many newer access points support Power over Ethernet (PoE). Using a PoE adapter, you can run current to your AP over an Ethernet cable. This is especially useful if you are connecting the AP to a broadband router to share an Internet connection.

In this case, you will only have to connect the router to the PoE adapter with an Ethernet cable and then run an Ethernet cable from the adapter to the access point. The access point will receive power as well as data over the Ethernet cable. This is possible because Ethernet cable has pairs of wires (4/5 and 7/8) that aren't used in data transmission. PoE equipment takes advantage of this to power Ethernet equipment. PoE adapters range in price from $30 to $60 and are available from most manufacturers of wireless gear.

Avoid mounting an access point or any antenna adjacent to an electrical outlet, conduit, or concentration of electrical lines. This includes your house's circuit breaker box or outlets in a utility room (often 220 V). While these sources of electrical radiation are normally very low frequency, around 50 HZ, I have seen them interfere with the operation of an access point (not with the signal, but with the operation of the device itself).

For best performance, keep the line-of-sight path between the AP and WLAN clients free of obstructions that might affect signal strength. Avoid placing the AP inside a cabinet or similar enclosed space.

Also, ensure that there is adequate space all around the access point to allow proper airflow to cool the unit. Make sure that the location you choose remains within the temperature and humidity ranges specified by the manufacturer. Don't place an AP where it will be in direct sunlight or adjacent to a heat source such as a furnace or heating vent.

Secret #34: Configuring an AP

Configuring an access point is a relatively simple task. Most manufacturers of Wi-Fi hardware have made an effort to keep this process uncomplicated and well within the abilities of the average computer user. In many cases it's easier to set up a wireless AP than it is to set up comparable Ethernet hardware.

You should collect some information before beginning. Having the following data handy will facilitate smooth installation of your access point:

♦ Your Internet Protocol (IP) address, supplied by your Internet Service Provider (ISP)

♦ Your Internet gateway address

♦ Your DNS server's IP address

♦ MAC address of your Ethernet card

♦ Any other networking information

You may not need all of this information during setup, but having it ready will save you the trouble of looking for it. If you are lucky, your ISP uses Dynamic Host Control Protocol (DHCP) (see the section titled "Internet Protocol Addresses" later in this chapter) and assigns all of this information dynamically, saving you a step during configuration. Your ISP supplies your DNS address; you can find your IP address and gateway in the networking control panel on your computer, or if your ISP is using DHCP you can discover your settings by doing the following in Windows:

1. Left-click the Start button on your taskbar.

2. In the Start menu, under Accessories select Command Prompt.

3. When the Command Prompt window launches, type **ipconfig -all** and press the Enter key.

4. The Command Prompt window will display your IP address, subnet mask, default gateway, DNS server, and your adapter's physical address (MAC address).

If you are using Mac OS X, you can find this information on the Network Screen.

cross ref I discuss and explain IP addresses in Chapter 5.

To facilitate setup and configuration, many APs have a Web-based configuration utility (see Figure 4-2). This means that once you have a wireless Network Interface Card (NIC) installed on your computer, you can connect to the access point through a Web browser (such as Internet Explorer) and configure it that way.

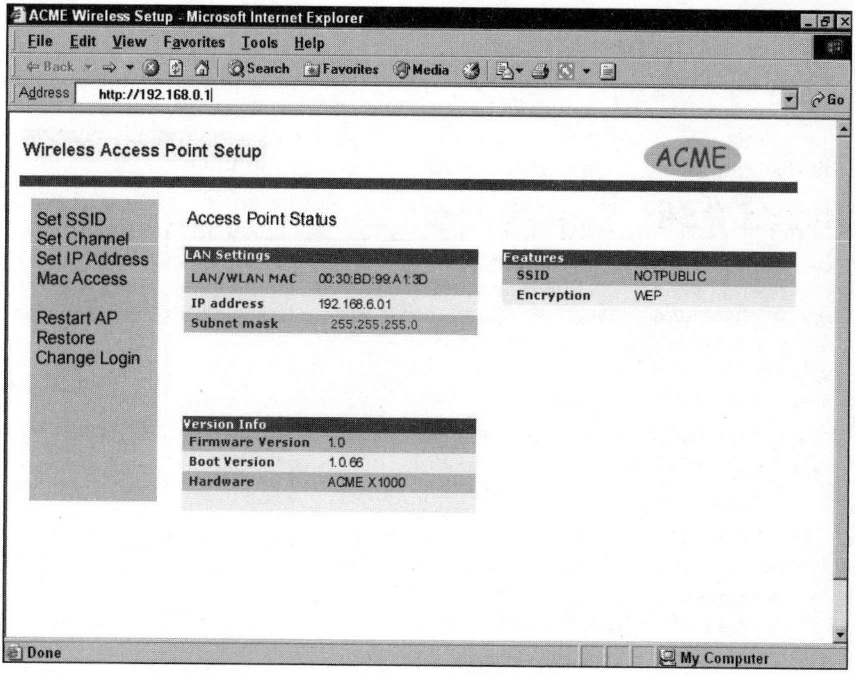

Figure 4-2: Web-based configuration of an access point.

note If your AP has an Ethernet port, it is advisable to connect the PC you will be using for configuration to it via an Ethernet cable. You can still use the Web-based configuration tool or manufacturer-supplied setup utility to connect; however, if you make a mistake during setup you can still communicate with the AP. If you aren't using an Ethernet cable during setup and you make a mistake, you will lose communication with your AP and most likely will have to reset the device and start over.

The setup process varies between manufacturers, so you have to consult the instructions that came with your particular AP. Generally, once you've plugged in the power and turned on the AP your wireless card should be able to "see" and communicate with it. To make this simple, manufacturers assign default settings to their APs. These settings include:

◆ The Service Set Identifier (SSID)
◆ IP address range
◆ Administrative username and password
◆ Radio Frequency channel

Service Set Identifier

The *SSID* is a name, up to 32 characters in length, used to identify a WLAN. The SSID is the network's name; this is useful for distinguishing WLANs operating in the same area. If your neighbors are also running a WLAN and you are in close proximity to them, you may end up accidentally connecting to each other's access points.

This is especially true if you are both using equipment from the same manufacturer and neither of you has changed the default SSID. The default SSID is unique to each manufacturer and makes it easy for you to quickly configure a card so that you can connect to the AP during configuration.

The default SSID can be used to identify the manufacturer of your AP. For example, most Linksys APs have "linksys" as the default SSID; some 3Com APs use "comcomcom." The default SSID is no secret; there are places on the Web where you can look up the default settings for just about every make and model of AP. When you are configuring your AP, remember to choose a unique name and change the SSID.

---

cross ref	To secure your network, you have to change the default SSID. I cover this in Chapter 15.

WLANs are composed of Basic Service Sets (BSS). A *BSS* is composed of an AP associated with one or more wireless devices that communicate through it. Multiple basic service sets can combine to form extended service sets (ESS). (You may hear the term *Extended Service Set Identifier [ESSID]* used in place of SSID.)

Internet Protocol Addresses

Many APs have router functions and are equipped with DHCP services (or you may have a standalone router with DHCP functions). To access the Internet, each client must have an IP address. DHCP automates this and assigns IP addresses to WLAN clients as they connect to the network. These dynamic addresses change each time the client connects to the WLAN, for instance after a reboot, or when you return home and reconnect your laptop to the network (see Figure 4-3).

With DHCP enabled, you don't have to assign a specific (static) address to each machine. DHCP assigns a random address within a specified address range. This is especially useful on large networks where users come and go a lot. ISPs use DHCP to assign dial-up users an IP address when they connect. After the user disconnects, the IP address can be recycled and assigned to another user.

Usually each AP has a static (unchanging) IP address assigned by default. For some units, DHCP assigns the IP. The AP also has a default *subnet,* or range of IP addresses available. If your unit has DHCP services, it assigns each client an address from this default range; if not, you have to do this manually.

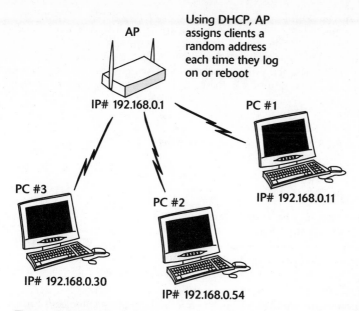

Figure 4-3: DHCP services.

In some instances you may wish to disable DHCP on your access point. This may be true if you have a broadband Internet connection with a router. In this case, the router may already have DHCP enabled and when you connect your AP to the router, the router will handle IP addresses for all of the devices on your WLAN. The same thing is true if you are connecting the access point to a wired local area network (LAN), which has a DHCP server.

---

cross ref

To secure your network, you have to change the default IP addresses and consider disabling DHCP. I cover this in Chapter 15.

I discuss and explain IP addresses further in Chapter 5.

If you have an IP address assigned by your ISP and you are using your AP as a router, you have to assign that IP address to the AP along with other information, such as gateway and subnet mask. Again, this depends on your particular setup, and your documentation and setup software generally leads you through this step-by-step.

Usernames, Passwords, and Encryption

Like SSIDs and IP addresses, your access point will have a default administrative username and password assigned at the factory. Even worse, some models have no password or user assigned. During configuration, choose a unique username and password for your AP. Don't leave the defaults in place, especially if they are blank.

If your AP supports it, and after you have completed the initial setup of your WLAN, enable encryption to protect your network traffic. Doing this after your WLAN is up and running will cause fewer problems than trying to do it during initial setup.

Contrary to what you might hear, with newer Wi-Fi equipment encryption does not cause noticeable slowing of most home networks, and it gives you an extra level of security. Although most Wi-Fi equipment supports Wired Equivalent Privacy (WEP) encryption, newer equipment supports the much stronger Wi-Fi Protected Access (WPA) encryption. Regardless of which type is available on your equipment, use it; encryption helps prevent accidental or casual connections to you network.

> **cross ref**   I discuss WEP, WPA, and encryption in Chapter 15

Radio Channel

Wi-Fi devices divide the frequency range they use into channels. For all of your Wi-Fi equipment to communicate, each Wi-Fi client adapter must be using the same channel as the AP that you want it to communicate with. When you set up your AP, you need to select a channel for it to use. If there are other APs operating on your network or on an adjacent WLAN (like your neighbor's), select a different channel for your AP.

Some access points automatically scan the available channels, looking for one that is free and that has the least interference. However, if this feature is not available you have to manually select the channel that your WLAN will use. This shouldn't be a problem. It's likely that you have most, if not all, of the channels available to you, and if you do experience problems you can try a different channel. Usually you can select a channel through the Web interface setup, but the user manual should also contain directions for doing this.

Secret #35: Setting Up Wireless Adapters and Network Interface Cards

For your client computers to connect to your WLAN, each of them must have a wireless adapter or wireless NIC. These adapters are small transceivers (radio transmitter/receivers) that allow your PC to send and receive radio signals. There are three main types of Wi-Fi adapters available for your WLAN: USB wireless adapters, wireless NICs, and PCMCIA cards.

A USB wireless adapter connects to your computer through its USB port. It is simple to install and enables you to adjust the location of the adapter to improve signal reception. You install a wireless NIC in a PCI slot within the computer, just like an Ethernet card; a wireless NIC installed within a computer saves desktop space. For a laptop computer, the best choice is a PCMCIA card adapter that fits in the laptop's PC card slot.

> **caution**   Always turn off the power to your computer when installing internal network adapters. You usually won't need to turn off the computer to insert PCMCIA cards or USB devices, but you may have to reboot to finish the installation.

Any time you open the case of a computer you need to take special care. Always turn off the power and unplug the cord. Don't force adapters into PCI slots, and be careful of dropping things like screws into the case. You also should wear an anti-static wrist strap to avoid damaging components with static electricity. See Chapter 17 for more information about protecting your computer from electrostatic discharge.

Wireless adapters have two modes of operation, *infrastructure* and *ad hoc* (as explained near the beginning of this chapter). This chapter assumes you will be using infrastructure mode and utilizing an access point. Installation of adapters is usually very simple. Once you install or connect the adapter to the client PC, Windows (assuming you are using Windows) usually recognizes the new hardware and prompts you to insert a disk with the appropriate drivers.

Even if you aren't using Windows, the configuration utility that comes with your adapter will lead you through the setup process and often automatically detects your access point and the channel that it is using. Manufacturers call the ability to automatically detect and select the channel *frequency-agility*.

Normally the software prompts you to select an SSID from a list of detected SSIDs. Assuming your AP is the only one in range, this will be a short list. You will then enter any other required information, such as encryption keys.

> **note**
>
> Windows XP has a feature called *Wireless Auto Configuration*. This is a useful feature if your wireless adapter supports it. Wireless Auto Configuration automatically configures your card to connect to a detected preferred network.
>
> This means that you can have several saved configurations (home, work, coffee shop, and so on) and Windows XP automatically configures your card to connect when it detects those networks. It also can prevent your computer from accidentally connecting with another network (like your neighbor's).

The software also may prompt you to select a data speed. This is the minimum speed required to connect to your WLAN. Usually your card performs this selection automatically, based on the signal strength that it detects. If your signal strength fluctuates you can set this speed manually to a signal level that your adapter can reliably detect. There also are good security reasons for setting a high minimum connection speed, and I discuss these in Chapter 15.

Adapter setup should be a relatively painless process. In the event that you do run into problems, review your documentation and visit the manufacturer's Web site for updates and helpful troubleshooting tips.

Secret #36: Installing Antennas

Chances are that you won't have to install any antennas for your access points or NICs. Most come with antennas already attached and ready to go. However, if you purchased external antennas to increase the performance of your WLAN, you have to properly attach and position these.

Whenever you purchase an antenna for an AP or NIC, make sure that it has a compatible connector. Manufacturers use different connectors, so the best way to find a compatible antenna is to purchase it from the manufacturer that produced your device. Some of the common types of connectors are N, RP-SMA, RP-TNC, Lucent, BNC, and MMCX. The documentation for your AP or NIC tells you which kind of connector you need.

insider
insight

Professionals no longer refer to connectors as male and female, because some connectors have reversed versions available, also known as *reversed gender*, and more often, reversed polarity (RP). Normally a male connector would have a center pin (like in coax cable for your cable TV box), and a female connector wouldn't. Reverse polarity connectors switch components between connectors, so a female connector might have the center pin from a male or vice-versa.

Plug and jack are the terms in use. The jack has no moving parts and the plug has active components such as a threaded rotating ring. Another way to distinguish the terms is to remember that the jack has the threaded rings on the outside of the barrel and the plug has the threaded rings on the inside of the barrel (see Figure 4-4).

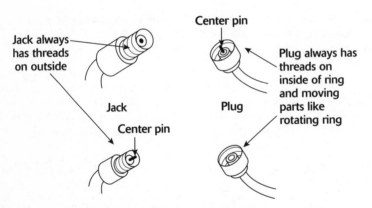

Figure 4-4: An example of a plug and a jack connector.

When you install an antenna, you also must check the maximum allowed cable length for the unit and antenna. A cable that's too long prevents the device from sending and receiving a radio signal. Different cables have different amounts of resistance to electrical current. Wi-Fi devices produce signals at varying strength, and some devices may not be able to operate with a longer cable because of the increased resistance. Do not exceed the maximum cable length listed in the documentation.

If you are installing an antenna outdoors, either to receive a signal from a fixed wireless service provider (WSP) or to extend the signal of your WLAN between buildings or to other parts of your property, you must take additional steps to protect your equipment.

The biggest threat comes from lightning strikes or damage from electrostatic discharge. You must properly ground an antenna, usually to the house's ground wire (see Figure 4-5). You have to do this in accordance with building codes, so check with your local government. If this isn't done you risk damage from lightning strikes and from static (and you'll probably void the warranty on some of your equipment).

caution Grounding an antenna through a house's electrical system is a job for a trained electrician or professional installer. I don't care how much of a do-it-yourself sort of person you are, if you attempt to ground your antenna this way and you make a mistake, you will ruin your equipment and possibly kill yourself.

Simply grounding an antenna to a ground rod isn't sufficient to protect the system. The charge at the ground rod won't be equal to the charge at the equipment end (access point) and you will most likely damage your equipment.

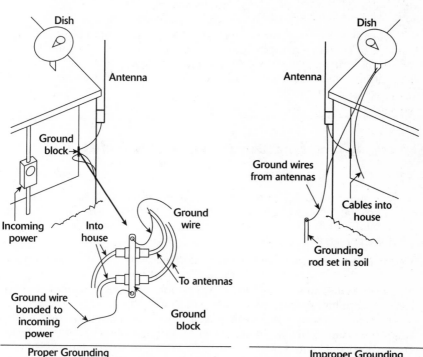

Proper Grounding   Improper Grounding

Figure 4-5: Grounding an outdoor antenna.

In an ungrounded system, a static electrical charge can build up from the atmosphere. This static charge can interfere with the WLAN signal and negatively affect the performance of your network. If you are experiencing static-related problems, you can manually ground the cable to discharge the static.

To discharge static on a cable, turn off power to the device and then disconnect the cable from it. Make sure that there is no power at either end of the cable, and then hold the cable in your hand and touch your thumb to the center pin. This discharges any static electrical charge through your body. You may then reattach the cable and restore power to the device (see Figure 4-6).

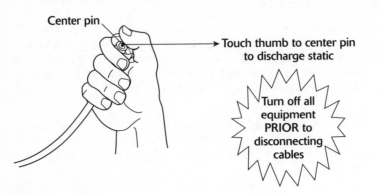

Figure 4-6: Discharging static from an antenna cable.

Besides grounding your antenna, you should install a lightning surge protector between the antenna and the equipment indoors. This operates much like the surge protector for your PC; if the current suddenly spikes, a fuse blows in the unit and interrupts the circuit, stopping the current from reaching your equipment.

Secret #37: Installing Network Printers

You can share printers on your WLAN in several different ways. Perhaps the easiest is to attach the printer to one of your WLAN client PCs and then share that printer with the rest of the network. Although this approach is simple, it has three potential drawbacks:

♦ The computer physically attached to the printer must remain turned on or other clients won't be able to use the printer.

♦ If clients print a lot of files, the performance of the computer sharing the printer may degrade (slow down or crash).

♦ If the printer is a multi-function device (printer, scanner, copier) and you connect it to a single computer, other clients may not be able to access all of its functions.

You also can make the printer available on a WLAN by adding a wireless adapter or connecting it to a wireless print server. You can usually configure wireless print servers and adapters the same way as an AP (which is what they essentially are)—using a Web browser interface or utility software provided by the manufacturer.

> note   If you are connecting an older printer or multi-function device through a wireless adapter or print server, be sure that it doesn't require proprietary software to operate. Often, software from older printers does not detect a network connection and may require that you connect the printer to the PC via a parallel port.
>
> Consult the documentation that came with the printer to determine if this is the case. This usually isn't a problem with newer printers, especially those designed with network support.

For specific instructions for sharing your printers, see "Secret #40: Setting Up Printer Sharing."

Configuring Software

Other than network settings for your AP and adapters, there isn't that much software that needs to be configured when you're setting up a WLAN. This section covers three types of software that you may have to configure.

Secret #38: Setting Up a Software Access Point

If you decided to use a software access point rather than a hardware AP, you have to set that up to get your WLAN up and running. The setup and installation depend on the SAP software that you have chosen and are different for every vendor. The parameters are similar to those required to set up a hardware AP and include:

- ◆ SSID
- ◆ Channel
- ◆ Encryption
- ◆ Network information

SAP software works by configuring your wireless adapter to act like an access point. Usually this means that the card handles radio functions, and the software handles most of the access point functions (routing, encryption, MAC address). Not all wireless adapters work with SAP software, so you have to make sure that you have a compatible adapter.

Because network adapters do not have the same power output as hardware access points, you may not be able to achieve the same speeds with an SAP that you would experience with a hardware AP.

Secret #39: Setting Up a Firewall

There are two types of firewalls, hardware and software. A software firewall resides on your machine, while a hardware firewall is a standalone device that connects to your network. Both do the same thing; they attempt to stop unauthorized traffic from entering or leaving your network or your PC.

This section provides instruction for setting up a personal firewall, which is a software application that you can use to protect your computer. In my opinion, even if you're running a hardware firewall on your network every computer you own should have a personal firewall installed. There are several on the market, including a couple that are free for home use.

While a hardware firewall is useful for protecting your network from threats that originate from the Internet, many threats originate within a WLAN, from wireless attacks or access points. A hardware firewall provides no protection against wireless intruders because these attacks originate on the wrong side of the firewall. This is why I stress the use of software firewalls to protect individual computers on your WLAN.

> **on the web** Zone Labs produces ZoneAlarm, one of the best personal firewalls available. ZoneAlarm costs $49.95 for a one-year subscription and you can download it at www.zonelabs.com.

Installation of a personal firewall is usually easy and is handled by an installer program or wizard. Exact installation instructions differ among firewall applications but there are a few common points that you should consider when installing any personal firewall.

1. Install a personal firewall after you have completed the setup of your WLAN. You want to be sure that everything is working properly before installing the firewall, so that you will know if subsequent problems are due to the firewall blocking connections or if there is a problem with the WLAN configuration.

2. Do not install more than one personal firewall on a computer. Running multiple firewalls does not make your computer more secure. The applications are likely to interfere with one another and crash your computer. They might also prevent each other from operating correctly, leaving your computer vulnerable.

3. Gather MAC and IP addresses from your WLAN clients before installing. Most personal firewalls install with a default setting that blocks all traffic from entering your computer. If you are sharing files or peripherals (printers), you need to tell your firewall which computers to let through. Depending on the firewall you are using, you need the IP or MAC addresses of computers that you want to allow to access your PC.

Personal firewalls are highly configurable, and many block outgoing as well as incoming unauthorized connections. You may find that your firewall is "noisy" at first. This means that you may see a lot of warnings and dialog boxes as each application tries to connect. Most firewalls quickly learn which of your applications should be allowed to connect to the Internet and which shouldn't. If you see a warning that a particular application has tried to access the Internet, do the following:

1. Determine what the application is. If you don't know what it is or what it does, look up the application's name through a Google search. Chances are you have a lot of spyware on your PC that you don't even know about. If you don't know what an application is, don't let it access the Internet.

2. If you know what the application is and what it does, and you feel comfortable letting it access the Internet, then configure your firewall to let it pass.

---

insider insight If you are running Windows XP then you already have a firewall on your computer. Windows XP comes equipped with the Internet Connection Firewall (ICF). ICF does a decent job of blocking incoming connections to your PC but does not block outgoing connections.

If you don't have a firewall installed, activate ICF. Microsoft provides detailed instructions for using ICF at `www.microsoft.com/windowsxp/pro/using/howto/networking/icf.asp`

Once you have installed your personal firewall, test it by visiting Gibson Research Corporation's "Shields Up!!" utility. Shields UP!! is an online utility that tests the effectiveness of your firewall.

---

on the web You can try Shields UP!! at `www.grc.com`.

Secret #40: Setting Up Printer Sharing

Once you've installed a printer, it's easy to share it. If you've decided to attach the printer to a WLAN client and share it that way, consult your operating system's help files for directions for sharing the printer. If you are using Windows XP, do the following to add a printer to the network:

1. Left-click the Start button; the Start menu will appear.
2. Left-click the Control Panel icon; the Control Panels folder will open.
3. Left-click the Printers and Other Hardware icon.
4. Under the Pick a Task heading, left-click Add Printer.
5. The Add Printer wizard will launch. Follow the steps to install a local printer attached to your machine.
6. During the printer install, you can choose to share the printer and assign it a network name.

If you want to share a printer that you've installed previously, open the Printers and Faxes control panel and do the following:

1. Right-click your printer's icon.
2. Choose Sharing.
3. Assign the printer a network name.

---

note   To share printers you need to have the File and Printer Sharing for Microsoft Networks network component installed. This component is usually installed and enabled by default. If you have disabled it you need to reactivate it before you can share a printer.

After the printer is shared or after it is available via a wireless print server or adapter, each client computer must install the remote printer to use it. For Windows clients, follow the procedure for installing a printer but select network printer instead of local printer in the Add Printer wizard. A list of available network printers will appear. Select the printer that you wish to install from the list. If Windows has a driver for the printer it installs it; otherwise, it will prompt you for a disk.

Troubleshooting Your WLAN

If you start to notice problems after you have your WLAN up and running, there could be a number of different causes. The problem could be due to RF interference, power outages, or configuration errors. Identifying problems on a WLAN can be frustrating for home users. Professionals have a number of high-tech tools available that can help them detect interference or analyze traffic on a network. These tools are very expensive and beyond the budget and technical expertise of most home users.

You also can use wireless sniffers like Netstumbler or Ethereal to help determine WLAN signal strength and detect RF interference. Sniffers also can detect if there are any nearby WLANs that might be affecting your network's performance.

Before you try to troubleshoot a problem, make sure that there really is one in the first place. If you think that something is affecting the speed of your WLAN, remember that in the real world you are likely to get actual throughput equal to less than half the advertised speed of your Wi-Fi gear. The speed drops off even further as you move clients away from your access point.

Try the following steps if you are experiencing problems with throughput:

◆ Try changing the channel on your access point. There may be interference or traffic on the channel you are currently using.
◆ Try relocating your access point or the clients.
◆ Check antenna connections and location.

If for some reason your access point or adapters stop working, check the following:

◆ Check to see that everything has power. It's easy to inadvertently unplug an AP.
◆ Make sure USB adapters are still connected to your USB port or hub.
◆ Check to make sure that none of the configurations has been changed.

Sometimes all you have to do is reboot equipment to get everything working again. Recently I was without power for about week, due to wildfires in Southern California. After the electric company restored the power, nothing wanted to work right. If you experience a loss of power, check the following:

◆ Check to see if your surge protectors have tripped. Often an electrical surge precedes a power outage.

◆ Check antenna connections for static charge. Use the technique outlined earlier in this chapter to discharge static.

◆ Make sure that no settings have changed or been erased.

In my case, my antenna connections and the cable between my satellite dish and router had built up a static charge that was interfering with the RF signals. When there is no power to any of your equipment, external antennas can collect a static charge. After a power outage you also can try turning all of your devices off and then rebooting them in this order:

1. Broadband router

2. Access points

3. WLAN clients (PCs, printers)

Sometimes all you need to do is to give everything a chance to reboot and the clients will recognize the access points.

Secret #41: Identifying RF Interference

If you suddenly start noticing problems with your network or you experience intermittent difficulty, RF interference may be affecting your WLAN. Identifying sources of RF interference isn't easy, especially if they originate from outside your home.

There are a number of things in your home that can cause interference. In Chapter 3 I identified the most common causes:

◆ Cordless phones

◆ Microwave ovens

◆ Wireless consumer electronics (speakers, cameras, walkie-talkies)

If you notice intermittent interference when one of these devices is in use, then it is probably the culprit. Another source of possible interference is an adjacent WLAN. If you suddenly start having problems with your network, check and see if there is another AP operating on the same channel.

You can use your adapter's configuration software to identify access points in the area. You also can use a wireless "sniffer" like NetStumbler to locate an AP interfering with your network. If there is another network interfering with your WLAN, try changing channels on your AP or moving it closer to your clients.

You also can try the diplomatic approach if you can figure out who is running the other WLAN. Perhaps you can work out a solution that allows both of your wireless networks to coexist peacefully.

insider
insight Make sure that all of your equipment uses the same 802.11x standard. This may seem like a silly thing to say, but it's not impossible for people to grab the wrong device at the store and not realize that they have an adapter operating at a different frequency than the rest of their equipment.

In addition, if you have an 802.11g access point and you are operating a mixed WLAN (that is, some adapters are 802.11g and others are 802.11b), you should be aware that some access points might slow down when supporting both standards simultaneously.

Secret #42: Configuration Errors

It's possible that software and hardware configuration errors could cause your network to behave erratically or not at all. Usually configuration errors prevent your devices from operating at all, but it's worth a review. If you have ruled out all other causes for your network trouble, try checking your AP and adapter settings and make sure that everyone is on the same page.

The following settings are common places you might find configuration errors:

♦ **SSID**—Often, when you are setting up several adapters or access points, you may forget to input the correct SSID or make a typo. Usually automatic configuration helps avoid this problem.

♦ **Wrong channel**—Check that all your equipment is set for the same channel.

♦ **Connection speed set too high**—If you set the connection speed manually, make sure that all of your clients can receive the signal at sufficient strength to connect at that speed.

♦ **IP addresses**— If you aren't using DHCP, make sure that you don't assign the same IP to two devices and that all of the gateway and subnet mask addresses are the same.

♦ **Antenna installation**—If you have added antennas to your equipment, make sure that the cables are not too long and that any directional antennas you have installed are facing in the right direction. You don't want to broadcast toward the kitchen when your clients are in the living room.

♦ **Adapters in wrong mode**—Make sure your adapters are in infrastructure mode. For example, if you change the adapter setting on your laptop to ad hoc mode so that you can connect with another laptop while you are away on business, make sure you change it back to infrastructure mode when you return home.

♦ **Adapter set for wrong network**—If you change the settings on your laptop's adapter to connect to another network, make sure you change them back when you return home.

Careful attention to detail will aid you in avoiding configuration errors. When you start to experience problems, check the obvious before you start looking for RF interference or outside problems.

Secret #43: Hardware Optimization Tips

There are ways to tweak software that can improve the performance of your network connections, especially your Internet connection. Because most of these adjustments are operating system- and vendor-specific, I can't review them all here. However, there are a few things that you can do that continually improve the performance of your hardware.

> **cross ref**
>
> I discuss broadband Internet connections and steps for optimizing them in Chapter 5.

The most important step you can take is to download driver and firmware updates. In fact, that's one of the first things that you should do after you set up your hardware. Visit the manufacturer's Web site and see if there are any updates available. Because your device has probably been in a warehouse or on a shelf for a while before you purchased it, chances are that there are updated drivers or firmware patches available that will improve the performance of your hardware.

> **insider insight**
>
> It's not hard, it's not soft, it's firmware. Firmware is software contained in programmable chips (EPROM, ROM, PROM) on a hardware device. These chips hold their software code even when there is no electrical current supplied to the device. An example of a firmware chip is the BIOS chip on your PC.
>
> Chips that contain firmware are programmable and can be *flashed* or programmed by users. Manufacturers can supply firmware upgrades as downloadable executable programs that improve the performance of their hardware. Firmware upgrades can extend the life cycle of hardware by adding new features or supporting new standards.
>
> An example of a future firmware enhancement to some Wi-Fi hardware is the new WPA encryption standard. Some existing hardware is upgradeable to the new standard through firmware upgrades.

You also should update your operating system. Microsoft makes regular updates to its operating systems and offers service packs or patches for users to download. Other vendors, including Apple Computer, do the same. These patches include updated drivers, system improvements, and security enhancements.

Depending on your Internet service and your hardware, there are changes you can make to settings that will speed up your Internet connection. Often this requires changing your computer's registry settings or your hardware's configuration. There are Web sites that offer utilities and instructions for improving performance, but unless you are very familiar with your operating system, I suggest that you don't mess with these settings.

caution

> If you decide to alter your registry settings, make sure that you back up your registry before you make any changes. This way, in the event the changes cause problems, you can restore your old registry settings.

Connecting
to the Internet

◆ ◆

Secrets in This Chapter

◆ ◆

haring an Internet connection is the number one reason that most people network their computers. It used to be printer sharing, which is still a close second, but with broadband Internet connections becoming more common, more people want to make the Internet available on every computer in their house.

Sharing an Internet connection isn't difficult. Depending on the type of Internet connection you have and how your home network is set up, there are a number of ways that you can do this. There are different services available, and understanding the differences will help you make an informed choice (if you actually have a choice).

Secret #44: Broadband Choices

The term *broadband* refers to the ability to transmit more data at higher speeds than was previously possible. There are several types of broadband Internet connections available for home users: cable, digital subscriber lines (DSL), wireless, and satellite. What type of service is available depends largely on your geographic location. In general, the further you are from urban areas, the fewer choices you have.

There are differences in performance and speed among the different types of service available. Even users of the same type of broadband can see a difference in performance based on their equipment, choice of ISP, and geographic location. The actual speed of broadband varies as well. When we talk about speed, we are actually talking about capacity and latency. (I discuss latency in "Secret #51: Network Requirements for Gaming," later in this chapter.)

The *capacity* of a connection is the total amount of data that a connection can accommodate at one time. For example, a connection that advertises 1 Mbps (megabits per second) has a maximum transfer *capacity* of 1 Mbps, not a speed of 1 Mbps. This means that the connection can never transfer more than 1 megabit of data during any one second of time.

When computer products and marketers advertise speed, they are really advertising capacity. Understanding the factors that affect broadband performance as well as the capabilities of different types of broadband helps you make smart choices and reduces your frustration level.

Cable

Cable is a popular choice for broadband Internet. It's much faster than dial-up, with advertised download speeds of up to 1 Mbps, and its price is usually reasonable when compared to other broadband options that range from $30 to $80 per month. The drawback is that cable Internet is not available everywhere because it is limited to areas serviced by cable companies that have made the necessary upgrades to their networks to support Internet service.

Cable television providers can deliver Internet over the same lines as your cable television signal because of the way they divide the signal. Cable companies broadcast their signals across a very wide-frequency band. The signal travels over a Hybrid Fiber Coaxial (HFC) network from the cable company's "headend" or distribution center to your home (see Figure 5-1).

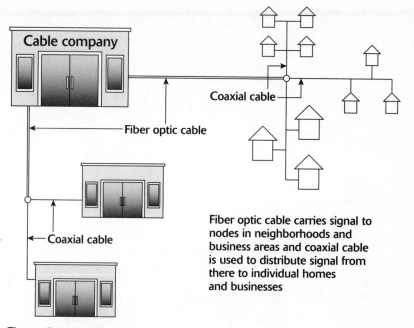

Fiber optic cable carries signal to nodes in neighborhoods and business areas and coaxial cable is used to distribute signal from there to individual homes and businesses

Figure 5-1: An HFC network.

Cable companies divide the total frequency band into channels by assigning each channel a small portion of the available bandwidth. They assign 6 MHz of the total signal for each television channel. The cable network can carry hundreds of 6 MHz channels. Usually, they assign one or more channels for the downstream data of Internet service (see Figure 5-2).

Cable channels

Cable channels	
Channel 100	⎯ 649.25 MHz 6 MHz
	⎯ 655.25 MHz
Channel 101	
	⎯ 661.25 MHz
Channel 102	
	⎯ 667.25 MHz
Channel 103	
	⎯ 673.25 MHz

Each cable channel is assigned a 6 MHz frequency band

Figure 5-2: Cable channels.

Cable Internet service providers install a device called a Cable Modem Termination System (CMTS) at the headend of their network. A CMTS interfaces with an Internet Service Provider (ISP) and encodes Internet data into an MPEG video signal carried in the cable company's broadcast stream. The CMTS also separates data received from customers' cable modems from the cable network and passes it on to an ISP.

At your end of the network sits your cable modem. The cable modem receives the signal transmitted over the cable line and decodes it into data packets recognizable by your computer. The cable modem usually connects to your computer via a standard Ethernet cable, although some modems can connect via a USB port. You may also be able to connect your cable modem to a wireless AP via an Ethernet cable, but some cable modems must be connected directly to a computer. Your modem also translates data traffic from your computer into an MPEG signal for transmission over the cable line on a specific channel. Put simply, the cable modem enables your computer to "talk" to the CMTS over the cable lines (see Figure 5-3).

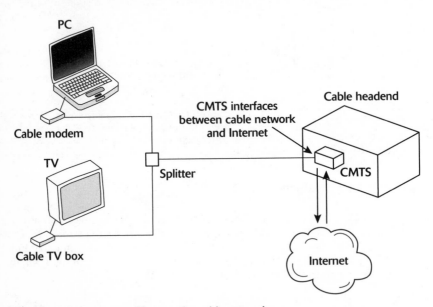

Figure 5-3: Internet traffic over the cable network.

The major drawback of a broadband cable connection is that all cable customers on a section of the network are sharing the same channel. As more people in your neighborhood sign up for cable Internet service, you will see your connection speed drop, especially at peak usage times. This is because more and more users are dividing the total capacity (often up to 30 Mbps) amongst themselves, which leaves less bandwidth for each individual customer.

Most cable Internet providers also limit the upstream data capacity to an amount significantly less than the advertised downstream rate, which is often less than 256 Kbps. For most users, this isn't an issue. Web surfing and e-mail require very little upstream bandwidth. When you view a Web page, most of the data travels from the Web server to your computer, not the reverse. Cable providers limit the upstream rate to prevent users from abusing the service by running Web servers from their homes. A Web server uses considerably more upstream bandwidth because it sends data to browsers when it serves Web pages.

Digital Subscriber Lines

Digital Subscriber Line (DSL) Internet services are broadband cable's chief competitors. DSL service operates over the same copper wires that bring phone service into your home. Because service isn't limited to areas where cable is installed, DSL service is potentially available to more households. However, there are limits to the technology that restrict its use to within a predetermined distance from a telephone company office or switch.

There are many types of DSL technology; the most common type available to consumers is Asymmetric DSL (ADSL). The connection is asymmetric because ADSL provides greater capacity for download than for upload. Symmetric versions of DSL do provide high capacity in both directions, but these are expensive and usually reserved for businesses.

Copper telephone wires are capable of carrying a lot more than the signal frequency used for voice phone calls. The DSL signal can share the same line as your telephone service because the phone company transmits the data signal at a much higher frequency than your telephone's analog voice signal.

Phone companies usually give their DSL customers low-pass filters to install on all the phone jacks that they aren't using for DSL service. These filters block all of the high-frequency DSL signals, which allows only the low frequencies used for voice calls to get through. This prevents interference on your voice calls.

Your phone company has to install special equipment at its telephone exchange and in your home to isolate voice and data signals from one another. At the telephone exchange, they install a device called a *DSL Access Multiplexer* (DSLAM). In your home, they install a DSL modem, which is actually a transceiver that transmits and receives high-frequency DSL signals (see Figure 5-4).

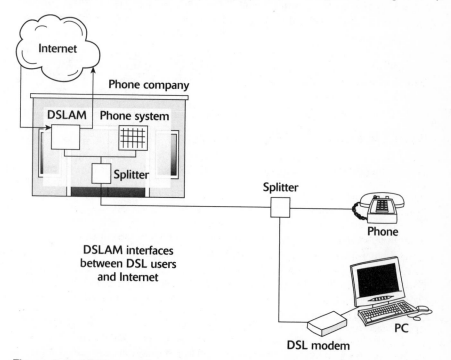

Figure 5-4: A DSL network.

The DSLAM intermixes and separates voice and data signals on your DSL line. The DSLAM also provides a connection point between DSL subscribers and the Internet. Unlike the CMTS on a cable network, the DSLAM provides a dedicated connection for each subscriber. Because of this, DSL subscribers don't experience a slowdown in service when multiple users are online. If the number of subscribers approaches the maximum capacity for a DSLAM unit, the phone company can upgrade or install additional DSLAMs.

In your home, the DSL modem separates the DSL signal from the voice signal on your phone line and converts it to data that your computer can understand. It also does the reverse by converting data into a DSL signal and transmitting it back to the DSLAM.

It may sound like DSL is the perfect broadband solution, and for some customers, it is. Unfortunately, there are limits to DSL technology that exclude millions of potential subscribers from using it. The major factor limiting DSL coverage is distance. DSL service is typically only available to customers less than 18,000 feet from a telephone exchange with a DSLAM. Often, this distance is less than 15,000 feet.

Part of the reason for this is that the telephone system uses Direct Current (DC) electricity to transmit its signals rather than the Alternating Current (AC) electricity that comes out of the outlets in your house. DC power can't travel as far as AC power. This is why the electrical company uses AC, even though it is far more dangerous than DC. If they used DC, they would have to have more power plants and transmission sites to carry the power to all of their customers.

Phone companies use DC to carry their signals because it introduces less signal noise onto the line than alternating current. Using DC also enables the phone company to store power in batteries and supply the phone system with a steady and quiet source of power even during a blackout.

Because DC has a short range, the phone company increases range by using devices called loading coils, as well as amplifiers and bridge taps. A DSL signal cannot travel through these devices so any customers with loading coils between their home and the telephone exchange cannot receive DSL service.

In some cases, DSL can provide a very fast alternative to cable, especially if the customer is close to the telephone exchange. Because the signal strength grows weaker as it gets further from the telephone exchange, customers at the limit of DSL's range experience significantly slower speeds. Depending on your geographic location and the carriers available, DSL service can range in price from $30 per month to over $50.

Wireless

Wouldn't it be great to have a high-speed wireless alternative to cable and DSL? It sure would, and, because this book is about wireless, it would be great if I could recommend a particular service. At this point, any wireless broadband service alternative would be great, but wireless broadband so far remains mostly hype.

---

note   Technically, satellite Internet access is wireless broadband, but what I'm referring to here are terrestrial technologies that don't use satellites to broadcast their signals.

A few startups are trying to bring "last mile" wireless broadband connections to residential users, but real solutions are at least a year away. Early attempts by industry leaders, including Sprint and AT&T, were failures: both companies abandoned their wireless broadband services.

Part of the problem was that the first generations of wireless broadband services were line-of-sight (LOS). These LOS services required that all customers have a directional antenna aimed precisely at the ISP's transmission tower (see Figure 5-5). The setup costs were enormous, and many customers simply had no LOS to the tower. Adding to the cost was the problem of scalability. When a tower reached its capacity, ISPs had to install additional towers. When the ISP moved customers to the new tower, they had to have their equipment realigned.

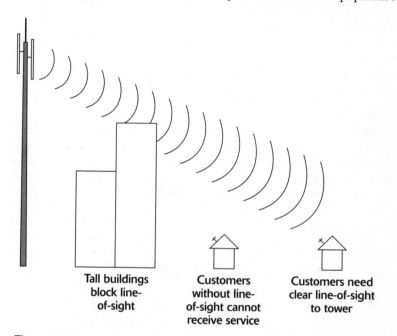

| Tall buildings block line-of-sight | Customers without line-of-sight cannot receive service | Customers need clear line-of-sight to tower |

Figure 5-5: Line-of-site wireless broadband.

New technologies are non-line-of-sight (NLOS), and they don't require that users have a clear LOS to their ISP (see Figure 5-6). There are several technologies competing to provide this service, but the IEEE 802.16 (WiMax) is starting to gain support from developers and manufacturers.

For now, residential wireless broadband Internet access isn't available in most areas, but you may see reasonably priced wireless ISPs emerge within the next couple of years.

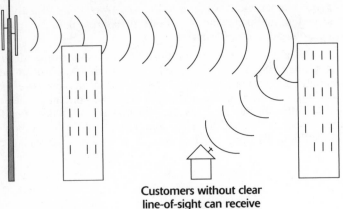

Customers without clear
line-of-sight can receive
reflected signals

Figure 5-6: Non-line-of-sight wireless broadband.

Satellite

If you live in an area where you are unable to get cable or DSL Internet service, and dial-up is just too slow for you, you have one alternative. You can sign up with a Satellite ISP. With a satellite dish, you can access the Internet at much higher speeds than with a dial-up modem. There are two types of service: two-way satellite service and one-way (also known as *satellite-return*). You must have a clear LOS to the southern sky—where the satellite orbits—to use either system.

Satellite-return service uses a modem to send upstream data, like page requests, to the satellite ISP's network operation center (NOC) and a satellite dish to receive downstream data (see Figure 5-7). This works out surprisingly well because most of the data flows downstream when you surf the Web. The draw-back is that this service isn't an always-on connection because you still have to tie up a phone line and dial-in. The upload speed also is slow because of the dial-up connection.

A two-way satellite connection uses the satellite dish to transmit and receive via a satellite (see Figure 5-8). Because data flows both ways via the satellite con-nection, the connection is always on, and the upstream speed is much greater than dial-up.

A satellite connection works surprisingly well; the big drawback is in the latency of the connection or how long it takes data to make a round trip. It takes much longer for a signal to travel to and from its destination via a satellite in orbit than it does to travel over a cable or DSL wire. Because of the latency issue, satellite connections do not work for Internet gaming, and you may not see much improvement in Web browsing over dial-up speeds. However, large files download much faster, often in excess of 500 Kbps.

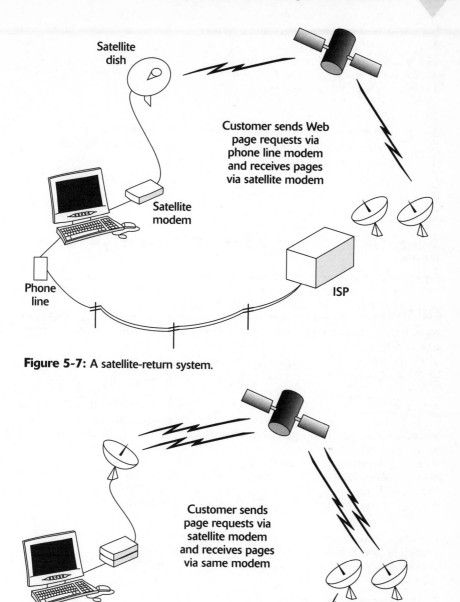

Figure 5-7: A satellite-return system.

Figure 5-8: A two-way satellite system.

The initial investment for a satellite system can be steep. It sometimes costs almost $800 with installation. The service itself can cost over $70 a month. You can't install a two-way system yourself; it must be precisely aligned with the satellite and properly grounded. If you live in an area where you can't get DSL or cable and want broadband access, consider trying satellite.

on the web	Interested in satellite broadband? The two main providers of satellite Internet service for home users are Direcway and StarBand. You can visit them on the Web at www.direcway.com or www.starband.com.

Secret #45: Sharing Dial-up Connections

If you don't have or can't get broadband Internet access, you can still share your Internet connection on your WLAN, but I wouldn't advise it. Even a good dial-up connection is slow, and, with more than one user online, it slows to a crawl. If you still want to make a dial-up connection available to the rest of the network, read on.

To share a dial-up connection, you can install connection-sharing software or use Internet Connection Sharing (ICS) that comes with Windows. ICS is functional and works reasonably well, but third-party software is often more configurable and efficient. Connection-sharing software essentially acts as a router and performs network address translation (NAT), which routes all IP traffic from the Internet to the appropriate computer on your WLAN (see Figure 5-9).

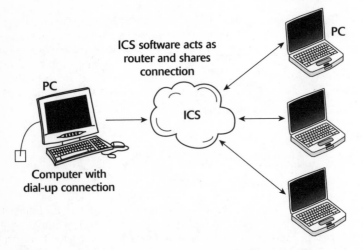

Figure 5-9: Using ICS to share a dial-up Internet connection.

After installing the connection-sharing software, you choose the connection that you wish to share (consult the software documentation) and configure network clients to connect to that computer for Internet access. The details of this depend on the software you are using as well as the type of AP that you have installed on your WLAN.

---

on the web	**Microsoft has instructions for using ICS at** `http://www.microsoft.com/ windowsxp/home/using/howto/homenet/ics.asp`.

Remember, for other computers to be able to connect to the Internet, the computer with the dial-up connection must remained dialed in and turned on.

Secret #46: Bandwidth and Access Policies

Depending on the ISP that you use for your broadband Internet connection, you may be subject to limitations on your bandwidth usage and connection speed. This varies among ISPs as well as types of connection.

Most DSL subscribers do not run into bandwidth limiting policies. Because DSL users have dedicated connections, they don't face the same problem as cable customers on crowded networks.

However, your DSL or cable ISP may place limits on upstream bandwidth and specifically prohibit your running a Web, file, or game server. This has become more of an issue as peer-to-peer file sharing networks become more popular. They also may place restrictions on customers reselling service or providing service to an entire network with a single subscriber account.

If you have a satellite Internet connection or connect through a campus network, you may be subject to a fair access policy. A *fair access policy* limits the amount of bandwidth any user may use in a given period. When a user exceeds their allotted amount of bandwidth, the ISP may restrict his usage for a short time. Activities like normal Web surfing use little bandwidth and are unlikely to exceed fair access limits. The bandwidth thresholds for a fair access policy vary between ISPs so you should examine your contract carefully.

Secret #47: Choosing How to Share the Connection

Like a dial-up connection, you can share a broadband connection via Internet connection-sharing software. However, this creates a bottleneck when WLAN clients try to access the Internet through the host computer. It's more efficient to share a connection through a broadband router connected to an AP or through an AP that had built-in broadband router functionality (see Figure 5-10).

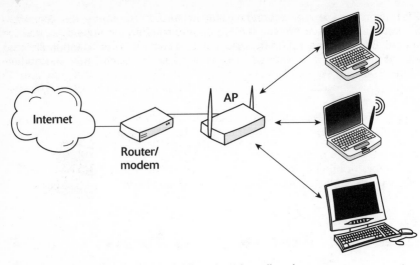

Figure 5-10: Using a router and AP to share broadband access.

The type of broadband modem that you have also affects how you share your Internet connection. The best type of modem is one that connects to your computer via a standard Cat5 Ethernet cable. With this type of modem, it's easy to share your connection simply by plugging the Ethernet cable into a router or AP/router.

Some cable and DSL ISPs have started providing their customers with modems that connect to a PC via a USB port. This is in their interest because a USB modem makes sharing your Internet connection more difficult. If you have a USB modem, you have to share your connection through Internet connection-sharing software or find a router that accepts a USB connection from the modem. There aren't many routers that work with USB modems, but manufacturers are beginning to catch on to the trend, and more should start appearing on the market shortly.

The newest hardware that is starting to appear on shelves combines the functions of a cable modem, router, and wireless AP all in one device. Obviously, if you have a WLAN and subscribe to a cable ISP, this would be a perfect piece of hardware for you.

Secret #48: Understanding Internet Protocol Addresses

Now it's time for your crash course in Internet Protocol. This is a brief, simplified introduction to what IP is and how your network and the Internet use it to function.

IP is part of the TCP/IP suite of protocols that have become the global standard for Internet communications. The TCP/IP protocol contains dozens of protocols, but the name refers to two of the most important—the *Transmission Control Protocol* (TCP) and the *Internet Protocol* (IP). The IP protocol provides addressing that makes TCP/IP communications routable. This means that all messages transmitted over a TCP/IP network are marked with the IP address of the destination network and station.

TCP/IP networks use a technology called *packet switching*. On a packet-switched network, computers divide data into smaller, individually addressed packets. Because each of these data packets contains a destination address, they can be switched or follow different paths to reach their destination. Contrast this with a circuit-switched network, like the telephone system, in which communications require a dedicated point-to-point connection (see Figure 5-11).

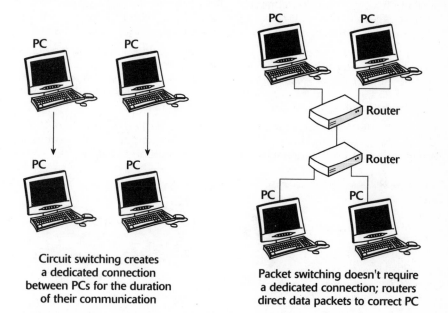

Circuit switching creates a dedicated connection between PCs for the duration of their communication

Packet switching doesn't require a dedicated connection; routers direct data packets to correct PC

Figure 5-11: Packet switching versus circuit switching.

A packet-switched network uses network bandwidth more efficiently because users can share bandwidth, all of them sending their packets at the same time. Routers direct each of the individually addressed packets to its proper destination, where the destination computer reassembles the packets into the original message. IP packets don't have to reach their destination in the proper order; each packet contains sequencing information in its address header.

Because of the way data travels over the Internet, each computer must have a unique IP address. An IP address is four sets of numbers separated by decimals. For example, your IP address may look something like this, 66.82.9.47.

IP addresses are divided into classes. Class A addresses start with a number range of 1–126. Class B addresses start with a number range of 128–191. Class C addresses start with a range of numbers from 192–223. (Don't worry about remembering this; it's just nice to know. There won't be a test later.)

The following address ranges are reserved for intranet (internal) addresses, which are used on internal networks like your WLAN. These address ranges aren't routable over the Internet.

♦ 10.0.0.0 to 10.255.255.255
♦ 172.16.0.0 to 172.31.255.255
♦ 192.168.0.0 to 192.168.255.255

To configure a network connection, you need to know three addresses:

- ◆ Your IP address
- ◆ Subnet mask
- ◆ Default gateway

Your IP address is the address of your computer and is assigned to you by your ISP. Technically, this is the address of your modem. When you share the connection on your network, your router gives you an intranet address. Your IP address can be permanent, or your ISP can dynamically reassign it each time you reboot or reconnect (using DHCP). An example IP address is 10.4.38.171.

Your subnet mask represents the portion of the IP address range that refers to subnet addresses. An ISP can divide its assigned IP address range into subnets. In this subnet mask example, 255.255.255.0, the first three numbers (255.255.255) represent the part of the IP address range that identifies subnets, and the last number (0) identifies hosts on that subnet.

This means that, with the example IP address 10.4.38.171, the numbers 10.4.38 identify the subnet. The number 171 identifies my computer on that subnet. A computer with the IP address 10.4.37.171 is on a different subnet (see Figure 5-12).

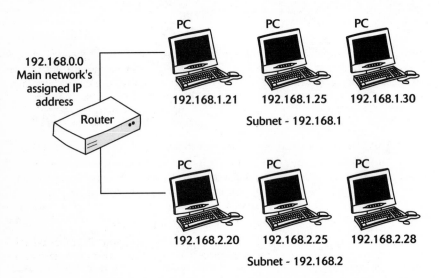

192.168.0.0
Main network's
assigned IP
address

Router

PC — 192.168.1.21 PC — 192.168.1.25 PC — 192.168.1.30
Subnet - 192.168.1

PC — 192.168.2.20 PC — 192.168.2.25 PC — 192.168.2.28
Subnet - 192.168.2

In this case, PCs on the same subnet share the same 3rd digit

Figure 5-12: Subnets.

The default gateway, for example, 66.82.157.37, is the address of the computer or router that you use to connect to the Internet. In most cases, your ISP provides you with the addresses you need to connect to its network, or a DHCP server assigns them automatically.

If you noticed that the IP address given in the example above is an intranet address, good job. You've scored extra points. Some broadband ISPs assign their customers intranet addresses and then have them connect to the Internet via router or server. This conserves public, routable IP addresses and provides some additional security.

Because the intranet address is not routable, the ISP must perform Network Address Translation (NAT). Using NAT, several customers share the same publicly visible IP address that the server assigns. The result is that the address is not unique to your computer.

This adds a layer of security because people outside the ISP's network cannot send traffic to your machine unless you request it. It also can wreak havoc with services that need to know the exact IP address of your machine, such as VPN.

Secret #49: Configuring a Router

Setting up a broadband router for your WLAN is easy. Most consumer hardware comes with configuration software or *wizards* that get you up and running in minutes. The process differs among manufacturers, but here are some common steps:

- ◆ Record your IP addresses (IP, subnet mask, and default gateway) and any other settings required by your ISP.
- ◆ Turn off the power to all of your hardware (modem, PC, and so on).
- ◆ Disconnect the modem from your PC, and connect it to your router (usually via an Ethernet cable).
- ◆ Connect the router to your AP with an Ethernet cable (unless, of course, your router is an AP).
- ◆ Turn on your modem, your PC, and then your router.
- ◆ To log into the router and run the setup software, your PC must be set up to acquire an IP address automatically (consult your OS documentation or help files).

When you run the setup software, it may prompt you for your Internet setup information; this is why you wrote it all down before you started. If you're lucky, your router will automatically connect with your modem and retrieve these settings for itself.

Because the setup is different for each make and model of router, make sure that you carefully review the instructions for your device before you start.

Secret #50: Configuring Networked Computers

Once your router is up and running, you need to configure your computers so that they can communicate with it. Chances are that your router has DHCP, so all you need to do is set each PC to acquire its IP addresses automatically and, voilà, you're on the Net.

If you don't have DHCP, you have to manually assign an IP address to each client. You need to determine the IP address range used by the router by using its configuration software, and you can then pick an IP address that falls in this range for each computer on your network.

> note
>
> If you are having problems connecting with Internet Explorer, make sure that you have it set up to use a LAN connection and that it's configured to automatically detect settings. You can find these options under the Internet Options menu item on the Connections tab.

You can configure your clients to improve Internet performance. Some Web sites that offer tips and tools for speeding up your Internet connections include:

◆ www.broadbandreports.com—This site offers reviews, tips, and user forums for broadband Internet, including satellite systems.

◆ www.speedguide.net—This site focuses on system performance and is geared towards a technically astute audience. There are useful tips and tools available here, but, if you're a novice, be careful and make sure you understand what you are doing before you attempt any of the tweaks.

◆ www.thedslzone.com—This site focuses on DSL and includes system tweaks and reviews.

◆ www.tweak3d.net—"Your freakin' tweakin' source" for hardware and software tweaks and reviews.

Remember to back up your system and registry often if you decide to test any of the tweaks available online.

Gaming with Your WLAN

Multiplayer gaming on your WLAN between family members or against opponents via the Internet is a great way to get even more enjoyment from your game console or PC. Facing off against friends and family via your WLAN is easy to accomplish. Let's get started so that you can start playing.

Secret #51: Network Requirements for Gaming

When it comes to playing games over a network, whether you're using a game console or a PC, one feature of your network and Internet connection is more important than anything else. Right now, you're probably guessing that it's bandwidth or, more exactly, capacity. You're wrong. The most important factor is the latency of your connection.

Games send a surprisingly small amount of data over a network—small that is—compared to what you might expect. The complicated stuff—graphics, sound, and video—resides on each individual's console or PC. The game doesn't need to send any of this over the network. What the game sends is information about players, including position, damage, score, inventory, and the like. For everyone to be able to play without the game slowing to a crawl, this small amount of data has to get to its destination quickly.

At the beginning of this chapter, I discussed capacity versus speed. I also mentioned latency. *Latency* is the time it takes for data to travel from your computer to its destination and back again. Latency is also known as *Round Trip Time* (RTT). There are several things that can contribute to high latency:

- A long or circuitous network route to the destination, which requires multiple "hops" along the way. Each computer or router that hands off the data to the next adds time.
- Network congestion.
- Interference on lines (DSL in particular).
- Signal transmission over a long distance; satellite users experience latency problems because of the time it takes their signal to travel through space and back (in both directions).
- Game server congestion.
- Improperly configured games.

Because of the high latency of satellite connections, they're useless for online gaming. If a salesperson tells you otherwise, they're either woefully ill-informed or dishonest. To play most online games, you need a RTT under 350 ms (milliseconds, or thousandths of a second). The RTT on most satellite connections is almost two seconds, sometimes longer.

Cable and DSL connections can suffer from high latency as well. Congested cable networks and signal interference on DSL lines can add RTT, which makes it hard or impossible to play online games. Even though there is little you can do to improve latency on your carrier's network, you can improve performance on your WLAN by not trying to play online games at the same time others are using the network to surf the Internet, print, or transfer large files.

You also should make sure that you configure your game correctly. Many games have settings that you can adjust to optimize them for the network connection you're using. Check the developer's site for configuration tips.

Secret #52: Hardware Requirements for Gaming

If you're playing a console game, you're covered. If you're playing a PC game, here are a few things you need beyond the hardware requirements listed on the game's box:

- At least a 1.5 GHz CPU; faster is better, and hyperthreading is great (however, you need XP Professional OS to take advantage of hyperthreading).

◆ A 128MB graphics card with hardware light and transform rendering.
◆ A hard drive with a short seek time, a large buffer (8MB or more), and a Serial ATA (SATA) connection.
◆ A PC with enough RAM to handle the game. RAM is cheap; buy a lot of it.
◆ The latest version of DirectX.

Make sure that you have all the latest patches and drivers for your system.

Secret #53: Adding a Game Console to Your WLAN

Game console makers are quickly adding networking to their products' list of features. Leading the way with this was Microsoft's Xbox. Sony's PlayStation and the Nintendo Gamecube are catching up, with multiplayer titles and networking support available.

Adding your game console to your WLAN is easy. You just need to add a Wi-Fi adapter. Microsoft recently announced an adapter for the Xbox, but both Linksys and NETGEAR already have game adapters available that work with all three consoles. The adapters connect to the console via an Ethernet cable, so if your console isn't equipped with an Ethernet port, you have to add that as well. Wireless game adapters range in price from $80 to $150, are self-contained, and don't require any drivers.

on the web	To learn about **Linksys Wireless G game adapter, go to** www.lynksys.com. **NETGEAR has information on using its products to network game consoles at** www.netgear.com/education/gaming.html. **For information on the Xbox wireless adapter, visit** www.xbox.com/en-US/hardware/ xboxwirelessadapter.htm.

Occasionally, you may experience problems between your router and your game console. The router may not recognize the console, or the console may not be able to acquire an IP address. Try this process to resolve the problem:

◆ Turn off all of your other WLAN clients.
◆ Turn off your console and router.
◆ Turn the router on.
◆ Turn the console (and adapter) on.
◆ Turn the rest of your clients on.

Sometimes, the game adapter has to establish its connection with the router before the other clients do. If this fix worked, you should only have to do this one time. If the problem persists, check the Web site of your router's manufacturer for troubleshooting tips.

Secret #54: Firewalls and Gaming

Many broadband routers have firewalls built into them. This is good because it adds an extra layer of security between your WLAN and the Internet. However, the firewall can occasionally get in the way of gaming by blocking software ports that a game wants to use.

Ports are numbered connections that computers use for different types of network traffic. For example, computers use port 80 for Web traffic and port 25 for e-mail. There are thousands of port numbers available, and a firewall closes most of them.

If a particular game requires a specific port be opened, you have to configure your firewall to allow traffic to pass through that port. How you configure the firewall depends on the model, but your documentation or the vendor's Web site should cover this. If your router and game software supports Universal Plug and Play (UPnP), then opening ports is easy because UPnP does it automatically when the game requires it. UPnP is a plug-and-play standard for network devices that allows them to be set up automatically with minimal user intervention.

It may be difficult to determine which port an application requires. In this case, you can try setting up a demilitarized zone (DMZ), as explained in the next section.

Secret #55: Setting Up a DMZ

When you can't figure out which port your game needs opened, you can opt to open them all, which in effect turns the firewall off for that computer. When you set up a DMZ, you're telling the router not to filter traffic to or from a specific machine on your network.

For example, if the IP address of your PlayStation's wireless adapter is 192.168.0.179, you can configure the firewall to filter traffic for every IP address but that one, which leaves the adapter free to connect on any port that the game needs.

A DMZ is the easy way to work around port issues, but it's not as safe as port forwarding. Opening up every port exposes you to more risk than selectively opening a couple of ports. Crackers and malicious programs (worms) will have more opportunities to compromise your network. Double-check your router's documentation, and consider port forwarding instead of using a risky solution like a DMZ.

Extending the Range of Your WLAN

Chapter
6

◆ ◆

Secrets in This Chapter

◆ ◆

Y ou may wish to have reception at all points over a large property or throughout a multistory building. Perhaps you'd like to sort through your e-mail backlog while sitting poolside in your favorite chaise lounge, or maybe you'd like to extend coverage to a garage or guesthouse. It isn't difficult to extend the range of a WLAN, and this chapter helps you make the right decisions when doing so.

Secret #56: Determining Where You Have and Want Connectivity

Before you start investing time and money extending the range of your WLAN, you need to determine two things: where you already have connectivity and where you want connectivity. You may already have adequate signal strength to sit by your pool and check your e-mail without having to buy any more equipment.

The easiest way to determine where you already have connectivity is to carry a WLAN client around your property and take note of where you can connect, the quality of the connection, and the connection speed. Of course, you need a laptop with a Wi-Fi NIC or a Wi-Fi-enabled PDA and a utility like Nestumbler, PocketWinC, Kismet, or ministumbler (see Figure 6-1).

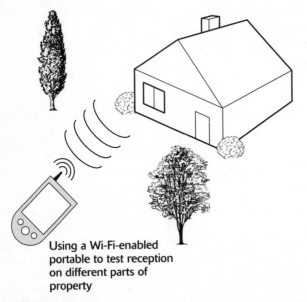

Using a Wi-Fi-enabled portable to test reception on different parts of property

Figure 6-1: Testing signal strength and coverage with a laptop or PDA.

Professionals use handheld wireless receivers for testing the signal strength in WLANs. These are very expensive, and, unless you are lucky enough to have a friend that owns one or belong to a wireless user group (WUG) that has one available for members, you won't be able to go that route.

If you don't have a laptop or wireless PDA and can't get access to an 802.11 wireless receiver, then you aren't completely out of luck. Kensington manufactures the Wi-Fi Finder, a credit card–sized device that detects the signal of 802.11b and 802.11g networks. The device doesn't work perfectly, but, if it's your only option, you should consider it. If you are using encryption on your network, the Wi-Fi Finder will not detect the signal, and it won't detect newer 802.11g devices or networks without a lot of traffic.

on the web For more information about the Wi-Fi Finder, visit www.kensington.com.

Secret #57: Locating Devices

If you want to extend your network coverage to a specific house, garage, workshop, or some other building, your best bet may be to set up a line-of-sight connection. This way, you can share your network between the two buildings without broadcasting to your entire neighborhood (see Figure 6-2).

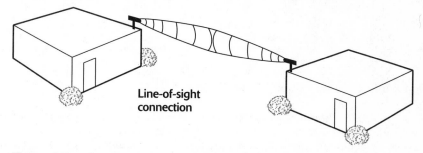

Line-of-sight
connection

Figure 6-2: A line-of-sight connection between two buildings.

Map out your signal and determine where you ultimately want to be able to connect. From that point, you can determine if you need additional equipment and what type of equipment you need to extend coverage to each area.

Assuming that you want to avoid having to buy additional equipment, you also can try relocating your existing equipment to improve coverage to the areas that you desire. This may be as simple as moving an access point closer to a window so that you can extend coverage to an area outside, such as a deck. Of course, after moving an AP, you'll need to check that you still have sufficient signal reception in the area that AP covered before you moved it.

Seasonal Considerations

When you initially designed your WLAN, you took the time (I hope) to minimize interference from construction materials, obstacles, and RF interference. Now that you're going to extend it, you need to take the time to do the same thing again.

If you're extending your Wi-Fi coverage outdoors, you still have to deal with obstacles and sources of RF interference. Position your access points so that your signal will pass through as few signals as possible. Vegetation, particularly trees and shrubs, can significantly reduce signal strength. This is because living plants are up to 90 percent water, and water is a resistor to 2.4 GHz RF signals. If you plan and extend a WLAN in the fall or winter, remember to take the seasonal foliage into account. You don't want to go through the trouble of relocating equipment in the winter only to have to move it again in spring. If there are deciduous trees or shrubs in the line-of-sight between your access point and clients, they will become a problem when they regain their foliage in the spring (see Figure 6-3). Just how much of an obstacle trees are depends on the number and type of trees and the density of the wooded area. To be safe, just plan your connections so that they avoid obstructions including trees.

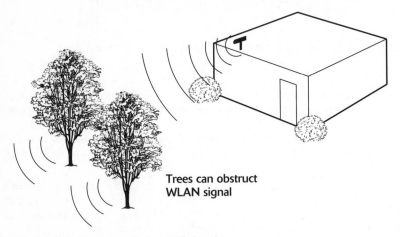

Trees can obstruct
WLAN signal

Figure 6-3: Trees can obstruct RF signals.

Because of their shorter wavelength, 5 GHz 802.11a signals have more trouble penetrating obstacles in the environment than 2.4 GHz signals do, so you'll have to be even more particular about placement of equipment for an 802.11a network.

Line-of-Sight and the Fresnel Zone

To limit propagation of your Wi-Fi signal all over the neighborhood and to take advantage of the increased gain of directional antennas (see the section titled "Antenna Options" later in this chapter), you can set up a line-of-sight connection between two sections of a WLAN or between two separate WLANs.

A line-of-sight connection requires an unobstructed view between transmission points that are free of obstacles in the signal path. An important consideration when establishing a line-of-sight connection between two points is the Fresnel zone.

The Fresnel zone (pronounced Fray-nel) is named after French physicist Augustin-Jean Fresnel. It refers to the pattern of RF radiation between a transmitter and receiver. Shaped like an elongated ellipse, the Fresnel zone between two antennas must be free of obstructions, or the signal will weaken dramatically (see Figure 6-4).

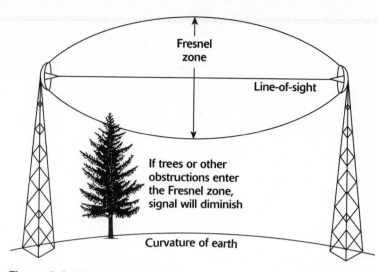

Figure 6-4: The Fresnel zone.

You can demonstrate a Fresnel zone for yourself using flashlights (see Figure 6-5). For the first demonstration, shine a single flashlight at a wall in a dark room. The brighter, focused circle at the center of the beam represents the Fresnel zone. Notice that, as an obstruction enters the Fresnel zone, it has more of an effect on the "signal" reaching the wall.

You also can take two flashlights and line them up so that they are pointing directly at one another in line-of-sight fashion. Turn on the lights, and you will notice that the center of the combined beam, which is slightly elliptical, is brighter. This is another illustration of the Fresnel zone concept.

Knowing the size of the Fresnel zone is important if you're setting up a link over a great distance. The size of the zone is determined by the distance of the link and the frequency of the radio signal. Antennas must be mounted high enough to allow the Fresnel zone to be clear of obstruction. Generally, 60–80 percent of the Fresnel zone must remain unobstructed.

At a mile, the Fresnel zone of a 2.4 GHz system is approximately 14 feet. At half a mile, it's roughly 10 feet. For shorter distances, you would be safe allowing 10 feet for the Fresnel zone, as long as it is clear of obstacles.

note
Careful planning and proper setup of equipment limits the number of people that can detect your signal and possibly compromise your WLAN's security.

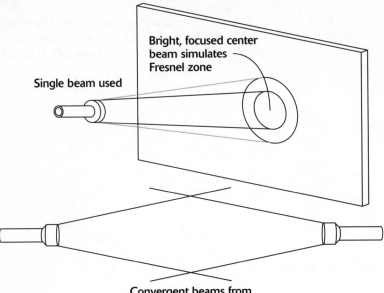

Bright, focused center
beam simulates
Fresnel zone

Single beam used

Convergent beams from
two flashlights can be
used to simulate Fresnel zone

Figure 6-5: Demonstrating the Fresnel zone with flashlights.

Secret #58: The 300-Foot Myth

By now, you've learned to take the advertised signal ranges of most Wi-Fi products with a grain of salt. That is, the advertised signal range rarely translates to the range that you will actually experience when you install the product. There are far too many variables that affect the range; most of these are the result of the operating environment.

Many advertisers claim that their devices can achieve between 150 feet to 300 feet coverage indoors. The advertised range may be achievable with an unobstructed line of sight between the access point and the Wi-Fi adapter. However, even then, you are likely to realize lower performance than expected. This can be attributed to a number of factors, including:

- ◆ Interference from other RF sources in your home
- ◆ Increased signal attenuation caused by obstacles such as walls and furniture
- ◆ Hardware and software configuration errors
- ◆ Exaggerated claims by manufacturer

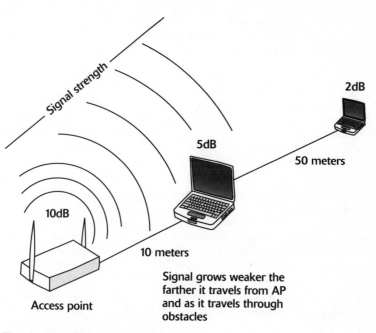

Figure 6-6: Signal attenuation.

Marketing departments always put forth a best-case scenario for signal range, which is often based on lab conditions that you aren't very likely to be comparable to those found in the typical consumer's home. Also, the results may be based on a particular equipment configuration, such as adding a ceiling-mounted, high-gain antenna. Remember, the advertised range is usually stated as "possible" or "up to" a certain number of feet; it's not guaranteed and never expressed as the minimum achievable result.

Signal range is important because it doesn't just affect the coverage area of your WLAN; it also affects quality of service (QoS) and the throughput. The further away that you are from an access point, the weaker the signal will be. Even though you may actually detect a signal 150 feet from an access point, the signal could be too weak to allow connection.

Secret #59: Determinants of Signal Strength

I'm not assuming you are an engineer, nor am I trying to turn you into one. So, I've tried to simplify the following description as much as I can. The good news here is that you don't need to remember this. It's nice to know, and you'll amaze your friends, but you can survive and extend your network without it. In fact, the secrets under the "Increasing Signal Strength" section that follows this one will help you handle the issues outlined here.

Decibels

You may be familiar with the term *decibel* as a measurement of noise level. Engineers express the strength of a signal in decibels (dB). In the early days of telephones, decibels were created as a way to measure the performance of telephone equipment and cables (and named after Alexander Graham Bell, the inventor of the telephone).

A decibel is a relative measurement between a reference input signal level and the output signal level. A bel is equal to 10 times the input signal level, and 1 decibel is 1/10th of a bel. One bel is the minimum level of change in sound levels that a human ear can discern, which means that your ear can hear the difference between a sound level of 1 bel and a sound level of 2 bels, but you can't hear the difference between 5 decibels and 7 decibels (although your cat or dog probably can). Many people experience pain when sound levels reach 130 dBs (unless they go to a lot of rock concerts and have become used to loud noises).

Decibels are the measurement that you will most likely encounter when you are extending your WLAN because the gain of an antenna system is typically expressed in decibels.

> note
>
> *Gain* is the amount that the power of a signal is amplified. For antennas, the gain is expressed in decibels. For example, if the signal output strength of an antenna is increased tenfold over the input power (10:1 ratio), you express the gain as 10 dB. If the output level of an antenna is equal to the input level (1:1), there is no gain in signal strength and you express this as 0 dB.

When you shop for a Wi-Fi antenna, you must select an antenna with the right amount of gain for your situation. Consider the coverage area that you need, as well as the distance between WLAN clients and the access point. Select an antenna with enough gain for a strong signal, but avoid using too strong of a signal, which may actually create problems due to reflections of the RF signal.

The problem caused by these reflections is called *multipath-interference*, or simply *multipathing*. Reflected signals arrive at the antenna at different times and at different strengths, cancelling each other out and resulting in a weaker signal. So, using too strong a signal in a small area can cause more problems than it would solve.

The antennas that come installed on many access points for home and SOHO WLANs are usually around 2 dB. For the average home WLAN, you'll seldom need more than a 6 dBi antenna—8 dBi maximum (see the related Insider Insight for an explanation of *dBi*). You can buy higher gain antennas; these are usually meant for outdoor use and longer distance links. For example, some 18 dBi panel antennas are rated for distances of up to 10 miles. So, an 18 dBi antenna is probably overkill between your house and garage.

insider insight

When you shop for Wi-Fi equipment, particularly antennas and connectors, you may see some measurements listed in dBm or dBi. The dBm measurement indicates decibels relative to one milliwatt (1/1000th of a watt), and dBi represents the gain on an antenna system relative to an isotropic radiator. Often, you'll see dBm used to measure signal loss from a connector.

An isotropic radiator is a theoretical ideal, a device that creates radio waves at 100 percent efficiency equally in all directions or (for reception) is equally sensitive in all directions. It's used as a standard test reference in laboratories, and products are compared against the performance of an isotropic radiator or *point source*.

The measurements dBi and dBm aren't terribly important where we are concerned; you really don't need to understand dBm and dBi unless you're designing antenna systems or if you're perhaps building your own "home brew" antenna.

Frequency

The frequency of Wi-Fi equipment also affects the range of the signal. A high-frequency signal requires more power to cover the same distance than a low-frequency signal. This can be seen in the range difference between 802.11b/g devices versus 802.11a devices. Because manufacturers don't want to increase power consumption of mobile devices, the result is a shorter range for the 5.0 GHz 802.11a signal.

High-frequency signals also are more susceptible to interference from obstacles than are low-frequency signals. The signal from 2.4 GHz and 5 GHz Wi-Fi devices are negatively affected by walls and other solid objects. The 5 GHz 802.11a signal has more problems with these obstacles than 2.4 GHz 802.11b/g signals do. Compared to Wi-Fi, low-frequency television signals have few problems going through walls and ceilings to reach your television.

Secret #60: Understanding Speed and Throughput

As signal strength grows weaker, the throughput of the connection decreases, and the latency increases. The decreased throughput and increased latency is a result of both the distance the signal must travel and the retransmission of lost and corrupt packets between the access point and the adapter.

insider
insight Because signals travel at the speed of light, latency increase due to distance is not noticeable on a WLAN. Latency caused by distance is only an issue if the signal is traveling extremely far, as with a satellite Internet connection. Even then, the latency increases only by a few hundred milliseconds.

Latency caused by retransmission of lost and corrupt packets increases because the weaker signal is subject to greater interference than a strong signal would be. Because of this, users at the edge of an access point's coverage area are more likely to experience "slower" throughput than those positioned closer to the access point.

This is the reason that you can set the minimum connection speed high as a security measure. Fast connections require a strong signal, and a strong signal usually requires that you be reasonably close to an access point. If you require WLAN clients to connect at a high speed, wardrivers are less likely to be able to connect without getting close to your home or building, and making themselves obvious.

Increasing Signal Strength

Now that you have more information than you wanted to know about the problems of signal strength, here are some suggestions for boosting your signal. Most solutions for extending a WLAN require increasing signal strength by some means. If done correctly, with full consideration for the risks and drawbacks, increasing signal strength is an easy way to increase the coverage area of your network. This section helps you decide whether this is the way you want to go, and, if so, how to determine the best way to achieve it.

Secret #61: Using Signal Amplifiers to Boost Signal Strength

One option for extending the coverage area of your WLAN is boosting the output power of your access point's signal. Amplifying the signal from your WLAN used to be a fairly advanced hack—not one to be undertaken by beginners unless they wanted to ruin their equipment. Fortunately, Linksys has begun to market a wireless signal booster for use with its access points and routers (see Figure 6-7). Other manufacturers are sure to follow suit.

Increasing the power of your signal increases your access point's range, which enables clients that are further away from an AP to connect at a higher rate than they were originally. However, amplifying your AP's signal is not a perfect fix and has its own drawbacks.

First, when you amplify the power of a signal, you also are amplifying any noise that was originally present in the signal as well. This usually won't cause problems for most clients on your WLAN, but it can affect connectivity and quality of service for clients with a weak signal.

Adding an amplifier to an access point only increases the output signal of that unit; it doesn't improve reception of the signal from wireless clients. If you are trying to improve service for clients with a weak signal, then an amplifier only takes care of half of your problem. Because Wi-Fi networking requires two-way communication, your best bet may be to add a high-gain antenna. An antenna doesn't add noise to the signal and improves reception of client signals at the AP.

> note   I discuss high gain antennas later in this chapter under the section titled "Antenna Options."

Boosting your signal also may extend it to neighboring houses or apartments. This can cause problems in two ways. First, it is more likely that your WLAN will be discovered and possibly used by wardrivers or neighbors. Second, you may interfere with the operation of a neighbor's WLAN and get an angry knock on your door (or head) as a result.

Both of these problems can be fixed—both by properly securing your WLAN and by using directional antennas to minimize propagation of your Wi-Fi signal outside the boundaries of your property.

> cross ref   For information on securing your WLAN, see Chapter 15.

Take care when boosting your signal or adding third-party-hardware or antennas to your access points. The transmission power of Wi-Fi products is regulated by the Federal Communications Commission (FCC), which has set strict guidelines for signal strength of all WLAN products. It's unlikely that the FCC will come knocking on your door, but be careful anyway.

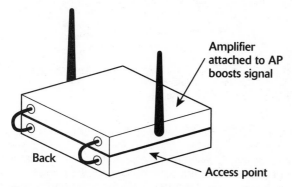

Figure 6-7: A signal booster (amplifier).

Secret #62: Using Wireless Repeaters to Boost Signal Strength

Another alternative to extending your access point's range is using a wireless repeater. A wireless repeater is a device that retransmits the signal from another access point on the same channel as the original signal. Today, many access points have a repeater option built into them; rather than having them run like a normal AP, you can put them into repeater mode and they will rebroad-cast signals from a central AP.

A wireless repeater can be a good solution to extend the range of an AP to areas of your house where the signal degrades due to distance or interference (see Figure 6-8). However, clients communicating through a repeater typically get only half of the normal throughput of the WLAN and sometimes less. This is because a repeater has to handle each packet of data twice when transmitting and receiving between the access point and the client PC. If you don't move a lot of big files around on your network, this won't be too much of a problem

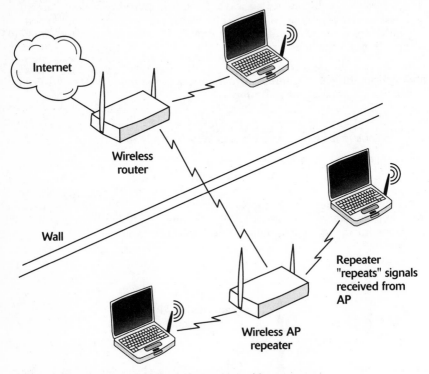

Figure 6-8: Extending an AP's coverage area with a repeater.

There is one thing to consider, though. When put in repeater mode, most access points no longer allow themselves to be administered via a wireless connection. You will have to connect to the repeater/AP through an Ethernet port to make changes or administer it. Keep this in mind when you are choosing a location for your repeater because you'll want to be able to reach it when necessary.

Antenna Options

The antenna is one of the most important parts of your WLAN. Without anten-nas, the signal wouldn't get anywhere and you certainly wouldn't receive any-thing. Still, most people have no idea how an antenna works or which antenna is right for a particular job. This section addresses both of these questions and helps you make the right choices.

Secret #63: How Antennas Work

Simply put, antenna theory is boring. If I were to go into great technical detail about how antennas work, your eyes would glaze over and you'd eventually start snoring. Because it's not my goal to create a 400-plus-page sleep-aid, I'm going to keep this description very simple. Of course, *simple* is a relative term. Still, the more you understand about the basic workings of antennas, the better you'll be able to choose the best antenna(s) for your WLAN.

When alternating current is applied to an antenna, electrons inside the antenna vibrate. The vibrating electrons create an oscillating electric field. Each electron has its own magnetic field, and as a result, the oscillating electric field, which is composed of electrons, creates an oscillating magnetic field. This gives us electromagnetic waves, or radio waves.

Radio waves radiate out from an antenna at the speed of light. The wavelength of a radio signal is determined by measuring the distance between wave peaks (see Figure 6-9). This distance is also known as a *wave cycle*.

Electromagnetic wave

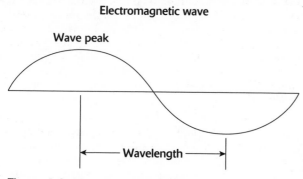

Wave peak

Wavelength

Figure 6-9: Measuring wavelength.

The frequency of a radio wave is the number of wave cycles that pass a given point in a fixed period of time. We measure frequency in hertz (Hz); one Hz is equal to one wave cycle passing a given point in one second. Because it takes longer for a long wave cycle to pass any given point than it does for a short wave cycle, we can say that low-frequency signals have long wavelengths, and high-frequency signals have short wavelengths (see Figure 6-10). So, our 802.11b signal has a short wavelength, which gives it a high frequency (2.4 billion cycles per second, to be exact).

At the receiving end, the radio signal causes the same thing to occur in reverse. The electrons in the antenna vibrate in reaction to the radio waves, and this is transferred to the radio receiver as an electrical signal, which can be heard or interpreted as data if the receiver is tuned to the same wavelength as the signal.

Long wavelength = Low frequency

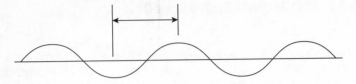

Short wavelength = High frequency

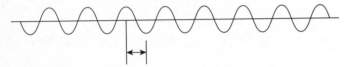

Figure 6-10: High- and low-frequency signals.

Are you sleepy yet? No? That makes one of us then, but let's continue. Earlier in this chapter, when I was discussing signal amplifiers, I mentioned that a high-gain antenna may be a better choice than an amplifier. There are two reasons for this. First, unlike an amplifier, an antenna does not add noise to a signal. This is because an antenna is a passive device; it doesn't provide any additional power to a signal. An antenna can only radiate power applied to it. Second, an antenna improves reception of weak signals from WLAN clients as well as increases broadcast strength. An amplifier does nothing to improve reception of weak signals from WLAN clients.

This is where the subject of antenna gain can start to get confusing. I defined gain as the amount that a signal is amplified. This is true for any electrical circuit where there is an increase in output power as compared to input power. It may seem that an antenna actually produces power itself and then broadcasts the stronger signal. An antenna cannot magically produce power; it's a simple device made of simple materials, usually metal.

An antenna produces gain by focusing the electromagnetic radiation into a tighter directional signal. A simple omnidirectional antenna has no gain; it doesn't focus the radio waves, and the signal retains the same power that it had coming into the antenna, minus any loss that occurs along the way due to resistance.

Think of signal gain from an antenna like light from a lighthouse. If a lighthouse didn't use focusing lenses (designed by our friend Augustin-Jean Fresnel), then the light would shine equally in all directions. This wouldn't be as effective for protecting ships. The lens focuses the light into a tighter and brighter beam. The lens is passive; it doesn't create additional light. Instead, it merely directs the existing light into a more concentrated and powerful signal.

A high-gain antenna works the same way. It doesn't create additional energy; it merely focuses the existing RF energy into a more powerful signal resulting in gain. High-gain antennas are directional. The amount of directivity of an antenna is its beam-width.

Secret #64: Types of Antennas

There are several types of antenna available for home Wi-Fi networks. The type of antenna you choose will depend on how you are planning on extending the signal to increase the coverage area. Some of the available antenna types are described in the following subsections.

Omnidirectional Vertical Polarity Antennas

This type of antenna is omnidirectional only on the horizontal plane. The signal spreads horizontally from the antenna, which narrows the vertical beam-width. This type of antenna is built into many access points and is sometimes called an *omnidirectional vertical gain* antenna (see Figure 6-11).

insider
insight
Most antennas used in WLANs have linear polarization, usually vertical. When you're extending your WLAN, make sure that your antennas have matching polarity. If the polarity of two antennas, especially directional ones, is misaligned, it will cause signal degradation.

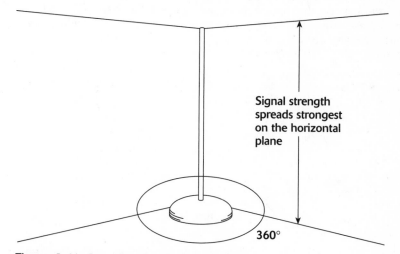

Signal strength spreads strongest on the horizontal plane

360°

Figure 6-11: Omnidirectional vertical polarity.

Panel or Patch Antennas

Flat panel or patch antennas are used to direct WLAN signals both indoors and out. Generally, they have a radiation pattern of less than 90 degrees, which makes them ideal for directing a signal into a specific room or section of a home. For indoor use, you should probably use the smaller panel sizes with a gain of 8 dBi or less. Larger panel antennas are good for bridging between buildings (see Figure 6-12).

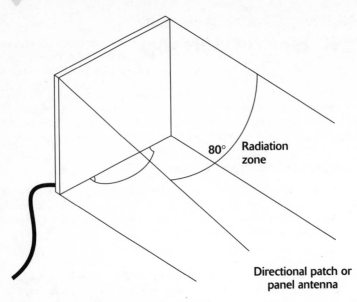

Figure 6-12: A panel or patch antenna.

Sector Antennas

Sector antennas are directional antennas with a beam between 90 and 180 degrees. These are useful for directing a signal toward a particular part of a building or property (see Figure 6-13).

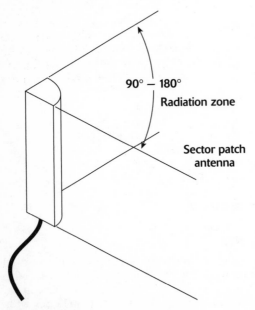

Figure 6-13: Sector antenna.

Ceiling Blister or Dome Antennas

This omnidirectional antenna with a 360-degree-radiation pattern mounts on your ceiling. The signal is directed out and down in a cone shape, which limits signal leakage to upstairs floors. These are primarily used for aesthetic reasons because they aren't very noticeable and look more like a small smoke alarm than an antenna (see Figure 6-14).

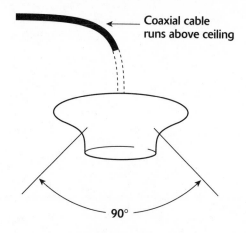

Coaxial cable
runs above ceiling

90°

Radiation cone

Figure 6-14: Ceiling-mounted blister antenna.

Slotted Waveguide Antennas

A slotted waveguide antenna is a highly directional, resonant antenna with a narrow frequency range. They are well-suited for use in a WLAN, and many people "home brew" or build their own waveguide antennas. You can buy one commercially or build one yourself using plans easily found on the Internet. Just do a search for "waveguide antenna," and you will find plenty of information and plans (see Figure 6-15).

Figure 6-15: Slotted waveguide antenna.

Yagi Antennas

A Yagi-Uda array, which is simply known as a *Yagi* antenna, is a highly direc-
tional antenna/high-gain antenna that is very popular among home brewers.
Like a waveguide, you can find plans for these antennas all over the Internet. A
Yagi is especially useful in a point-to-point connection (see Figure 6-16).

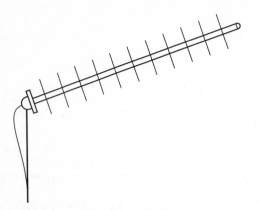

Figure 6-16: A Yagi antenna.

Home Brew (Pringles Can)

There are a lot of plans for "cantennas" on the net. They are easy-to-build, and
they get the job done. Designs vary, with some cantennas being closer to Yagi-
style antennas and others acting more like waveguides. The design that popu-
larized the use of cans was the Pringles cantenna, which is made from a
discarded potato chip can. Cantennas are directional antennas—easy to build
and very cheap. If you're the do-it-yourself type, you'll want to try this, but you
should take care because, if done improperly, you could damage your hardware
and void your warranty (see Figure 6-17).

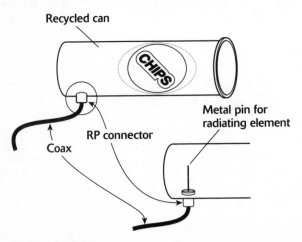

Figure 6-17: Home brew cantenna.

on the
web If you're interested in making your own antennas, consider visiting these sites for more information:

www.netscum.com/~clapp/wireless.html

www.geocities.com/lincomatic/homebrewant.html

www.turnpoint.net/wireless/cantennahowto.html

Cables and Connectors

Most antennas in WLAN equipment use reverse polarity connectors. Unlike regular connectors, these reversed polarity (RP) connectors, which are also known as *reversed gender*, have the center pin switched so that it is in the opposite connector from the "normal" polarity connectors.

The reason for this was simple; the FCC didn't want you to start modifying your WLAN equipment with higher-gain antennas, so they required all manufacturers to use non-standard, proprietary connectors to make it harder for the average person to modify an access point.

Unfortunately for them, the FCC failed to consider the power of a free market economy. If people want to modify their equipment, someone is going to manufacture what they need and sell it to them. As a result, reverse polarity connectors are no longer an oddity; they are a standard.

When you choose to upgrade your antenna, check what type of connector is on your WLAN, and purchase (or build) an antenna with a compatible connector. In fact, make sure you can upgrade your antenna in the first place. Some access points don't have a connector for an external antenna. If this is the case, you may have to consider upgrading to a newer access point.

When you are connecting an external antenna, keep the length of the coaxial cable to a minimum. Your manufacturer's documentation should tell you what the maximum cable length is; make sure you don't exceed it. Using an excessively long cable can actually end up reducing your signal rather than increasing it.

Client Antennas

The antennas that come with many wireless NICs, especially PCMCIA cards, are terrible. The typical laptop NIC has a tiny integrated bulge antenna, which is practically worthless. Unfortunately, most PCMCIA NICs don't allow for the connection of an external antenna.

If your desktop's NIC has an external connector, you can get an appropriate antenna to improve its signal strength and reception. A good choice would be a simple omnidirectional dipole antenna, which is available at most stores that sell Wi-Fi equipment. Upgrading your AP's antenna is a good centralized way to start, but, if your performance is still lacking, consider upgrading your client antennas, too.

Secret #65:   Bridging Two Networks

Normally, when you think about bridging two networks, you think about connecting them through a wired bridge, such as when you hook up an AP to share your broadband Internet connection via a router.

Actual wireless-to-wireless bridging is a new thing, made possible by the new Wireless Distribution System (WDS) standard. WDS allows traffic to flow from one AP to another as if it were traveling from Ethernet port to Ethernet port on a wired network. Best of all, your AP can function like an AP at the same time (see Figure 6-18). It doesn't have to be locked into a dedicated role, like an AP used as a router.

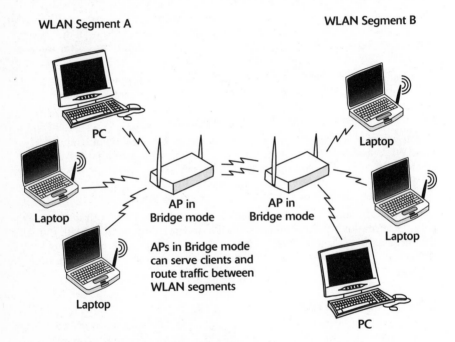

WLAN Segment A

WLAN Segment B

PC

Laptop

Laptop

AP in
Bridge mode

AP in
Bridge mode

Laptop

APs in Bridge mode
can serve clients and
route traffic between
WLAN segments

Laptop

Laptop

PC

Figure 6-18: Wireless bridging using WDS.

You also could use two APs using WDS to extend coverage between two buildings by attaching a directional antenna to each AP or allowing for line-of-sight through a window over short distances. If you use APs combined with directional antennas, they won't be able to serve clients unless the clients are in the path of the directional signal. Still, with the price of access points dropping, this could be an easy way to connect two WLAN segments over a greater distance and with better performance than other options.

Part III

Mobile Wireless

Choosing the Right Mobile Device and Service

◆ ◆

Secrets in This Chapter

◆ ◆

W hat do you want to do with a mobile device? Are you interested in messaging or wireless e-mail? Do you want to take and share photos, or play games? If you see your phone as an opportunity to accessorize, you'll want a model with interchangeable faceplates. Perhaps you just want reliable cell coverage, or wireless Web access.

With the exception of a notebook computer, wireless devices are not direct substitutions for a desktop PC. Personal digital assistants (PDAs), Pocket PCs, and Web-enabled Phones all have different capabilities. Not all phones are customizable, and not all PDAs are created equal.

Secret #66: Determining Your Mobile Needs

Choosing a mobile device, whether a cell phone or PDA, can be a very frustrating experience. Service providers offer different plans and features and require different devices to use their network. Many consumers purchase a cell phone and sign a contract only to find out later that they want additional features or capabilities, but these just aren't available with their provider.

You can avoid problems like these by deciding a few things in advance, before you head out the door to get that new phone or other wireless device. Start by determining what you need to be able to do. The needs you identify here should be deal-breakers; don't sign a contract until you are positive that these features are available and included in the service you choose. Knowing how you will use your device will help you make the best choices. Ask yourself the following questions:

- Do I really need a mobile wireless device?
- Where will I use my device the most?
- Where will I call the most?
- How many minutes will I use each month?
- What time of day will you make the most calls?
- What is my budget for the device and service?
- What features must the device and service have?
- Do I need wireless Web access?

Do You Need a Mobile Wireless Device?

I know this seems like a silly question for me to be asking, but it really is the fundamental thing that you have to ask yourself. I'm not selling devices or wireless services, so I have nothing invested in your answer. Of course, if you already have a cell phone you've probably answered this question already. If that's the case go ahead and move on to the next question.

Still here? Okay then, let's take a good look at your lifestyle. Just how mobile are you? Do you spend a good deal of time on the road, away from home? If you do, how often do you wish you could get in touch with someone, or wish you were available for others to contact? Most of us tend to want more connectivity; good evidence of this is the amount of growth in the cellular industry.

According to the Cellular Telecommunications and Internet Association (CTIA), as of June 2003 there were more than 148 million cellular subscribers in the United States. Subscriptions to mobile services have grown steadily, about ten percent per year, since 1985. To support this growth service, providers have invested over $134 billion in improving their networks and services, with investment growing on average 13.3 percent a year.

With this sort of growth, having a cell phone has become the norm and we're expected to be reachable at all times, particularly in our professional lives. However, what's expected of us doesn't always translate directly as something we need. Chances are you need a cell phone if you answer yes to any of the following questions:

- Does your profession require that you be reachable when you're out of the office?
- Do you travel frequently, either locally or long distance?
- Would you feel safer if you, or a loved one, had a way to call for help in an emergency, even (especially) when on the road?
- Do you need a way to check messages, e-mail, or other information while you're away from home or the office?

Again, if you answered yes to one or more of these questions, then a cell phone or similar mobile device would be a sound investment. Even if you feel you need a mobile device only for your piece of mind, there are service plans or prepaid options that would make it worth your while.

Where Will You Use Your Device?

You've decided that a mobile device is a good investment. Now, to be sure that you choose a service that lives up to your expectations, you need to determine where you will be using your device most of the time. Not all services operate in every location, and quality of service varies from place to place.

Make a list of places where you or your family members will most likely use your phones. These might include:

- At school or work
- During your commute (using a hands-free headset of course)
- While traveling

Make sure that you choose a service provider that has good coverage in the locations where you will be using your phone most often. If you need to use your phone at work, make sure that you'll have coverage there. It won't do you any good if it works at home but can't connect, or drops calls while you're in the office.

If you travel frequently you'll want to check on the roaming charges, and that you'll have coverage in areas that you normally travel to. Not all carriers offer nationwide coverage (see "Secret #74: Determining Coverage Areas" later in this chapter).

Where and Who Will You Call the Most?

Cellular plans differ on charges for long distance and local calling. Some plans offer free calling to other cell phones from the same carrier, in the same geographic area. Others offer free calls to friends and family. If you seldom make long distance calls, or rarely call long distance from your cell phone, you may save money by signing with a local carrier, perhaps your local phone company.

How Many Minutes Will You Use Each Month?

How much time do you spend on the phone now? Do you think it will increase significantly if you get a cell phone? Do you plan on using other features like messaging, e-mail, and Internet often? All of this can add up quickly, and you may be surprised by how much time you'll spend on the phone.

Carefully estimating the number of minutes you need helps you select the best plan. Choose a plan that gives you adequate minutes so that you won't exceed your allotted time each month or end up paying for minutes you'll never use. Some service providers have started rolling unused minutes over to the next month, allowing customers to save what they don't use, but the majority of carriers don't do this yet.

What Time of Day Will You Make the Most Calls?

Consider what time of day you place most of your phone calls now. Will adding a cell phone change this significantly? If you currently make most of your calls in the evening, will having a cell phone encourage you to place more calls during the day?

The time of day that you place the majority of your calls is important for two reasons. First, it will affect the kind of plan that you sign up for. If you make most of your calls around lunch time, it doesn't make sense for you to sign up for a plan that charges you extra for unlimited minutes after 7 p.m. You'd be better off paying for a plan that gives you more time during the day.

Second, if you make the majority of your calls around peak calling times, let's say Friday evenings around 7 p.m, or at lunchtime on weekdays, then you'll want to make sure that the carrier you choose has enough network capacity to handle the traffic during peak hours. If they don't, you'll suffer from dropped calls, or be unable to call when you need to.

You also should take into account where you intend to make most of your calls from. If you place most of your calls at work around noon and your carrier doesn't have enough network capacity in that geographic area, you're out of luck. Remember, network capacity depends on the number of cell sites or cell towers in a given geographic area that are available to serve customers.

What Is Your Budget?

Determine how much you can afford to spend before you head out to sign up for any mobile service. Just like on a car lot, the sales people are going to do their best to get you buy as much as they possibly can. Decide how much you are willing to pay for a phone and monthly service.

Remember, even though some plans offer a free phone when you sign a contract you could end up paying more for that phone over the life of the contract than you would for purchasing a phone outright. In fact, you may be able to save money if you purchase your own phone and sign up for a shorter contract.

If you do decide to purchase your own phone, purchase it from the carrier you intend to sign up with. If you purchase it elsewhere, make sure the carrier supports that model of handset and will activate the phone. Carriers often use proprietary technology, and a phone purchased elsewhere might not be supported by your chosen carrier.

When faced with high-pressure sales tactics and a bewildering array of features and plans, deciding on a budget ahead of time can help you narrow the choices quickly.

What Features Do You Need?

Digital cell phones are feature rich. Unlike older analog phones, today's cell phones offer everything from text messaging to gaming all in one device. Some newer smart phones also are full-fledged PDAs. Also, you may find that even though some advanced features sound good, you'll never use them. Choose the features that you must have and the deal breakers that you'll definitely need before you sit down to decide on a phone and service plan.

Not all phones have every feature, and not all service plans include the features you want even if your phone supports them. Consider the following features and the likelihood that you'll use any of them:

- ◆ E-mail
- ◆ Paging
- ◆ Games
- ◆ Instant messaging (real time, not basic text messaging)
- ◆ Call forwarding
- ◆ Conferencing
- ◆ Chat
- ◆ Internet access
- ◆ Photo or multimedia messaging
- ◆ Two-way radio or walkie-talkie
- ◆ Polyphonic ring tones (cool ring tones of your favorite songs)
- ◆ Security features such as locking mechanisms and biometric authentication (fingerprint readers)

The following are usually standard features available with most phones and service plans:

- ◆ Text messaging
- ◆ Call waiting
- ◆ Voicemail
- ◆ Caller ID
- ◆ Operator assistance
- ◆ Directory assistance

When you're deciding on extra services, pay careful attention to any additional costs that may be associated with each. Some features, like Internet access or e-mail, may add substantial cost to your plan and count against your total minutes as well.

Comparing Mobile Devices

Mobile devices have different capabilities; some are feature rich, like cell phones and PDAs; others, like pagers, offer fewer features and almost no interactivity. You've taken the time to decide what you need your device to do; now we'll look at some of these devices and see which ones best fit your lifestyle and needs.

Secret #67: Choosing a Mobile Phone

Once you've decided on the features that you need, you can look for a service provider. Your choice of service provider will affect which models of cell phone you can choose from. Carriers use different technologies, and as a result each carrier usually has a selection of phones that will work with its service.

Carriers buy phones in bulk from cell phone manufacturers. They give basic phones away for free with a contract, and heavily discount high-end models when you sign with them. How can they afford to do this? It's simple; they charge extra fees for services like e-mail and Web browsing, often on top of the per-minute charge you pay when using these services. They also make up the cost when you go over your allotted monthly time and over the life of the contract.

Other than the obvious requirement that a phone have all of the features that you want, there are some other features that you should consider:

◆ **Battery life**—Select a phone with a battery that holds a charge for a significant amount of time. You don't want to run out of power during a call.

◆ **Car power adapter**—You want to be able to charge your phone in your car.

◆ **Hands free headset**—Depending on where you live, a headset may be required by law if you plan on making calls while driving.

◆ **Hands free speaker kit**—An alternative to wearing a headset, the speaker kit lets you make calls while driving.

◆ **Battery charger**—This is a must, and should be included with your phone. A good battery charger has a place to dock your phone and one or two additional batteries.

◆ **An extra battery**—Consider this insurance, as well as a convenience. You'll be sure to have at least one charged battery on hand so that you can always use your phone.

◆ **Car antenna**—You can get antennas that will improve your cellular reception when you are placing calls on the road.

◆ **Interchangeable faceplates**—If you accessorize with your phone, you may want a model that has interchangeable faceplates so that your phone will always match your couture.

◆ **Data cables**—Almost any cellular phone can be used like a cellular modem, albeit a very slow one. If you want to dial up on your laptop via your cell phone, you are going to need a data cable.

◆ **Bluetooth accessories**—You can get Bluetooth wireless headsets and hands-free kits. Many new phones are now Bluetooth-ready.

◆ **Carry cases and holsters**—A case will protect your phone from scratches and damage.

◆ **Cameras**—Some cell phones have camera attachments available that enable you to take and send photos.

Consider getting a flip phone with a folding microphone or earpiece that covers the keypad when not in use. This will help prevent "pocket dialing," accidentally placing a call when keys on your phone are pressed while in your pocket or in your purse. As much fun as it may be for someone to talk to the inside of a purse (and I have done this many times), it will waste your minutes and eventually annoy everyone on your speed dial list. You can lock the keypad when your phone isn't in use, but in practice most people get sick of doing this and simply stop. Get a flip phone, it's easier.

Digital versus Analog

With over 80 percent of the U.S. cell phone market now digital, analog service is dying. Still, in rural areas there are a lot of analog cell sites. If you live in, or travel through rural areas, a phone that works with both digital and analog services can be a lifesaver. Recently, after being evacuated from my home during some of the worst wildfires in the history of southern California, having a phone that worked with analog towers allowed me to connect and place calls while other evacuees were without cell service or landline phones.

One thing to remember about analog service is that while you are connected through an analog cell site, you won't be able to use all of the nifty digital features of your phone. That means no text messaging, e-mail, Web browsing, or instant messaging. It also means no sending or receiving digital photos, or using walkie-talkie features. You also may incur roaming charges while using analog service. Still, it's a nice backup to have when digital service is unavailable.

Gaming on Your Phone

Some newer cell phones enable you to download and play simple video games. This can be a fun way to kill time while sitting in an airport, or a really boring meeting. Depending on your carrier, games may be free, or you may be charged a per-download fee plus airtime. The big thing to remember is that playing games runs your battery down faster than placing calls does.

Most games aren't especially advanced; they're more along the lines of an old Atari system, but they can still be addictive. Recently Nokia introduced the N-Gage. The N-Gage has games with graphics that are on par with the original Sony PlayStation. It's an MP3 player, and when you're sick of your MP3s it also has a built in FM radio. Oh yeah, it's a fully featured cell phone too. The N-Gage also has Bluetooth wireless support built in for head-to-head game play between N-Gage units, and supports e-mail and Web-browsing.

Accessing the Internet on Your Phone

If you want to have access to the Internet from your wireless device, you have to choose between Wireless Application Protocol (WAP) devices or devices like PDAs that can give a better approximation of "real" Web-surfing. WAP devices deliver Web pages as text, based on Wireless Markup Language, which is a streamlined version of HTML designed for the tiny screens on most mobile phones (see Figure 7-1).

WAP devices surf the Internet via a WAP gateway that delivers WML pages and encodes and decodes HTML into WML for delivery to tiny screens. When a cell user requests a Web page, the page request is directed through a WAP gateway which then requests the page from a Web server. The Web server delivers the page to the WAP gateway, which then translates the page into WML and delivers it to the cell user's phone (see Figure 7-2).

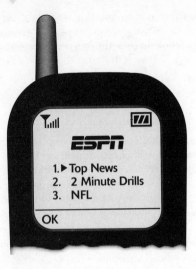

Figure 7-1: An example of a WAP Web page on a cell phone.

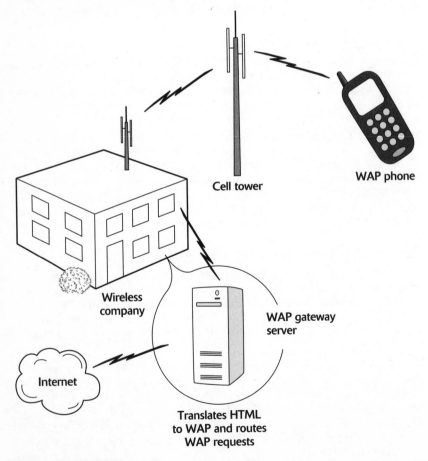

Figure 7-2: A WAP gateway.

With larger, color screens, PDAs and some smart phones can deliver a Web-browsing experience closer to that of a PC. Even though the graphical interface is better on these devices, the overall speed of browsing is much slower than with a Wi-Fi or broadband connection.

Depending on your service plan, additional charges may apply to Web browsing, as well as time charges. Review your plan carefully to keep from exceeding your allotted minutes.

Secret #68: Camera Phones and Privacy

As camera phones and photo messaging become more popular, there is a growing recognition of the privacy issues that surround these unique devices. Because of their small size, and the fact that some models are indistinguishable from regular phones (see Figure 7-3), they can be secreted into areas where a camera wouldn't normally be permitted.

Figure 7-3: A camera phone from Sprint.

This is leading to new sets of rules, and sometimes an outright ban on cell phones in some places. This is especially true in health clubs and gyms, and many of them are requiring patrons to check their cell phone at the front desk if they have built in cameras. This is in reaction to cases where customers have been secretly photographed, sometimes in the nude, and had their pictures circulated on the Internet.

Some corporations, fearing corporate espionage, have banned camera phones in factories and laboratories and on tours of their facilities. Other businesses are sure to follow suit, if only to avoid legal liability. As this issue becomes more prominent, look for the government to step in with tougher privacy laws.

Secret #69: Consider a PDA

There are several advantages to using a PDA over a standard cell phone. A PDA gives you access to your files, calendar, contact lists, productivity software, and with a cellular or Wi-Fi connection, e-mail and Web browsing.

There are a lot of PDAs on the market, with varying capabilities. In the U.S. the market is split between PDAs running the Palm OS and those running Microsoft's Pocket PC operating system. Both operating systems have their advantages and disadvantages, and there is a wide range of devices running each. If you're trying to decide which type of PDA is best for you, consider the following points.

Price

Palm devices tend to be cheaper than Pocket PCs. The Palm OS needs less memory and processor speed than Pocket PCs do, and this is reflected in their price. There are some entry-level Pocket PCs that are competitive in price with Palms, and some high-end Palms that cost as much as Pocket PCs, but for the most part you'll pay more for the higher power and extended functionality of a Pocket PC device.

Size and Weight

Most Palm devices are smaller and lighter than Pocket PCs, although not by much. Pocket PCs tend to have bigger and better displays than Palms and don't necessarily slip into your pocket as easily as some slimmer Palm PDAs do. Newer Pocket PCs are getting smaller and this difference will be less of an issue.

Input Methods

Both Palm OS and Pocket PC PDAs enable you to input data by writing on the screen with a Stylus. Palms use a system called Graffiti, which in earlier versions of the Palm OS required learning a new system of block letters that was different than the normal alphabet. Newer Palms use Graffiti 2.0, which doesn't require you to relearn the alphabet.

Pocket PCs have three options for inputting characters by writing. One option is similar to the original Palm OS graffiti, so Palm users can transition to a Pocket PC and use a familiar system. Pocket PCs also recognize standard block alphabet and cursive handwriting.

Both Palms and Pocket PCs have onscreen keyboards that enable you to tap in your letters with a stylus. There also are options for portable keyboards that you can use while your PDA is in a cradle, or QWERTY keyboards, either built into the PDA or available as a clip-on accessory, that let you type with your thumbs. Hey, I do that on my laptop.

Applications

The big advantage of a Pocket PC is that it includes pocket versions of major MS Office applications. A Pocket PC integrates with Word, Excel, and Outlook with no problems. Because over 90 percent of us are using MS Windows, this is a big deal. You can create, view, and edit Word documents on a Pocket PC as well as manage your Outlook contacts, e-mail, and calendar.

There are third party applications available for Palm PDAs that enable you to view and work on Word documents, or to get information from Outlook, but they don't work nearly as well as a Pocket PC, and they never will. Because Pocket PC is a Microsoft product, it only makes sense that it will always do a better job of integrating with Windows.

Palms do have a lot of software available, and a base of dedicated software developers that continues to extend the capabilities of the Palm platform. As a personal information manager, a Palm is easier to use and more intuitive than a Pocket PC. It takes fewer clicks to get what you need, and you'll be a Palm pro in no time. A Pocket PC is a little more involved, but if you're a Windows power-user the learning curve will be shorter for you than for most Pocket PC users.

Battery Life

The major issue with any portable device is battery life. Palms win here hands down because they need less memory, smaller processors, and tend to have smaller displays so they use less power. Depending on the model, Palms can go for several days to a month without replacing batteries or recharging, while Pocket PCs usually only last as long as a typical laptop, three or four hours.

When you shop for a PDA, make sure that it has a battery that you can replace. Some PDAs with rechargeable batteries don't have removable batteries, so you'll have to plug in or dock your PDA to recharge it. Removable batteries will allow you to keep a fully charged spare on hand, so you won't have to stop and recharge. Some Palms use AAA batteries, which makes finding replacements cheap and easy.

Secret #70: Capabilities of Smart Phones

Smart phones combine the functions of a PDA and a cell phone, giving you the best of both worlds (see Figure 7-4). Like PDAs, you'll have to choose between Palm OS-powered smart phones or smart phones that run Microsoft's Windows Mobile OS. All of the same considerations apply when choosing between the two, although with smart phones there are a couple of extra issues to consider.

Your choice of smart phone depends on the cell carrier that you choose. Just like standard phones, carriers support specific models so you'll have to choose from what they offer. Smart phones are all digital; I haven't found a model that also supports connecting via an analog cell site. This shouldn't be a problem if you're in a major U.S. city, but if you travel throughout the U.S. you need to be aware that you'll be unable to use the phone outside of your carrier's digital network.

Figure 7-4: A smart phone from Sprint.

Other than Palm OS and Windows Mobile smart phones you also can consider Blackberry wireless handhelds. Known for its two-way messaging and e-mail devices, Blackberry also produces wireless handhelds that include voice, SMS messaging, and e-mail. These devices aren't full-fledged PDAs; they're more wireless organizers and don't have anywhere near the functionality of a Palm or Windows Mobile smart phone.

Secret #71: Pagers as an Alternative

Okay, I'm sort of kidding here, a pager really isn't an alternative to a phone or PDA. However, if you're carrying around a phone, a PDA, and a pager and want to consolidate a few features, you should take a look at some of the two-way paging devices offered by different manufacturers, including Motorola and Blackberry.

These devices offer paging, two-way messaging, and e-mail all in one package. However, for e-mail you may have to use an e-mail address provided as part of your service. This may not make a difference to you, but it does require that you inform all of your contacts of yet another e-mail address you've acquired.

Secret #72: MSN Smart Watches

Yes! I can get a watch just like Dick Tracy had. (Now all I need is a flying car, and I'm all set.) Well, the watch is almost like Dick Tracy's; for now it's a receive-only device, but it's still cool. Starting in the fall of 2003, Microsoft began rolling out its MSN Direct service, which delivers information to MSN Direct wireless wristwatches via the DirectBand Network.

Subscribers can get personalized weather, sports scores, stocks, appointment reminders, personal messages, and more, all delivered to MSN Direct enabled watches. The watches aren't big clunky looking things either; they're being made by Fossil and Abacus. In fact, Fossil is making the "Fossil Wrist Net Dick Tracy" watch, a stylish revisiting of the super-sleuth's wrist communicator.

The DirectBand Network initially covers the 100 largest cities in the U.S. and Canada. It works by broadcasting MSN Direct information on FM radio subcarrier channels. These FM channels are sometimes used by FM radio stations to broadcast their call letters, and occasionally song titles for display on newer car radios. MSN Direct is leasing this space to broadcast the MSN Direct service to enabled devices. Right now that means watches, but additional devices may be available in the future.

Secret #73: Mobile Phones and Hearing Aids

Digital mobile phones, GSM phones in particular, can cause problems for people with hearing aids, especially older hearing aids. Hearing aids receive the magnetic field from phones as hissing or static, and it can be quite painful for the person wearing the hearing aid. This also makes it almost impossible for people who rely on hearing aids to use mobile phones.

Generally, to cause a problem the phone has to be within a few inches of the hearing aid, so there are things that hearing-impaired persons can do to reduce interference and use mobile phones. This normally involves using a hands-free kit or neck loop to keep the phone away from the hearing aid.

Newer, digital hearing aids don't normally have a problem with mobile phones, and in-canal hearing aids work a little better with phones than behind-the-ear units. Unfortunately, other than testing it, there isn't any way to be sure that a phone won't interfere with your hearing aid. When you are buying a phone or signing up for a service, ask to test the phone at the store prior to purchasing it. This way you'll be sure that your phone will be usable.

Choosing a Mobile Service Provider

After you've decide what you need, and you have an idea about what sort of device you are looking for, you can set out to find a suitable cellular carrier.

When you're shopping for your new phone and plan, don't believe all the sales pitches you hear about coverage, number of subscribers, and call quality. Marketing departments are always going to present a best-case scenario, and because quality of service can vary so widely between carriers in a particular geographic area, you're going to have to do a little investigating to be sure that you don't sign a two-year contract for what could end up being a digital paperweight.

The biggest reason for varying service and coverage is that the industry is continuing to build out and upgrade its networks. According to the CTIA, as of June 2003 there were almost 148,000 active cell sites in the United States. The number continues to grow by over 12 percent each year. As more cell towers are installed, service continues to improve.

Unfortunately, even when they want to add cell sites and improve service, cell carriers can't always find a suitable place to install them. This is usually due to NIMBYism (Not In My Back Yard) of some sort. As an example, some communities in San Diego have been complaining about poor cell coverage, dropped calls, and what they perceive as the cellular industries' overlooking their needs. In reality these same communities vehemently oppose every attempt by carriers to locate cell sites in their communities to improve their reception.

Secret #74: Determining Coverage Areas

Many factors affect quality of service in wireless coverage areas; these include distribution of cell sites, topography of the surrounding landscape, and the number of subscribers served by any individual cell tower. Unfortunately, there isn't any way to discern any of this from brochures or commercials. Most carriers have coverage maps on their Web sites. Usually you have to input your zip code, and you are shown a coverage map. The quality of the maps ranges between generalized maps that don't show detail below the level of entire states, to detailed neighborhood coverage maps. The coverage maps are usually accompanied by a handy disclaimer stating that the map indicates general areas of coverage and doesn't represent guaranteed service areas or quality of service.

How do you determine which carrier has the best service in your area? The best resource for determining which cell carrier has the best coverage in your area is the people around you: friends, neighbors, coworkers, and family. Because the most important thing is that you get the best coverage and call quality, take an informal survey of all of these people. Start by asking them about the following things:

- ◆ Coverage and quality in your neighborhood
- ◆ Coverage and call quality at work
- ◆ Dead zones where they can't connect
- ◆ Problems at peak call times
- ◆ Dropped calls
- ◆ Quality of customer service
- ◆ Coverage in other areas that you frequent, including other cities if you travel for business frequently.

Make sure that you ask about performance during peak hours, particularly during the times that you've determined you'll be using your phone the most. In some urban areas, especially business districts, cellular traffic during peak times can make it almost impossible to place or receive a call. You may find that while one carrier has good capacity and coverage near your home, it has lousy coverage where you work. Your coworkers or friends that work in the same area will be your best resource for determining this.

Nationwide Coverage

All of the major cellular companies have coverage in major metropolitan areas, so if you travel to major cities on business you should have no problem using your phone. However you should review your contract to determine whether you will be charged a roaming rate while traveling. You may be able to sign up for a nationwide plan that eliminates roaming charges.

If you do get a nationwide service plan that doesn't charge for roaming, check to see if it lets you roam on another provider's network when your carrier isn't available. If your carrier doesn't have an extensive network, you need to be able to connect through another provider's network when you travel or you'll have less ability to receive and place calls.

Using Your Cell as Your Primary Phone

A growing number of people are canceling their wired telephone service and using their cell as their primary phone number. This has some advantages, one being that you only have one phone number and one place to check messages. If coverage is good at your house, then this may be an option. Remember, cell service isn't as reliable as landline service, and if you use your cell as your only phone it can get frustrating quickly. You'll also need to keep a close eye on battery life.

If you don't have phone service, your options for Internet connection are more limited. You can still get DSL or cable if they are available, but if they aren't you'll be locked into satellite Internet or checking e-mail via your mobile device. If you get DSL service you may have to get a phone reinstalled. Some DSL carriers may require that you have a phone, stating that they use the phone number as the account number.

From a purely technological point of view this is ridiculous; DSL doesn't require a phone account to operate. Recently state regulators stepped in to one instance in Georgia and instructed DSL providers to stop requiring phone service as a prerequisite for DSL connections. This will probably result in phone companies creating some sort of bundling offers that make DSL without phone service more expensive than simply including a landline phone.

Secret #75: Examining Service Plans

When you are deciding which carrier to use, don't be lured in by offers that sound too good to be true. Often there are hidden charges, or better deals that you may miss in your haste. Study the plan thoroughly and consider the following things before you sign anything.

Promotions

Everywhere you look you are going to see great deals and special offers. Like anything else you buy, you're probably going to see the best deal right after you sign with a different company. Often these deals include a "free" or reduced-cost phone in exchange for signing a lengthy contract. Usually by the end of the contract you've paid for the phone twice with hidden fees and higher per-minute rates.

Your plan may offer special features free-of-charge for a specified period, but what will these features cost when that period expires? Will you be able to cancel them without penalty?

By-the-Second Billing

Most cellular plans are billed by-the-minute. That is, if you make a call that lasts for one minute and one second, you'll be charged for a two-minute call. Would you pay for three gallons of gas if you pumped two gallons and one ounce? No you wouldn't, and you shouldn't have to pay for cell time that way either.

There are by-the-second billing plans available, where you'll only be charged for the actual amount of time that you spend on the phone. The by-the-second rate usually begins after the first minute; anything less than 60 seconds and you'll still pay for at least one minute.

You can save a lot of money this way if you make a lot of short local calls every month. If most of your calls are long conversations, or long distance, you won't see much of a saving.

Pre-Paid Wireless

Pre-paid wireless service has some advantages. You never have to worry about overtime charges because you buy minutes in advance, and you aren't locked in to a one- or two-year contract. However, you'll usually pay more per-minute than you would if you signed a contract, and you'll have to buy your own phone.

If you have bad credit or no credit, then pre-paid is likely the way you'll have to go. Some carriers may give you service with bad credit, but you'll have to pay a hefty deposit fee.

Secret #76: The Fine Print

As with any contract, when you sign up for cellular service, there is plenty of fine print. Being aware of some of the more common clauses found in cellular contracts puts you in a better position to negotiate or choose a better deal.

Activation Fees

A common "gotcha" is activation fees, charges you incur by signing up for a service and having them turn on your phone. Sounds ridiculous doesn't it? That's because it's the equivalent of charging someone to flip a switch. I can't think of too many other businesses that penalize customers for bringing them business.

Most carriers waive activation fees if you sign a contract. What many people don't know is that they will also waive the activation fees if you insist upon it. They want a new customer, and because you have so many other service providers to choose from, most waive the fee because they know the competition will.

Roaming

This is a quick way to run up a big cell bill if you aren't careful. You can get plans that offer no-roaming charges, but be careful; this usually refers to roaming within your carrier's own network and doesn't cover roaming on another provider's network or analog cell sites.

Choose a carrier that doesn't charge for roaming within their own network; most of the big cell companies don't. You should also double-check the roaming feature of your cell phone because you may have choices that you can set to prevent inadvertent roaming charges. Often you can choose among the following:

- Only use the (insert provider name here) network
- Analog roaming where available
- Automatic setting

The problem with an automatic setting is that your phone may connect to an analog tower and go into roaming mode even when your provider's network is available. This can happen if the signal from an analog tower is slightly stronger than one from your own carrier's network. Choosing analog roaming may cause the same problem if you wander into an area where there is a strong analog signal. The safest setting is to leave your phone locked to your carrier's network.

note   To provide greater connectivity, many phones come with default settings that allow automatic choice of roaming. Double-check your setting.

Overtime Charges

Boo, hiss, everyone hates being charged an arm and a leg for going over your allotted time. Sometimes the per-minute charge is more than double the cost of the per-minute charge on your land phone, so read your contract carefully and get a plan that gives you enough minutes to prevent overcharges without wasting money on minutes that you don't use.

This can take some fine-tuning, but some cell companies allow you to increase or decrease the minutes on your plan as you go. Just be aware that doing so may extend your contract. You also can consider pre-paid service to avoid overtime charges.

Some companies have started to allow consumers to rollover their unused minutes from one month to the next. You can't keep them indefinitely, and there's a limit to how many you can rollover each month, so review your plan. Still, this is a great way to save money and avoid overtime charges.

Early Termination Fees

Every contract has these clauses. I repeat, *every* contract. This is how cellular companies subsidize all those free phones that they give away. If you don't fulfill the contract you can pay anywhere from $150 to $500 in penalties. There are usually no exceptions to the early termination penalties, even if you terminate because of poor service. This is why the mobile phone industry is such a buyer-beware marketplace.

Most contracts make no exception for poor service, the company's inability to live up to its part of the contract, or even death of the cell phone user. That's right: If you die, your family may have to pay over a hundred dollars to cancel your cell phone service.

Read your contract carefully, and insist on having the details of the plan explained to you. You are responsible for any agreements you sign, no matter how unfair or unethical they are. If you need to cancel a cell contract because the service if poor, discuss it with your cell provider, and if they won't do the right thing, call the Better Business Bureau (BBB), your local newspaper or news program's consumer advocate, or if your state has one, the consumer affairs department.

Secret #77: Number Portability

Starting in November 2003, the FCC implemented the new Local Number Portability (LNP) rules. You are now able to take your phone number with you when you change cellular services. Switching services doesn't mean switching numbers. Initially this service was available only in the 100 top metropolitan statistical areas (MSA) in the U.S., but carriers were given six months to make it available nationwide. By May 24, 2004, cell phone users across the country should be able to switch numbers when they switch services.

Even though you can now switch your service and keep your number, you are still bound by any contracts you have signed. Most likely you will have to pay penalties for early termination. Your old carrier may charge a fee for porting your number; the fees are likely to vary, so check with your new provider prior to porting. However, your provider cannot hold your number hostage until you pay porting fees. You can still transfer the number to a new service even if you owe your previous carrier porting fees.

You also can transfer your wired phone number to your cell phone if you should decide to forego having a landline phone. This service will take a little longer to implement, so you will want to plan accordingly. Also, porting your landline number will change your long distance provider to your cell company; so you must plan for that as well

You can only port your number to a carrier that serves the same geographic area. For example, if your number is (619) 555-1111, you can't switch to a carrier in the 313 area code and keep the same number. The new carrier must provide service in your area in order for you to keep the same number.

The FCC also recommends that you do the following when porting your number to a new carrier:

- ♦ Compare rates and coverage prior to switching (we might have never thought of that one).
- ♦ Review your contract. You should be aware of porting and cancellation fees.
- ♦ Don't cancel your old service prior to signing up for your new one. This may cause you to lose your number.
- ♦ Contact your new carrier. Let the new carrier initiate the porting process.
- ♦ Bring a copy of your current phone bill to the new carrier to assist them when dealing with your old company.

Even though you can port your phone number, this doesn't guarantee that you can keep your old phone. Chances are your old phone is incompatible with another carrier's network, so you'll have to purchase a new one. Your carrier will activate the new phone with your old number.

---

on the
web
For more information on LNP regulations, visit the FCC Web site at www.fcc.gov/cgb/NumberPortability/.

Staying Connected on the Road

Chapter

8

◆ ◆

Secrets in This Chapter

◆ ◆

Connecting to the Internet with a mobile device, whether it's a phone, PDA, or notebook, gives you real-time access to news and information, shopping, and services no matter where you are. This chapter demystifies wireless Web terms and technologies and provides you with the information you need to make informed decisions and select the solutions best for you.

Examining Wireless Web Technologies

If you want to stay connected with wireless while you're on the road, you have two main services to choose from. You can access your e-mail and the Web via a Wi-Fi service or subscribe to a digital cellular service with Web and e-mail access. A Wi-Fi connection lets you surf the Web and download e-mail at fast speeds, but it requires that you be in the proximity of a Wi-Fi hotspot. Cellular, while slower (for now), gives you greater mobility and for the time being a much larger coverage area.

Secret #78: How the Wireless Web Is Different

Besides the obvious difference, the wireless Web differs from the regular World Wide Web primarily by the content that can be presented on mobile devices. The wireless Web isn't a separate entity. When you access the wireless Web you're accessing the regular Internet, just via a different route.

To deal with the limitations of cell phones and similar small-screen, low-power devices, wireless Web content is composed in (or converted to) the Wireless Markup Language (WML). Most wireless Web pages are produced separately from the regular Web site. Many major Web sites and portals provide Web pages written in WML to be accessible by mobile devices, in addition to the "same" pages in standard HTML for standard screens (see Figure 8-1).

Figure 8-1: A Web site viewed on a cell phone with a WAP browser. Unlike HTML, WAP pages are little more than text and usually have no graphics.

If you're using a PDA or smart phone, your wireless Web experience will be quite different from Web surfing on your PC. If you have an older PDA, you'll be browsing via a WAP interface, just like on a cell phone. Newer PDAs have larger screens, typically with a screen resolution of 320 x 240 pixels, compared to a minimum desktop PC resolution of 640 x 480. These newer PDAs and smart phones can run Web browsers that present a wireless Web experience much closer to what you have come to expect from a PC or notebook, only much smaller. This gives users of PDAs and smart phones easier access to a wider variety of Web content.

---

insider insight

You may wonder what the difference is between a smart phone and a PDA with cellular voice services built in. The answer is: not a whole lot. A smart phone is usually smaller, looks like a phone, perhaps even a "clamshell" flip-phone, and has a smaller screen and less computing power. A smart phone is a full-fledged PDA with cellular technology built in. It looks like a PDA, and it has more memory and a bigger, often color screen. Both PDAs and smart phones are available in Palm OS or Windows (Pocket PC, Windows Mobile) versions and can usually use popular PDA software.

Regardless of the way you choose to access the wireless Web, the advantage is clear: freedom to access information where you need it and when you need it. This is the true power of the Internet beginning to be realized; we live in an information-based economy, and on-demand information in the palm of your hand is as empowering as it can get.

No more plugging in and dialing up. No more running home or to the office to check and send e-mail. You won't have to miss a beat; just log in from wherever you are and get what you need. With enhanced digital cellular networks and new Wi-Fi services appearing, the connection speed is going to keep increasing. Before long you'll be able to get most, if not all, of your Internet services via your wireless device, including streaming media.

Secret #79: Deciding What You Want to Do with a Mobile Device

As with everything else we've looked at thus far, your first step is going to be deciding what services you want and what you want to accomplish with wireless Internet access. Consider the following services:

- E-mail
- Information services (such as stocks, weather, news)
- Instant messaging or chat (not SMS)
- Shopping

E-Mail

E-mail is the application that drove people to adopt the Internet, and now it's doing the same for wireless services. Ask anyone why they a want wireless Internet device and they'll probably answer that they want access to e-mail while they are away from home or the office. Adding e-mail service to a phone with voice mail essentially lets you take your office with you (see Figure 8-2).

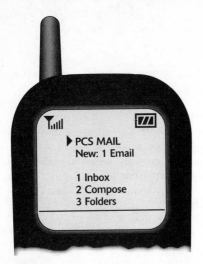

Figure 8-2: E-mail via a mobile phone.

Many cell carriers provide e-mail service as part of their contracts. Often you also can check your phone's e-mail via a Web interface on the carrier's Web site, allowing you to have one e-mail address and to access it everywhere, even from your home PC.

Information Services

Many portals, including Yahoo! and MSN, offer Web alerts and information services that you can sign up for. You visit the site and select the updates that you want to receive. These are then sent to your phone as text messages. Some carriers charge for text messages or count them toward your on-air minutes.

You also can access this information via your phone's (or PDA's) Web browser. Rather than receive multiple text messages throughout the day, you can log in and check information when you want to.

Instant Messaging and Chat

Instant messaging and chat are other popular reasons for getting a mobile Internet connection. I'm not referring to simple text messaging here; I mean full-fledged IM, like MSN Messenger. If you have a Web-enabled PDA or smart phone, you can log into your MSN messenger account and chat and IM your contacts just like you would from your PC.

This differs from simple text messaging because it's an interactive two-way process. Your contacts or "buddies" can see when you're online and contact you in real time. With the regular Simple Messaging Service (SMS) available on most phones, people can send a message to your phone, but they have no idea when you receive it because if your phone is off or out of your coverage area, the message is saved at an SMS server and forwarded when you're available.

Shopping

You probably aren't going to do a lot of shopping via a WAP browser on your phone, but if you have a Web-enabled PDA or a smart phone you can shop online just like you would on your laptop or desktop PC. It is possible to shop via WAP, but the experience isn't the same, and you don't have the option of viewing photos of products (see Figure 8-3).

Figure 8-3: Shopping at Amazon.com via a WAP browser.

In a pinch you can certainly buy what you need or check the status of an order, but you'll probably want to do your online shopping from your PC or laptop.

Browsing with a Mobile Device

As you've seen, browsing the World Wide Web on a mobile device is a different experience than it is using a standard PC and browser. Because of a number of factors, which I'll explain shortly, mobile devices don't lend themselves well to casual Web surfing. To get the most out of them you should take the time to plan and prepare in advance. Know what you need, where to get it, and organize your bookmarks ahead of time. Being prepared will save you time and money, ensuring that you get the most out of your investment in a wireless device and service. First, you need to decide whether a PDA or a smart phone best suits your browsing needs.

Secret #80: Browsing with Your PDA

PDAs are incredibly useful tools and pack quite a bit of computing power considering their size. Even the very first Palm OS PDAs had more computing power than the Apollo 11 command module. Some PDAs have more raw computing power than the computers on the space shuttle, which were designed in the 1970s. Today, top of the line PDAs are more powerful than some older PCs.

How you choose to connect to the Internet with your PDA partially depends on what is available in your area, with the choices being between Wi-Fi service or a cellular connection. Wi-Fi service is usually available in places where you'll most likely need to access it, such as hotels, airports, restaurants, and convention centers (see Figure 8-4). Wherever large numbers of people congregate is a likely place for a Wi-Fi hotspot.

---

note   A *hotspot* is the coverage area of a Wi-Fi access point. While you are in the hotspot, you can connect to the access point and surf the Web or check e-mail.

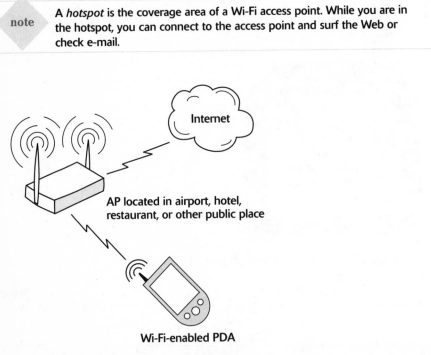

Figure 8-4: Connecting with a PDA via a hotspot.

Wi-Fi connections are multi-megabit, blazing fast compared to cellular connections. The downside is that the coverage area is smaller and you have to locate hotspots to connect (see Figure 8-5). In spring 2003, Sprint PCS began rolling out a nationwide Wi-Fi service, with a plan to set up 2,100 hotspots by 2004.

---

cross ref   Table 8-7 contains a list of Web sites that can be used to locate hotspots in your area.

Wi-Fi services offered by carriers like Sprint makes locating access points easier by providing software that detects compatible hotspots and automates connections. Sprint also plans to make a directory of hotspots available via customers' devices. This directory will be updated online and downloaded to devices when they are connected. Users will be able to view the directory offline and locate local access points.

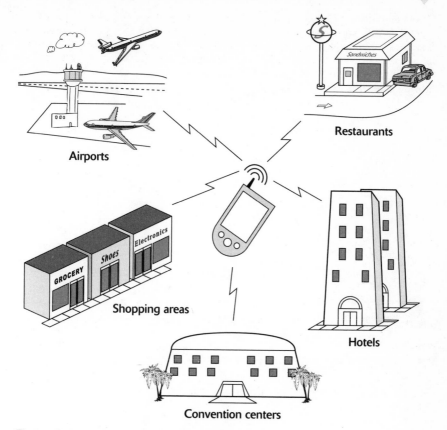

Figure 8-5: Likely places for Wi-Fi hotspots.

Connecting via Wi-Fi requires you to purchase a Wi-Fi card or a PDA with Wi-Fi support built in. Wi-Fi is a distinct technology from digital cellular PCS services and requires an adapter with 802.11b/g/a support. Your service provider will inform you of the exact 802.11 standard that it supports.

You also can choose to connect to the Web via a cellular connection (see Figure 8-6). Cellular connections are slower, but they still usually surpass the speed of a dial-up modem. To connect via a cellular connection, you must buy your device from your service provider. The PDA will have a cellular phone integrated into it, and it will have voice service in addition to wireless data services.

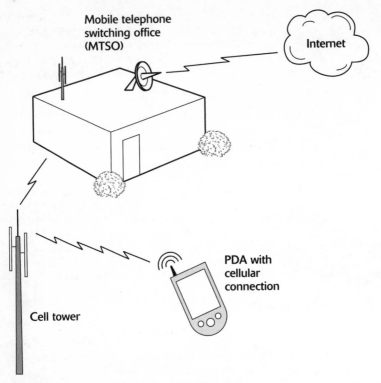

Figure 8-6: Connecting with a PDA via cellular.

Secret #81: Browsing with Phones

Your browsing experience will vary among phones. Some have larger screens, and others have better keypads. The speed of the average WAP phone is around 19.2 Kbps, not quick by anyone's standard, but because WAP is all text, it's not a problem. Speed isn't the issue when browsing with a WAP phone, the interface is.

Depending on your phone model, your display may show as little as three rows of text, each only twelve characters across. All the information you browse on the Web has to wrap to fit in this space. You're going to be doing a lot of scrolling to view information and read e-mail. Some newer phones open up to reveal a larger horizontal display that makes WAP browsing a little more enjoyable (see Figure 8-7).

Figure 8-7: A phone with a large horizontal display.

The other drawback with most WAP phones is entering data via the phone key-pad. If you've programmed names and contact information into your phone, you know how annoying this can be. It can get tedious when you have to enter user names and passwords using tiny keys so that your finger can't hit just one at a time. Typing in several Web addresses this way can tip a sane person over the edge.

Secret #82: Considering Security and Airtime Charges

If WAP browsing is a feature available on your phone, smart phone, or PDA and is supported by your service, you should be able to connect with little or no setup. Depending on the security that your carrier uses, your first connection to the wireless Web may entail your phone downloading a cryptographic key to establish a secure connection. Depending on the size of the key, this could take up to a few minutes. This is an important step; having your wireless Web data encrypted protects any information that you send to or receive from Web sites.

---

cross ref   I discuss encryption in Chapter 16.

You also may see a reminder about airtime charges when you start your WAP browser. Don't forget, when you connect to the wireless Web, you're making a call and airtime charges apply. There also may be additional service charges, and you may have a base amount of Web time allotted to your account each month. Exceed this time and you could incur significant overtime charges.

Secret #83: Time- and Cost-Saving Tips

Because airtime charges can add up quickly if you use the wireless Web fre-quently, any steps you take to streamline your browsing process can save you a significant amount of money. A good start is to avoid having to re-input Web addresses every time you surf. Most phones have a "Favorites" type of feature that lets you save Web addresses so that you can get to them quickly on subse-quent visits.

---

note   Not all phones enable you to input Web addresses; some only enable you to select from a list that you have set up via your carrier's Web site.

You also may be able to set your bookmarks and preferences for Web sites via a Web page using your PC (see Figure 8-8). This way you can sit down and input all of your Web addresses, contacts, and e-mail addresses without adding to your airtime. Your provider may have the most popular wireless portals and sites bookmarked already. Check the list and add any sites that you frequent to save time when you're browsing with your phone.

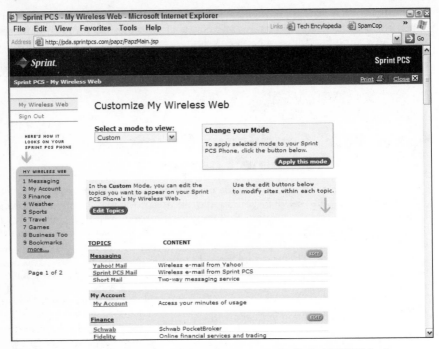

Figure 8-8: Setting up wireless Web preferences on the Sprint PCS Web site.

Once you've signed into some sites you can remain logged in, even between wireless Web sessions. This can keep you from having to enter a long user-name/password combination when you visit the site again. (Be careful about doing this; you don't want to lose your phone if you've remained logged into an e-mail account like Yahoo! mail, or MSN Hotmail or a shopping site like Amazon.com. Whoever finds your handset would then have access to those accounts and all of the information contained in them.)

Secret #84: Using Search Engines on the Wireless Web

Finding information isn't any harder on the wireless Web than it is on your PC. Google has a WAP page so you can perform Google searches from your phone (see Figure 8-9). Google is the default search page on the Sprint PCS wireless Web; you don't even have to enter the address, just select the search feature.

The Google WAP page has limited functionality compared to the HTML version, and it doesn't support some advanced features like spellchecking. Another difference is the search results; the Google WAP page only returns results for pages that you can access from a WAP browser. Makes sense, doesn't it?

---

cross
ref   Appendix B contains some useful search sites for mobile devices.

Figure 8-9: The Google WAP page in action.

Information on the wireless Web is also organized into several portals that make finding related information easier. An example of a wireless portal is the MSN Mobile portal. The MSN Mobile portal lets you access Hotmail, Messenger, MSN alerts, ring tones, and more. The site is organized so that you can get around quickly and easily. A WAP portal can help you save time by giving you access to things that you need all in the same place.

Secret #85: Useful Sites on the Wireless Web

The wireless Web can help you stay connected to customers, check e-mail, and even track shipments. Whether you're using a mobile phone or a PDA, there are sites that will help you be more productive and successful. Tables 8-1 through 8-5 list some of the more popular and useful sites grouped according to function or service. Appendix B also contains a list of useful resources for mobile devices.

Table 8-1: Travel

Site	Address	Description
MapQuest	www.mapquest.com	Driving directions
Sabre/Travelocity	www.sabre.com	Travel information in real-time
MyPNA	www.mypna.com	Traffic information and directions
OAG Mobile	www.oag.com	Worldwide flight statuses and schedules
GetThere.com	www.getthere.com	Flight statuses and schedules
Expedia.com	www.expedia.com	The world leader in online travel

Table 8-2: Finance

Site	Address	Description

Hoover's Online	`http://catalyst.`
	`2roam.com/www.`
	`hoovers.com`
		All the business information you need

Bloomberg News	`www.bloomberg.com`	Financial info and business analysis
Forbes.com	`www.forbes.com`	Home page for the world's business leaders
CBS Market Watch	`http://cbs.` `marketwatch.com`	Interactive financial news

Table 8-3: Weather

Site	Address	Description
The Weather Channel	`www.weather.com`	Weather forecasts for over 40,000 cities
Go2weather	`www.go2.com`	Get weather information via Go2online

Table 8-4: News and Information

Site	Address	Description
CNET	`www.cnet.com`	The latest in tech news and information
Real Cities Local News	`www.realcities.com`	Local news and information
CNN	`www.cnn.com`	National and international news
MSNBC	`www.msnbc.com`	National and international news
The New York Times	`www.nytimes.com`	The NY Times, when and where you need it
USA Today	`www.usatoday.com`	National and international news and headlines
The Washington Post	`www.washingtonpost.` `com`	News and information on Washington and the world

Table 8-5: Tools and Reference

Site	Address	Description
Google	www.google.com	Search the mobile Web
ConvertIT.com	www.convertit.com	Conversions
Dictionary.com	www.dictionary.com	Definitions and translations

Public Networks and Hotspots

Wi-Fi hotspots are popping up all over the country. Some of these are part of branded commercial services; others are free or part of a community Wi-Fi project. Before you connect to any of these Wi-Fi hotspots, you have to find them.

Secret #86: Finding Public and Community Networks via Wireless User Groups

Across the country, businesses and communities are making public wireless access available. In coffee shops, restaurants, airports, and campuses people are able to connect and access the Internet and e-mail. Currently, there are over 12,000 hotspots in North America and 28,000 worldwide. Analysts expect over 200,000 hotspots worldwide by 2008.

Often, public networks are initiated by the local Wireless Users Group (WUG). If there is a WUG in your area, it can be a great source of information about local hotspots and any community networks. Table 8-6 lists some of the largest and better-known WUGs in the country.

Table 8-6: Wireless User Groups

Site	Address	Description
Bay Area Wireless Users Group (BAWUG)	www.bawug.org	This group promotes wireless use in the San Francisco Bay Area. BAWUG is one of the first and largest WUGs in the U.S.
Southern California Wireless Users Group (SOCALWUG)	www.socalwug.org	This group serves the greater Los Angeles area.
Dallas Fort Worth Wireless Users Group (DFWWUG)	www.dfwwireless.org	DFW area group, one of the largest in the country

continued

Table 8-6: *(continued)*

Site	Address	Description
NYCwireless	www.nycwireless.org	Members of this group in New York City provide free wireless Internet access to their communities. One of NYCwireless's stated goals is to bring broadband wireless Internet access into underserved communities in its area.
San Diego Wireless Users Group (SDWUG)	www.sdwug.org	SDWUG is an open group dedicated to promoting wireless LAN technology. SDWUG members also have started planning and implementing free public hotspots.

WUGs are great sources of technical information as well as an excellent place to meet other Wi-Fi users and participate in projects that benefit your community.

Secret #87: Other Sites for Locating Hotspots

If you sign up for a commercial Wi-Fi service, you'll have access to updated lists of hotspots that are part of your ISP's network. However, the Internet has some useful sites for locating both commercial and free hotspots. Table 8-7 lists some of the most popular of these sites.

Table 8-7: Hotspots

Site	Address	Description
Jiwire.com	www.jiwire.com	This is one of the most complete databases of worldwide hotspots on the net. The name means *Joining Invisible Wire*. Jiwire.com's database shows hotspots in your area, which service runs them, and the cost (if any) for connecting.
Wifinder.com	www.wifinder.com	Wifinder is an independent Wi-Fi directory for both commercial and free Wi-Fi hotspots.

Site	Address	Description
RedDotSpots.com	www.RedDotSpots.com	This is an open directory of free, wireless hotspots. It's not as extensive as the previous sites, and it relies on users to register their own hotspots.

In 2003, McDonald's Corporation began to offer wireless service in some of its restaurants. This service, named McD Wireless, offers users high-speed wireless Internet access while in McDonald's restaurants. Starbucks Coffee has teamed with T-Mobile to start offering Wi-Fi access in its coffee shops. Like McDonald's, these are subscription services, and you can buy access for about $10 per day or for a monthly subscription.

Secret #88: Getting Connected to Hotspots

To connect to most commercial hotspots, you'll need to subscribe to a wireless ISP and buy the appropriate adapter for your device. Don't run out and get the adapter just yet; your ISP may have specific requirements, or it may not support your new 802.11a card at all its sites. There are several wireless ISPs to choose from. Table 8-8 offers some of the bigger ones, with the widest coverage areas.

> **insider insight** Many of these companies have agreements or partnerships with one another, and others are direct investors in other Wi-Fi services. For instance, Sprint partners with Wayport, yet is a direct investor in Boingo Wireless.
>
> Most of the major cellular companies are launching Wi-Fi services, so competition should start heating up here very soon. This should mean better deals for wireless consumers and perhaps bundled services (Wi-Fi + Cell).

Table 8-8: Wireless ISPs

Site	Address	Description
Boingo Wireless	www.boingo.com	As of October 2003, Boingo had over 5,000 hotspots worldwide. Boingo's hotspots include about 3,500 cafes, 1,300 hotels, 200 office buildings, 28 airports, and 11 convention centers in 19 countries. You can subscribe through Boingo or one of its many major ISP partners.

continued

Table 8-8: *(continued)*

Site	Address	Description
Wayport	www.wayport.com	Wayport provides high-speed Wi-Fi Internet access in more than 600 hotels and 12 airports nationwide. Wayport also provides service to more than 70 McDonald's locations in the San Francisco Bay Area.
Sprint PCS	www.sprintpcs.com	Sprint is aggressively expanding its Wi-Fi services as a complement to its enhanced digital PCS services. Sprint's Wi-Fi offerings will be available at over 2,100 hotspots in the U.S. by spring 2004.
T-Mobile HotSpot	www.t-mobile.com/hotspot	T-Mobile HotSpot claims to have the world's largest Wi-Fi network. It provides high-speed Wi-Fi Internet access in airports, Starbucks coffeehouses, and Borders Books & Music stores.
Verizon	www.verizon.net/wifi/	Verizon is beginning to launch its own Wi-Fi service, starting in New York City. Interestingly, Verizon is offering the Wi-Fi service to Verizon online customers at no additional cost. Hopefully this will spark competition among ISPs and we can all benefit.

Working with Mobile E-Mail and Messaging

Chapter

9

◆ ◆

Secrets in This Chapter

◆ ◆

E-mail is the original "killer app," the solution that convinced millions of people to get connected and adopt the Internet and related technologies. Today, it is one of the main reasons why people consider investing in a mobile wireless device.

Wireless E-Mail Options

For many people, having access to e-mail while traveling is not just a luxury, it's a requirement. The device you use will dictate what sort of e-mail solution is available.

Secret #89: Mobile Devices and E-Mail Limitations

Although wireless e-mail is different in many ways from wired e-mail, it's essentially the same technology delivered in a different way. To illustrate this let's review how e-mail works, and then we can compare it to wireless e-mail and see where it's different.

An e-mail system requires two types of applications to function: an e-mail server that receives and forwards messages and an e-mail client that enables the user to compose, send, receive and read e-mail from the server. Microsoft Outlook is an example of an e-mail client, as is Qualcomm's Eudora.

Generally, there are two types of e-mail server standards in use: POP3 and IMAP. Post Office Protocol 3 (POP3) servers are very common and many ISPs use them. A POP3 server receives e-mail messages from the Internet and holds them until you connect and download your messages and attachments. POP3 servers are simple and don't offer as many features as IMAP.

Internet Message Access Protocol (IMAP) servers offer users more options. IMAP enables users to browse headers and then decide which messages to download. An IMAP server also enables users to archive messages and store them in personalized folders (though these features depend on your ISP or mail administrator making them available).

To send and receive e-mail you need to have an e-mail address and account. An Internet e-mail address is divided into two parts: the username and the domain. For example, in the e-mail address jackm@myisp.com, jackm indicates my username and myisp.com indicates the domain of my mail server. Using this address format, mail servers can forward mail to one another.

insider
insight When designing the first e-mail system in 1971, Ray Tomlinson chose the symbol @ to separate the username and domain in e-mail addresses. At first this choice wasn't popular because the @ was a control character used in some early computer systems. Inserting an @ sign caused the computer to delete the previous line of text. This problem was remedied by programmers and the @ sign remains in use to this day.

The @ sign, pronounced "at," is officially known as the *commercial at* and rarely the *asperand*. Computer users located in countries other than the U.S. have had to assimilate and name this new symbol, which prior to the Internet, may not even have existed on their keyboards. While some countries adopt the English *commercial at* or just "at," some have created their own unique names for the symbol.

Here are some examples of names that users in different countries have adopted for the @ sign:

- In Dutch the @ is called an *apestaart (monkey's tail)* or *apestaartje (little monkey's tail)*.

- In Hebrew it's called either *shablul* or *shablool (snail)*; and sometimes *shtrudl (strudel, the pastry)*.

- In Hungarian it's slandered and called the *kukac (worm or maggot)*.

- The Taiwanese sometimes call it *xiao lao-shu (little mouse)* or *lao shu-hao (mouse sign)*.

- In Japan it's called the *atto maaku (at mark)*.

When you send an e-mail, your mail server uses the domain portion of the e-mail address to do a Domain Name Service (DNS) lookup and find the Internet Protocol (IP) address of that domain's mail server. Once it locates the IP address it contacts the addressee's server and attempts to deliver the e-mail. The addressee's server checks the username portion of the e-mail address, and if it recognizes the username, it delivers the message to the appropriate mailbox (see Figure 9-1). If the receiving mail server doesn't recognize the username it sends an "undeliverable mail" message back to you via your server.

If you want to attach a file to your e-mail, let's say a picture or movie, your e-mail client software has to encode it so that it can be transmitted as part of the text message (see Figure 9-2). For outgoing mail, servers utilize the Simple Mail Transfer Protocol (SMTP). SMTP is a protocol that describes the format of text messages and how they are transferred over the Internet. Because SMTP was only designed for ASCII text messages, a method for encoding e-mail attachments into ASCII text is needed. Today the most common method for transmitting non-text attachments is the Multipurpose Internet Mail Extensions (MIME). MIME encodes attachments so that they can be transmitted as part of an SMTP message.

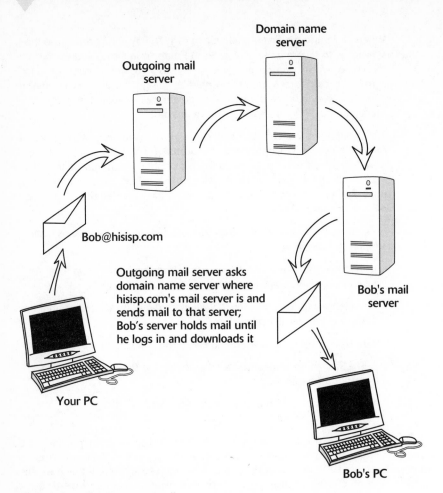

Figure 9-1: Sending an e-mail.

When MIME encodes an attachment, the message is converted to ASCII text. This text can be transmitted via the SMTP protocol and decoded back into the original. In Figure 9-3 you can see a JPEG file that I want to attach to an e-mail.

When I attach this photo to an e-mail, MIME encodes it and converts it into a series of ASCII characters. If we were to view the MIME attachment without decoding it back into a JPEG, it would look something like this:

```
MIME-version: 1.0
Content-type: multipart/mixed;

IyEvYmluL3NoCgojIy91c3IvWDExUjYvYmluL1ggJgojI3NsZWVwIDE1CiMgIHhOZX
JtIC1zYiAtZ2VvbWVOcnkgODB4MjQrMTAwKzEOMCAmCnhob3N0NOICsKeHN1dCBz9mZg
p4c2VOcm9vdCAtc29saWQgJyM2NjY2NjYnCm9jbG9jayAtZ2VvbWVOcnkgMTAweDEw
MCsxMCsxMjIAgJgp4bG9hZCAtanVtcHNicm9sbCAxICLnZW9tZXRyeeSA2MHg4MCsxMC
syMzAgJgojICB4c2VOcm9vdCAtYml0bWFwIGNoYYWluMi5ibXAKIyMvdXNyL29wZW53ZW53
aW4vYmluL29sdndtCi91c3IvWDEx L2Jpbi9mdndtCgo=
```

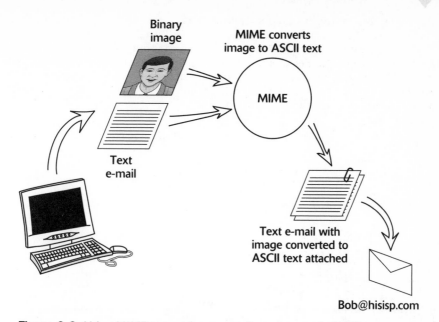

Figure 9-2: Using MIME to transfer an e-mail attachment via SMTP.

Figure 9-3: A JPEG file before MIME encoding.

Wireless e-mail basically works in the same manner as wired e-mail, although most mobile devices don't support attachments the same way a PC or laptop would. This has nothing to do with the delivery methods (wireless versus wired), but with the lack of storage and memory on most mobile devices. Some PDAs can receive and view attachments, depending on the type of attachment and the application required to view it. For example, a Pocket PC device can open a Microsoft Word document sent as an attachment, provided it has Pocket Word installed.

When you send or receive an e-mail through your mobile device, your message goes through your carrier's network, cellular, or Wi-Fi, and then through your carrier's mail server. From there it travels the same route that an e-mail from a desktop PC would take (see Figure 9-4). Sometimes, depending on the type of mobile device and service you are using, e-mail received for your address is routed through a Short Messaging Service (SMS) system for delivery. This is often the case with mobile phones.

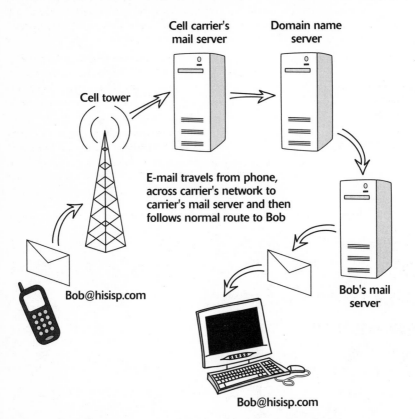

Figure 9-4: Sending an e-mail from your mobile wireless device.

Most mobile phone carriers include e-mail either as part of their basic phone service or sometimes for an additional charge; either way, airtime charges usually apply when you are retrieving your e-mail. For example, as a Sprint PCS customer I have e-mail included as part of my service.

The e-mail address for a mobile device is formatted the same way as any other e-mail address. In the case of Sprint PCS, my e-mail address is nottelling@ sprintpcs.com; nottelling is the username and the domain is sprintpcs.com. Any other Internet mail server can locate and send mail to sprintpcs.com.

Secret #90: Web-Based E-Mail Solutions

Because most mobile devices have at least a WAP browser, one alternative to the e-mail service provided by your cell carrier is to use a Web-based e-mail client. You can access your e-mail, and many Web-based e-mail services will send alerts to your mobile phone to let you know when you have new e-mail. Both Yahoo! mail and MSN Hotmail support mobile devices.

A Web-based e-mail service also solves another problem for many mobile users: storing contact information for a large number of people. While some devices, a PDA for instance, can store a large number of contacts in great detail, the average cell phone is limited in the amount of contact information it can store. Some cell phones don't store e-mail contacts at all.

A Web-based e-mail client usually enables you to store and manage your contacts on the Web site and to access your address book from your mobile device when you are composing e-mail. Some of the e-mail accounts provided by cell carriers also have a Web-based interface where you can manage your e-mail and address book (see Figure 9-5).

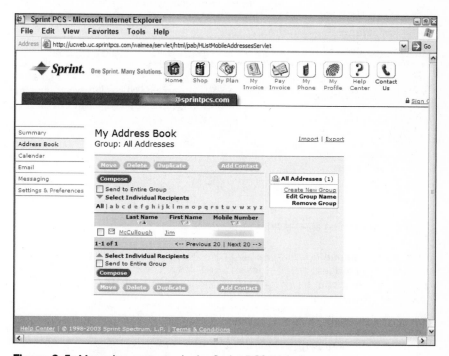

Figure 9-5: Managing contacts via the Sprint PCS Web site.

Storing and managing your contacts via a Web site is also safer. If your mobile device is lost or stolen, your contact information isn't on it. Your information will be safe and sound on a server, and you won't lose a thing. This also is more convenient when you are switching to a new phone; you don't have to reenter all of your contacts on a new device. Just use the new device to access your online address book.

Secret #91: Managing Multiple Accounts

Let's face it; the big drawback to all of this communication is that most of us have several e-mail accounts. Either we've collected them along the way and just never closed the old ones, or we keep getting new ones every time we sign up for a service or get a new device. I have several accounts: my work address, my cell phone account, my home ISP, a Hotmail account, and so on.

At some point checking each of these accounts gets far too tedious, even if the majority of them are only checked occasionally. If the majority of your contacts use your work or home e-mail address, what good does it do you if you get a cell phone with a mobile account? Do you want everyone you know to start using the mobile e-mail address? You probably don't, especially if you need to receive e-mail attachments.

If you really need wireless access to your work address, what can you do if your corporate e-mail server doesn't support your wireless device? Many companies that have implemented wireless e-mail use solutions like the RIM BlackBerry server that requires each user to have a BlackBerry device to access their e-mail (see Figure 9-6). This may not be an option where you work, and even if it is you may not want to have to purchase yet another device.

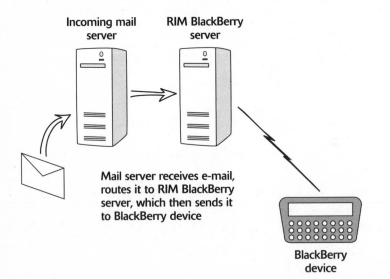

Figure 9-6: Getting e-mail via a RIM BlackBerry device.

One alternative is to use a Web-based service that can check all of your e-mail addresses and consolidate your messages in one place (see Figure 9-7). An example of this type of service is legmail.com. This service can check your POP3 e-mail server and online e-mail accounts like Yahoo! and Hotmail. It consolidates all the mail in one inbox, and you can view and reply to the mail from one place. You can also reply using the return e-mail address of the account where the mail was originally sent.

note   If you decide to use a service like legmail.com, make sure that the service is accessible from your mobile device, especially if it's a WAP device.

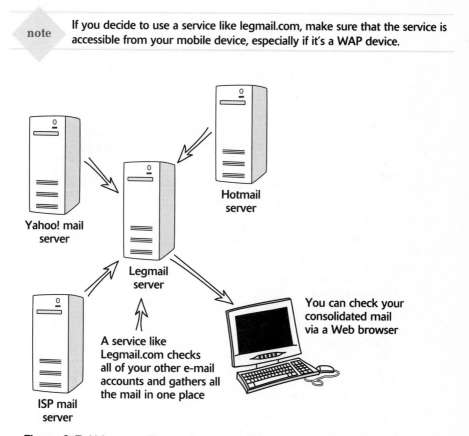

Figure 9-7: Using an online service to consolidate your e-mail.

A second alternative is to use an application called a redirector. A *redirector* is an application that you install on your PC. It monitors your incoming mail and forwards it to client software on your mobile device. Your PC has to remain on and connected to the Internet for a redirector to work. Depending on the redirector, you can view and reply to e-mail messages as if you were sitting right at your PC. Some redirectors also enable you to redirect e-mail from Web-based e-mail and POP3 servers all to one device (see Figure 9-8). An example of a redirector is Visto MessageXpress, available at www.visto.com.

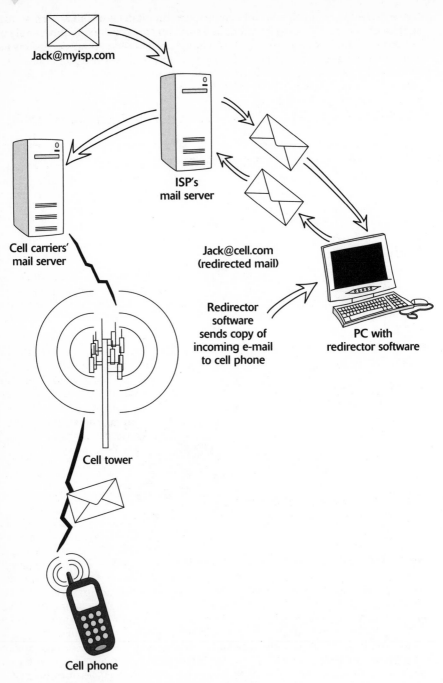

Jack@myisp.com

ISP's
mail server

Cell carriers'
mail server

Jack@cell.com
(redirected mail)

Redirector
software
sends copy of
incoming e-mail
to cell phone

PC with
redirector software

Cell tower

Cell phone

Figure 9-8: Using a redirector to forward e-mail.

You also can set up your e-mail client to forward a copy of the e-mail to your mobile device. If you use Microsoft Outlook you can accomplish this simply by setting up a rule to forward e-mail to your device when certain conditions are met, such as when you have activated your out-of-office notification.

Secret #92: Mobile E-Mail Tips and Etiquette

E-mail etiquette becomes even more important when you're dealing with limited message sizes and the tiny screens of mobile devices. Most of the common-sense rules for e-mail sent to and from a desktop PC apply when you're e-mailing someone via their mobile. However, some deserve special emphasis because not following them can really irritate mobile e-mail customers.

Rule #1 Keep It Simple

Keeping your message short and sweet is always a good idea, especially because most of us have a decreasing amount of time to spend reading an increasing amount of e-mail. The per-message allotment is getting shorter, so the best thing you can do is stay on topic, be brief, and wrap it up. This is especially true for e-mail sent to a mobile device.

Mobile devices usually have small screens, and viewing long e-mails can get tedious because the user has to keep scrolling, or worse, downloading the message one section at a time. Often there are limits on the amount of text that can be sent in a single e-mail. If you're sending a text message via e-mail, this message will certainly be limited to approximately 160 characters.

Also, mobile phone users are usually charged airtime when they are accessing e-mail on their cell phones, so remember that the recipient is paying to be able to read your e-mail, and the longer it is, the more time and money that they will spend reading it.

Rule #2 Don't Shout

USING ALL CAPS IS NEVER A GOOD IDEA. IT'S HARD TO READ AND IT LOOKS LIKE YOU'RE SHOUTING ALL THE TIME. On the small screen of a mobile phone, it can be even harder to read and is certainly more annoying. If you use all caps, you will seem unprofessional, inconsiderate, and immature. Personally, I would read about a sentence of an all-caps e-mail before moving on to less aggravating messages.

Rule #3 Don't Write in Code

You want to save time and keep your message brief; perhaps you're composing your e-mail on your own cell phone and hate using the number pad to key in your text. Abbreviating words is fine, and in this case makes sense, but make sure everyone knows what the heck you are saying. Use abbreviations that everyone understands; don't invent your own on the spot and expect your readers to decipher it. A good source for commonly-understood abbreviations is the instant messaging shorthand glossary at the end of this chapter.

Secret #93: Fighting Spam

Spam wastes your time, and when you're using your mobile device, it wastes your money. Of course I'm not talking about Hawaii's favorite canned meat. I'm talking about unsolicited commercial e-mail, junk e-mail in fact. Once your e-mail finds its way onto a spammer's list, your inbox is inundated with spam advertising—from personal enhancement ads to car loan notices and everything in between.

Many e-mail service providers provide some sort of anti-spam service that filters out spam messages with varying degrees of success. If you have access to one of these services I suggest that you use it, but monitor it to make sure that it doesn't mistake your legitimate e-mail for spam. Spam filters usually move suspected spam to a junk folder where you can view it at your convenience, just to make sure that no real mail gets deleted by mistake.

The best way to reduce spam is to prevent your e-mail address from getting on a spammer's e-mail list in the first place. When one spammer has it, they will all get it sooner or later. Also, once you're on a list there's no way to get off of all of them; you're going to get spam forever. There are a few ways that you can avoid getting on spam lists.

   ◆ Don't ever give out your real e-mail address when filling out online forms, especially when you're entering contests or claiming "free" prizes.
   ◆ Don't post your e-mail address to Web sites or discussion and news groups.
   ◆ Don't post to discussion or news groups from your real e-mail account.

Consider setting up a throwaway or junk e-mail account that you can use as the address you give out when you sign up for stuff online. This way once the address starts finding its way onto spammer lists, the spam doesn't wind up in your real inbox. Periodically, you can log in and check the spam account to delete piled up messages and make sure that no important mail is waiting there among the spam. Also, if you use a free e-mail service you'll have to log in periodically to keep the account active.

If you participate in Usenet or other discussion groups, don't post from your real e-mail account. Spammers use automated software that scans groups and compiles lists of e-mail addresses. Post from your throwaway account, and keep your inbox spam-free.

The automated software that spammers use also can detect and copy e-mail addresses from Web pages and the bodies of news postings. If you post from your junk account but list your real e-mail address in the message body you'll end up on the junk e-mail lists. If you must post your real e-mail address, obfuscate it so that the spammers scanning software won't recognize it as an address. For example, if your e-mail address is you@yourisp.com, you could post it as "you at yourisp dot com" or "youNOSPAM@yourNOSPAMisp.com." Either one would be decipherable by a reasonably intelligent human being, but not by a spam-bot.

Besides filtering, another step that you should take is to report spam. Rather than ducking and hiding we should start hitting back. Many spammers use (abuse) someone else's mail server, often without their knowledge. If you take the time to report the spam, mail administrators can take action and stop spammers from abusing their servers. Web sites that use spam to advertise may be in violation of their service agreements and reporting the spam can get them shut down.

The best reporting tool I have found is Spamcop.net. Once you register, you can report spam through an online form or by forwarding spam to an e-mail address that they assign you. You also can get a spamcop.net e-mail address, which spamcop.net monitors to filter out spam. In the three years that I have been using Spamcop.net, I have seen about a dozen "spamvertised" Web sites get shut down as a result of my reporting them.

on the web   You can visit Spamcop and start fighting spam at `www.spamcop.net`.

Secret #94: Alerts from the Web

In addition to checking your e-mail, you also can take advantage of services that send alerts directly to your mobile device to inform you of breaking news, stock prices, weather, appointment reminders, or other information that you desire. You can even have alerts sent to your device to let you know when you have received new e-mail or even e-mail from a specific person.

Many online services offer mobile alerts, including Yahoo! and MSN mobile. You can have MSN Mobile alerts delivered free of charge; all you have to do is set up a passport account and log in to set up the MSN Mobile to work with your device and service.

on the web   To set up an MSN Mobile account, visit `http://mobile.msn.com`.

When you set up alerts, make sure that you pay attention to how often you'll be receiving them. Some carriers only allot a specific number of free messages per month, after which you'll be paying for each message you receive. Check to see how many messages you're allowed prior to subscribing to an alert service

Having Fun

CMIIW (correct me if I'm wrong), but messaging is probably one of the most convenient and fun uses for a mobile device. While e-mail may be the original "killer app," messaging is a close second, and now popular chat services like Yahoo! and MSN are expanding from the PC and onto mobile devices.

Secret #95: SMS Explained

Short message service (SMS) is a text messaging service that enables you to send and receive short e-mails via your cell phones. SMS is similar to e-mail in that messages are stored at SMS centers and then forwarded to your cell phone whenever it's available (see Figure 9-9). SMS messages are usually limited to 160 characters in length.

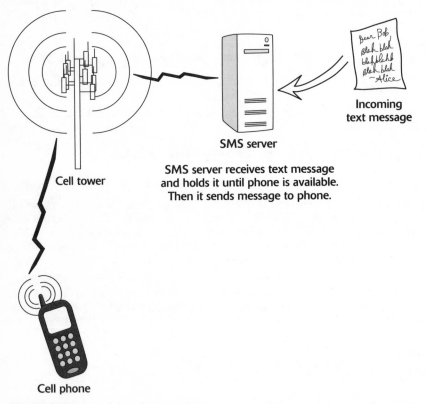

Figure 9-9: The short message service.

You also can use your e-mail software to send SMS text messages to mobile phone users from your desktop e-mail client. To do this you'll need to know the correct domain to send the e-mail to as well as the recipient's cell phone number. As an example, if you wanted to send a text message to a friend who is a Sprint PCS customer, you would format the address as cellphonenumber@ messaging.sprintpcs.com.

Your e-mail server can find the messaging.sprintpcs.com server on the Internet and send your e-mail to it. The messaging server forwards the e-mail to your friend's phone as a text message. Here are the messaging addresses for some of the larger cellular carriers:

- ◆ Nextel: number@messaging.nextel.com
- ◆ Cingular: number@mobile.mycingular.com
- ◆ T-Mobile (USA): number@tmomail.net
- ◆ Virgin Mobile (USA): number@vmobl.com
- ◆ AT&T wireless: number@mobile.att.net
- ◆ Verizon wireless: number@vtext.com
- ◆ Verizon (formerly Airtouch): number@airtouchpaging.com

Generally, you are allowed about 20 characters for the "from" line and 160 characters total for the entire message, including the heading. Some carriers allow more and some less; you'll have to check the carrier's Web site for message size.

Secret #96: Examining Instant Messaging

The difference between instant messaging (IM) and SMS messaging is that IM enables people to interact in real-time. Using IM you can see when your friends are available and message them. IM is two-way; you can carry on a conversation through text. Examples of IM clients on the desktop are MSN messenger and Yahoo! messenger.

Some mobile devices support instant messaging. The type of messaging depends on your service and your device. Some carriers enable users to IM with other handsets on their network, while with other devices you can actually interact with MSN messenger and Yahoo! messenger users. Interacting with users of MSN and Yahoo! services requires that you sign up with one of the services and that you have a compatible device.

Even if you don't have a device capable of using IM, you can set up your MSN or Yahoo! account to enable people on your friend list to send text messages to your cell phone while you're away from your PC. Essentially, the IM service forwards any instant messages to your phone as SMS messages (see Figure 9-10).

Secret #97: Investigating Wireless Chat

Chat takes place in real time just like IM does; the main difference is that chat enables more than two people to interact at once. There are several chat clients available for mobile devices. Many of them integrate with Internet chat servers and enable you to use an existing chat account. The type of chat available depends, as always, on the device and service that you have.

Many carriers have added chat services and created chat rooms accessible by their customers through a WAP browser. Sprint PCS includes chat in its wireless Web service. Most carriers have some sort of chat available to WAP-enabled phones: chatting burns minutes and carriers don't care how you use minutes; they just care that they get used. Be careful when you're chatting and using IM; you don't want to go over the minutes on your plan or you'll incur overtime charges.

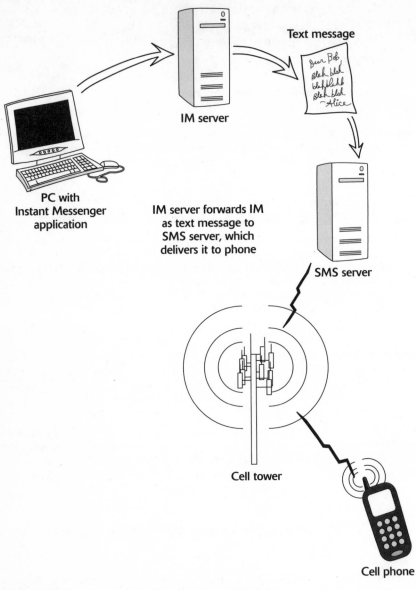

Figure 9-10: Sending SMS messages via an IM client.

Secret #98: Speaking the Language

Because most of us can't type 80+ words a minute, we need some way to make IM and chat more enjoyable and less like a Mavis Beacon typing exercise. The Internet community slowly evolved its own shorthand to deal with this, which resulted in a collection of abbreviations and emoticons, also known as *smileys*.

According to most accounts, emoticons (emotion icons) first appeared in e-mail messages back in 1979. More accurately though, these were the first ASCII emoticons, as users of Control Data Corporation's early Plato system were creating emoticons in the early 1970s.

Chances are that you've seen and used plenty of emoticons, but here are a few of the most prevalent ones in use today:

- :)—the ever-present smiley to indicate happiness
- : D— the big grin smiley, for really happy people
- : O— indicates surprise
- :(— unhappy
- :\— sideways smile, "oh well"
- ;)— a wink and a smile
- >:(— ok, now I'm mad

Use emoticons sparingly outside of IM and chat; remember, people had no problem conveying emotion through writing prior to the Internet. For brevity on mobile devices emoticons are fine; just don't overdo it. The same thing can be said for IM abbreviations; they're fine for IM, but don't start using them all the time in e-mail and documents.

IMSHG (Instant Messaging ShortHand Glossary)

There are a lot of abbreviations used in IM and chat rooms. Table 9-1 shows just a few of the more common ones, but you're sure to see variations on these, and you'll probably understand them when you encounter them in the context of a chat conversation.

Table 9-1: Common IM/Chat Abbreviations

Term	Meaning
@	At
1	One
2	To or too
2day	Today
2moro	Tomorrow
2nite	Tonight
4	For
7K	Sick (this is a good thing)
AFAIC	As far as I'm concerned
AFAIK	As far as I know
AKA	Also known as
ASAP	As soon as possible

continued

Table 9-1: *(continued)*

Term	Meaning
B	Be
BBL	Be back later
BBS	Be back soon
BRT	Be right there
BCNU	Be seeing you
B4	Before
BWD	Backward
BBFN, BFN, or B4N	Bye bye for now / bye for now
BRB	Be right back
BTDT	Been there, done that
BTW	By the way
C	See
CMIIW	Correct me if I'm wrong
CU	See you
CYA	See ya
CUL8R	See you later
CW2CU	Can't wait to see you
DOIN	Doing
EOL	End of lecture
FAQ	Frequently asked questions
FITB	Fill in the blanks
F2T	Free to talk
FOAD	F***** off and die (unfortunately you may see this a lot in chat rooms)
FUBAR	F***** up beyond all recognition
FWD	Forward
FWIW	For what it's worth
FYI	For your information
GAC or GACD	Get a clue, or Get a clue, Dad
GAL	Get a life
GALD	Get a life, Dad
GMTA	Great minds think alike
Gr8	Great
HND or HAND	Have a nice day
H8	Hate
HTH	Hope this helps

Term	Meaning
H4U	Hot for you (common in chat rooms)
IAC	In any case
IAE	In any event
ICCL	I couldn't care less
IDK	I don't know
IYSS	If you say so
IHTFP	I hate this f***** place
ILUVU or ILU	I love you
ILUVUMED or ILUMED	I love you more each day (usually elicits the awwwww response)
IMHO	In my humble opinion
IMNSHO	In my not so humble opinion
IMO	In my opinion
IOW	In other words
IRL	In real life
IYKWIM	If you know what I mean
JM2C or JM2CNTS	Just my two cents
KIT	Keep in touch
KISS	Keep it simple, stupid
L8	Late
L8R	Later
LUV	Love
LOL	Laughing out loud or, less often, lots of luck
LDR	Long distance relationship
LTNS	Long time no see
MMD	Make my day
MMDP	Make my day, punk (a la Clint Eastwood)
MOB	Mobile or actually mob
MSG	Message
MYOB	Mind your own business
MTE	My thoughts exactly
NE	Any
NE1	Anyone
NO1	No one
NRN	No reply necessary
O	Hug or Oh

continued

Table 9-1: *(continued)*

Term	*Meaning*
OIC	Oh, I see!
OTOH	On the other hand
PAW	Parents are watching, usually followed by GALD
PCM	Please call me
PITA	Pain in the a** (common in chat rooms)
PLS	Please
PPL	People
PS	Post script
PRT	Party
QPSA	Que pasa?
QL	Cool
R	Are
RGDS	Regards
ROF	Rolling on the floor
ROTFL	Rolling on the floor laughing
ROTFLMAO	Rolling on the floor laughing my a** off
ROTFPMPL	Rolling on the floor p***ing my pants laughing (only for very funny jokes)
RU	Are you?
RUOK	Are you okay?
SIT	Stay in touch
SOME1	Someone
STATS	What are your stats (age, sex, location)
STRA	Stray
SWAK	Sealed with a kiss
THNQ	Thank you
THX	Thanks
TIA	Thanks in advance
T2GO	Time to go
TTFN	Ta ta for now
TTUL8R or TTUL	Talk to you later
TUVM	Thank you very much
U	You
UR	You are or your
U2	You too
WAN2	Want to?

Term	Meaning
WAN2TLK	Want to talk
W	With
W8	Wait
WTG, W2G	Way to go
WKND	Weekend
WTTW	Word to the wise
WUF	Where are you from?
WYSIWYG	What you see is what you get
X	Kiss
XLNT	Excellent
YR	Your
YTLKIN2ME	You talking to me? (Robert DeNiro a la "Taxi Driver")
YYSW	Yeah, yeah, sure whatever
YYSWD	Yeah, yeah, sure, whatever Dad

Getting the Most Out of Your PDA

Chapter
10

◆ ◆

Secrets in This Chapter

◆ ◆

This chapter offers some recommendations for putting your PDA to its fullest use. It begins with suggestions for choosing useful accessories and then turns to software to enhance your PDA's capabilities.

Choosing Accessories for Your PDA

You can make your PDA more functional by selecting the right keyboard, adapters, and data storage accessories.

Secret #99: Keyboards for Your PDA

Perhaps the most important thing to consider when shopping for PDA accessories is how you will input your data. After all, in order to get the most out of your investment you need to be productive while using it. It's hard to be productive when you can't get ideas and information into your PDA in a timely fashion. Also, you're less likely to use your PDA if you don't enjoy using it.

Ideally, inputting data should be straightforward and intuitive—more like typing and less like programming your VCR. The handwriting recognition on PDAs, specifically the Graffiti alphabet on Palm OS, leaves most people wanting something else. Many people give up trying to learn and use Graffiti, which usually means they end up using their PDA less and less. Slowly a powerful and expensive personal computing tool turns into a powerful and expensive paperweight.

Perhaps the easiest and most intuitive method for PDA data input is a keyboard. Most people can type faster than they can print, which means that even if handwriting recognition is perfected, a keyboard will always be the quickest way for you to get ideas and information into your PDA (aside from speech recognition, which is highly problematic and takes a great deal of processing power).

With a good keyboard, a powerful PDA becomes a reasonable substitute for a laptop, especially on a plane. You can write memos and work on documents, update contact information, and compose e-mail. A good keyboard will make you more productive with your PDA and you'll be less likely to end up with a $500 paperweight or doorstop.

There are many portable keyboards available for PDAs, although not all of them are created equally. Some of the cheaper portable keyboards are awful; they just don't live up to even low expectations. This is an important point because a bad keyboard isn't better than no keyboard at all; it's worse. Some of the more clever keyboard technology looks great on paper but will actually slow you down due to increased error rates and unresponsive keys, especially if you are a proficient touch typist.

When you set out to find a keyboard for your PDA, there are some things you should consider. First of all, try it out before you purchase it. This is important because you want to be able to evaluate the feel of the keyboard before you invest around $100 for one.

Consider the feel or tactile response of the keys when you use it. Do they feel right? If the keys don't *give*, or have a similar range of motion to a regular keyboard, you may have trouble adjusting to it. Check the key spacing. Are the keys situated far enough apart for you to be able to work comfortably? The key spacing on most keyboards is standardized to facilitate touch-typing by large and small hands alike.

Check the layout of the keys as well. Is it the standard QWERTY arrangement that most of us are used to? Does the keyboard include all the keys you would normally find on a full-sized model? Some smaller keyboards save space by omitting some keys, like function keys, and combining their functions with other keys.

Still other designs reduce the number of keys, leaving out almost half of the keys. To type letters on these keyboards, you combine different combinations of keys, like chords on a piano. These are called *chording keyboards;* they are counterintuitive and require a high learning curve. Most people would be better served by a traditional keyboard.

When you're trying out the keyboard make sure you can touch-type with a minimum number of errors. Some keyboards have a built-in cradle for your PDA, which supplies power as well as a way to plug the keyboard into the PDA. Check that the position of the PDA's screen is comfortable when you're typing.

Still other keyboards are wireless. They take advantage of the *infrared* (IR) wireless port built into most PDAs. This can be more convenient than cables or using a special cradle. The drawback is that because of the position of the IR port on most PDAs, usually on top, the workaround required to connect a keyboard using IR usually undermines the benefit of having a wireless keyboard in the first place.

Some infrared wireless keyboards have you point the PDA's IR port at the keyboard's IR port. This leaves the screen upside down, which requires you to install software that rotates the image on the screen 180 degrees. This also means that the PDA is lying flat, so you'll be looking straight down on the screen or, even worse, at an angle.

Determine just how well the keyboard works with your particular model of PDA. Not all keyboards are compatible with every type of PDA, so double-check that they work together. Confirm that the keyboard has its own power source to avoid having it draw power from your PDA.

Finally, check the keyboard's sturdiness and the quality of its construction. This is certainly a case where you get what you pay for. Cheap keyboards are usually produced cheaply, out of inexpensive lower-quality plastics and mechanisms. If you travel a lot, you will spend more money replacing cheap keyboards than you would initially spend for a high-quality keyboard that withstands the rigors of travel.

There are many unique keyboard designs available for PDAs, reflecting the number of ways manufacturers have tried to solve the portability problem of adding a keyboard to a PDA. The following sections describe the main types of PDA-compatible keyboards.

Thumb Keypads

The smallest keyboard option available for a PDA, a *thumb keypad,* fits over the bottom of your handheld and allows you to type using both of your thumbs. For a generation that has grown up playing with the Nintendo Game Boy, this might not be such a bad solution. Although slower than touch-typing on a real keyboard, a thumb keypad maintains the reason for having a PDA in the first place—namely, portability.

Using a thumb keypad, you don't have to set up your PDA and keyboard on a flat surface. However, a thumb keypad isn't good for long messages; it's designed for inputting quick notes and e-mails as an alternative to using Graffiti or other handwriting recognition systems. The size and design of thumb keypads also create the potential for repetitive motion injuries. I've noticed pain and strain on my wrist and thumbs after prolonged use.

Folding Mini-Keyboards

Mini-keyboards that fold up for easy storage when traveling are convenient options for people desiring a keyboard for data input. However, because of their smaller key size and smaller key spacing, it's almost impossible to touch-type on them. When open, these keyboards are significantly smaller than a full-size keyboard and may even make a laptop keyboard seem huge in comparison.

These are really only useful for short messages or documents; with anything longer you'll notice that you type far more slowly than you normally would, as well as make many more errors. If you have large hands, consider something closer to a full-size keyboard; otherwise you'll spend too much time cursing and retyping mistakes.

Flat, Roll-Up Keyboards

This is a neat idea that looks cool on paper but just doesn't work. These keyboards are solid state with no moving parts. Usually made out of a single piece of rubber or plastic, they have sensors contained in the "keys" that detect the tap of a finger. A few of them even have partially raised keys and attempt to mimic the feel of a real keyboard. The main advantage of this type of keyboard is that it's spill-proof and can be rolled up into a compact package for easy storage.

Unfortunately, there isn't any tactile feedback because the keys don't move. They typically aren't very responsive either. You really have to tap hard on most of these keyboards. It's actually very much like pressing the buttons on your microwave oven's touchpad; touch-typing is impossible and the error rate is high. These aren't very comfortable to use and you must operate them on a perfectly flat surface.

Chording Keyboards

Designed to be compact and usable with only one hand, chording keyboards typically have very few keys, sometimes one for each finger and thumb. Unlike a typical keyboard, where each key you depress represents a character, chording keyboards require you to depress multiple keys either simultaneously or in sequence to type a character, much like a stenography machine.

Chording keyboards are ergonomic and lightweight. Some are smaller than the PDA itself. It is possible to type quickly and accurately using a chording keyboard, faster even than with a standard keyboard. The problem is that the learning curve is quite high; you essentially have to forget everything you know about typing and relearn from scratch.

Virtual Keyboards

Technologies of the future, *virtual keyboards* resemble something straight out of science fiction. Although some products are just starting to appear—unveiled at trade shows like COMDEX—I have a healthy skepticism regarding just how useful they will actually be.

A virtual keyboard is a device that projects a keyboard into the air or onto a flat surface and monitors the position and movement of your fingers as you "type." This is a very neat idea but it lacks practicality in at least one aspect.

Human beings require tactical feedback, especially when typing. Our hands are extremely dexterous and sensitive. We expect feedback when we use our fingers. Tapping into thin air does nothing for us in this regard.

For the same reason that it's hard, if not impossible, to touch-type on a roll-up keyboard, virtual keyboards might become a cool gadget for bleeding-edge early adopters and tech-junkies, but they'll end up gathering virtual dust when people actually want to get something done.

Full-Size Folding Keyboards

The best of both worlds—a full-size keyboard that collapses into a compact package for travel—is the holy grail of PDA input devices. Fortunately, this technology exists and it won't take a quest for you to acquire one. Several companies produce these keyboards with the same layout, key size, and key spacing as a standard keyboard. You can touch-type with no problems.

This is really the best option for entering lots of text into a PDA. With a full-size folding keyboard, you'll be able to use your PDA for many of the same purposes you may have used your laptop in the past.

Secret #100: Power Adapters for Travel and Road Trips

Besides data input, power issues are another chief issue for PDA owners. If you use your PDA extensively, you need to recharge it often—not always a convenient option. Fortunately, there are a number of new products that make it easy to recharge your PDA while you're out and about.

When you're shopping for batteries and adapters, it's important that you get the correct voltage for your device. If you select an adapter that has too high a voltage output, you will damage your PDA, perhaps even destroy it. Most PDAs use five volts (5V) or less. Power input as high as 7V can short them out. To be safe, purchase adapters and chargers marketed specifically for the make and model of your product.

---

on the web | The following Web sites sell power adapters, inverters, and chargers for mobile devices: www.targus.com, www.instant-power.com, and www.handango.com.

When you look at batteries and chargers, you'll see them rated with the acronym *mAh*, which stands for milliampere hour, or *Ah*, representing a 1000th of an ampere hour. This is a measurement of the charge that a battery will hold and how long a device can run off it. If you know how much energy your device uses in milliamperes, you can figure out how long it will run off a single charge based on the mAh rating of the battery. The average PDA battery is around 700–900 mAh and lasts a few hours.

One of the big hassles for PDA owners is having to pack the PDA's cradle for recharging and synching. This just adds to the list of peripherals that you have to schlep around with you when you travel. Manufacturers have solved this with several new adapters that allow you to charge and synch a PDA using a laptop or desktop's USB port without a cradle (see Figure 10-1).

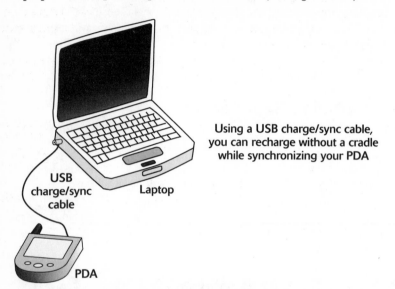

Using a USB charge/sync cable, you can recharge without a cradle while synchronizing your PDA

USB charge/sync cable

Laptop

PDA

Figure 10-1: Charging and synching with a USB cable.

You can combine this type of cable with other adapters to allow you to recharge from a wall outlet or a car's cigarette lighter. This means no longer having to carry your PDA's cradle just to recharge it. The small size of these cables makes them convenient to carry.

If you don't have access to an outlet, either in a car or building, or to a USB port on a computer, there are some products that will still enable you to charge your PDA. These products are all portable and will get the job done in a pinch.

The first of these alternatives is an instant-charger or an air-powered charger. These devices use a zinc-air cell that produces electricity when exposed to air. Typically these devices can charge a cell phone or PDA up to three times before being disposed of. They cost around $13 and replacement cartridges sell for about $10 each.

on the web   For more information about zinc-air recharging systems, visit www.instant-power.com.

Another alternative is using an adapter that allows you to use AAA batteries to recharge your PDA. Several of these are available on the market. Each device has a battery compartment that holds four AAA batteries and an adapter that attaches to your PDA. When selecting one of these devices, make sure it has a *voltage reduction circuit* (VRC) that regulates the electrical output to ensure that the batteries do not damage your PDA.

The final alternative is solar power. There are portable solar devices available for PDAs and cell phones that allow you to charge your phone wherever you have access to sunlight. These devices fold down to a size that is easy to transport. If you're visiting a sunny climate, like southern California or Africa, this may be a good way to recharge your PDA when you're on the road.

There are some interesting future power sources in development. While some of them may never become viable consumer products, a couple of them are sure to wind up in commercial products someday.

The loudest industry buzz concerns *fuel cells*. These are self-contained devices, similar to batteries, that produce electricity from hydrogen and oxygen (water is the waste product). Toshiba and NEC are prototyping a fuel cell–powered laptop.

Researchers at Birmingham University in the U.K. have produced micro-engines smaller than a fingernail that can run on lighter fluid. One of these tiny engines produces almost 700 times more power than a similar-sized battery and only needs refueling about once every two years. Researchers are predicting that these will replace batteries in portable devices by 2010.

Don't hold your breath. We still don't have holographic data crystals, which were supposed to replace hard disks within five years (a claim almost eight years old now) or the flying cars that science promised when I was a kid.

Secret #101: Wireless Adapters

Mobile wireless adapters come in three basic flavors: Bluetooth, Wi-Fi, and cellular. If you want to connect to a cellular network or to Wi-Fi access points, you need a wireless adapter to do so—that is, unless your PDA has wireless capabilities built in. In addition to the type of wireless that an adapter supports, there is various adapter hardware to choose from, and not all PDAs support every type. You need to consider the compatibility of each type with your PDA.

The main types of adapters are *Compact Flash* (CF) and *Secure Digital* (SD). The next section covers these types in more detail but for now you need to know which type of card your PDA accepts to avoid buying the wrong one. The type of card slot your PDA is equipped with is usually listed on the package, in the user manual, and, for some devices, printed on the adapter slot.

note   You can use CF and SD cards to provide storage or, in the case of wireless adapters, PDA cameras, and even PDA music players, to add functionality to your PDA. The CF and SD standards describe the physical dimensions of the card and the electrical interface, not the card's function.

There are other types of cards, such as Type II and Type III PC cards (PCMCIA), but these are not supported by the majority of PDA manufacturers. For a while, CF cards were the dominant adapter, but SD card adapters have caught up and may eventually surpass them in popularity.

Many newer PDAs have Bluetooth functionality built into them and a few even have integrated Wi-Fi, so you won't need to buy a separate adapter. If you choose a Wi-Fi-enabled PDA, pay attention to which standard it supports. An 802.11b or 802.11g PDA will be able to connect at more hotspots than an 802.11a-enabled PDA will.

There are cellular adapters available for PDAs, too. These are usually CDMA, GSM, or GPRS. If you choose a cellular adapter, you will have the widest coverage and will be able to connect in more places than with Bluetooth or Wi-Fi, but you will also have to subscribe to a cellular carrier that supports the device you have purchased. If cellular is the way you want to go, choose a carrier first and then get the device.

Secret #102: Storage

Since PDAs don't have a lot of storage built in, there are a number of storage options for PDA users. Most of them come in the form of removable memory cards, like the CF and SD cards I mentioned previously. The storage on a PDA is a form of read-only memory (ROM) that is nonvolatile, meaning that it doesn't lose its information when it loses power, like your computer's random access memory (RAM) does.

The ROM chips used in PDAs are called *flash memory*. Unlike older ROM chips, their information can be rewritten, or "flashed," by the user. There are two types of flash memory used today: NOR (Not OR) and NAND (Not AND). NOR and NAND are types of Boolean logic used to create logic gates on chips. NOR flash memory can store and execute software. This is the type of flash memory used in PDAs, cell phones, and digital cameras. The device's software resides and operates in NOR memory; this ability is known as *execute in place* (XIP).

NAND memory stores data but does not execute programs. Software stored in NAND memory must first be copied into NOR flash memory or RAM. NAND flash memory is faster, cheaper, and more durable than NOR, and can be written up to one million times. The flash memory in most removable card media is NAND flash memory.

Storage media come in a wide variety of adapter cards. Installing a card is as simple as inserting it into the proper adapter slot on your PDA, which will recognize the storage card and allow you to format it as well as copy files to it. You can leave the storage card in for as long as you need, or remove it for convenient storage. You can also purchase card readers that hook up to your computer using the USB port so that you can copy files from your PDA to your PC with the storage card.

CF cards range in price from $10 (32MB) to over $450 (2GB). SD cards range from $15 (32MB) to over $270 (512MB). *Multimedia cards* (MMCs) and *Memory Sticks* (MSs) have a similar price range. To determine which type of card your PDA supports, consult the PDA's user manual or product information. In some cases, the card type is printed on the PDA's card slot. You can also visit the manufacturer's Web site to find out which card your PDA supports.

Compact Flash

CF was introduced by SanDisk Inc. in 1994. It is very popular among manufacturers of everything from cameras to PDAs. Because CF cards use the same electrical interface as PCMCIA cards, but have fewer pins, they can be used in PCMCIA slots with an adapter.

The newest type of CF card, *Compact Flash Type II* (CF2), is slightly thicker than the original cards, which allows more electronics to be included in each card. Some manufacturers, including IBM, have begun to produce micro-miniature hard disks enclosed in CF2 cards.

Because both cards use the same electrical interface, a CF1 card fits into a CF2 device and still operates, but a CF2 card is too thick to be inserted into a CF1 slot.

Secure Digital

This type of card is becoming very popular, with many PDA manufacturers opting to adopt SD cards over CF cards in their newer models. Because SD cards are quicker than other memory cards, they are popular as storage media.

SD cards are similar to MMCs, but thicker. SD card readers accept MMCs, but not vice versa. In 2003, a newer Mini SD card was introduced which is less than 40 percent of the size of the original SD card, but fully compatible. SD card readers accept Mini SD cards. Full-sized SD cards are available with capacities of up to 1GB, while Mini SD cards are available up to 256MB.

PCMCIA

Some PDAs have PCMCIA card slots that support PC cards, but these are not nearly as common as SD or CF cards. PC cards are 16-bit devices, more often seen on laptops than PDAs. PC cards are one way to extend the functionality of laptops. The most common PC cards are Type II cards, which are 5.0mm thick and used for LAN adapters and storage in laptops.

There is also a Type III PC card that is 10.5mm thick and used for wireless adapters, hard disks, and other devices. Type II cards will work in Type III adapters, but not vice versa. Toshiba has proposed a Type IV card, but it hasn't been accepted as a standard yet.

Memory Stick

The MS is a flash memory card produced by Sony and used in many of its products. MSs are smaller than a stick of gum and are also used in IO devices, such as mini-cameras for some Sony PDAs. MSs are not widely used outside of Sony's products.

Multimedia Cards

Multimedia cards, or MMCs, are widely used and compatible with many SD card readers. They're supported by many device manufacturers and are often used for delivery of PDA software. Multimedia cards use either NOR or NAND flash memory, depending on the intended use of the card. NAND cards are the choice for memory expansion.

There is also a secure version of the MMC that protects copyrighted material, and can be used in e-commerce transactions.

Microdrive

Microdrives are microminiaturized hard disks, some less than the diameter of a nickel, that you can use for storage in portable devices. Compared to flash cards, they are faster and can store more information. These smaller drives conserve power compared to larger hard drives, although they still have the disadvantage of being mechanical, rather than solid state, and are more susceptible to damage and mechanical failure as a result. Microdrives also produce heat, another disadvantage compared to solid state flash memory.

Secret #103: Automotive Accessories

There are several clever accessories for your car that extend the usefulness of your PDA. Because your PDA can interface with a GPS module, you can use it as a navigation aid. Of course, you can't really drive around town while holding your PDA in one hand and steering with the other.

The answer is a PDA mount for your car. There are several types of these mounts available, all of them designed to hold your PDA in position on or in front of your car's dashboard for easy viewing.

> caution
>
> **Don't attempt to use your PDA while driving your car! Using it as a GPS display is one thing; trying to send e-mail or surf the Web is another. Your message to Aunt Minnie or the recipe for crème brûlée can wait until you reach your destination.**

Generally, there are five types of mounts: One fits into a cup holder and extends upward to hold your PDA at a suitable height for viewing, another attaches to the vents in your car's dash, and a third uses suction cups to attach to your car's windshield. These are fine, but none of them are especially sturdy. That will become evident the first time the suction cups come loose during a turn and your PDA bounces off the dashboard or, worse, dashes your head.

A fourth type of mount uses strong adhesives to attach to your dashboard. These are generally sturdier than the prior three types of mounts, and far less likely to fly off in a turn. You can also get mounts that bolt to the floorboards or beneath your dashboard.

Mounts that bolt in place are the sturdiest of the lot. They often incorporate other features as well, such as a keyboard or peripheral ports for charging your PDA and cell phone. Some high-end mounts provide an interface with your car's stereo system so that you can use your PDA as a digital audio player.

Choosing Software for Your PDA

At some point, we've all been there—stuck in an airport with 10 minutes to find a connecting gate, a cup of coffee, and a restroom. It's times like these that you're glad you own that PDA—that is, if you have the right software. Whether you use a Palm OS handheld, Pocket PC, or smart phone, there is software that will let you find your way (and a restroom) in almost any major airport in the world. Your PDA isn't just for storing contacts and keeping a calendar anymore; put it to work and make it earn its keep.

Secret #104: GPS and Navigation Software

A PDA is a great way to find your way around a new city or tourist attraction. Combine it with a GPS module and you'll never be lost again. More importantly, you'll never need to ask for directions.

There are a number of useful GPS and navigation applications available for both Palm OS and Pocket PC devices. Tables 10-1 through 10-4 list some of the more popular ones for each.

Table 10-1: Palm OS GPS and Map Software

Application	Address	Information
Tracker	www.gpspilot.com	Navigation and log tracking
TripPilot	www.gpspilot.com	Driving directions and route planning
GPSatlas	www.gpspilot.com	Digital atlas for planning trips around the world, downloadable maps
Mapopolis Navigator	www.mapopolis.com	Turn-by-turn driving directions
Outdoor Navigator GPS Maps	www.maptech.com	Detailed topographic maps for North America
TUBE New York Pro	www.visualit.co.uk	NYC subway maps, also available for London, Paris, Seoul, Washington D.C., and more
TravelMateUS-Airports	www.travelmate.com	Up-to-date information on U.S. airports, amenities, ATMs, parking, terminals

Table 10-2: Pocket PC GPS and Map Software

Application	Address	Information
Microsoft Pocket Streets	www.microsoft.com/mappoint/pocketstreets	Integration with GPS, street maps for entire U.S.
Vito SmartMap	www.vitotechnology.com	GPS navigation and map software

continued

Table 10-2: (continued)

Application	Address	Information
Navio for Pocket PC	www.tinystocks.com	GPS positioning, including altitude, route tracing, course plotting
TUBE New York Pro	www.visualit.co.uk	NYC subway maps, also available for London, Paris, Seoul, Washington D.C., and more
Airport Map Pack I & II	www.handango.com	Maps of six major U.S. airports

Table 10-3: Palm OS City Guides and Entertainment

Application	Address	Information
Vindigo 2.0	www.vindigo.com	Local guides to restaurants, clubs, movies, and more
ZAGAT TO GO for Palm OS 2004 Restaurant and Entertainment Guide	www.zagat.com	The most comprehensive restaurant guide available for Palm OS
Mapopolis Platinum PlaceGuide Subscription	www.mapopolis.com	Restaurant, gas station, bank, and hotel listings for cities all over the U.S.

Table 10-4: Pocket PC City Guides and Entertainment

Application	Address	Information
Vindigo 2.0	www.vindigo.com	Local guides to restaurants, clubs, movies, and more
KnowPlaces	www.brightangle.com	Detailed maps of popular tourist destinations, including Disneyworld, Mall of America, National Museum, and more
ZAGAT TO GO for Pocket PC 2004Restaurant and Entertainment Guide	www.zagat.com	The most comprehensive restaurant guide available for Pocket PC

Secret #105: Software for Data Input

The handwriting recognition software that comes with PDAs is adequate, but there are better options available. You can also get note and keyboard applications that make inputting data on your PDA a little easier. Tables 10-5 and 10-6 list some of the better applications.

Table 10-5: Palm OS Data Input Software

Application	Address	Information
Decuma OnSpot	www.decuma.com	Handwriting recognition for Palm OS; much better than Graffiti
CIC JotComplete	www.cic.com	Natural handwriting recognition for Palm OS
The Pad	www.mapopolis.com	Note-taking software for Palm OS

Table 10-6: Pocket PC Data Input Software

Application	Address	Information
CalliGrapher	www.phatware.com	Natural handwriting recognition for Pocket PC
MessagEase	www.exideas.com	Powerful onscreen keyboard for Pocket PC
Decuma OnSpot	www.decuma.com	Advanced handwriting recognition for Pocket PC
PhatPad	www.phatware.com	Handwritten notes for Pocket PC

Secret #106: Useful Utilities

There are many useful utilities for both Palm OS and Pocket PC devices. Tables 10-7 and 10-8 offer just a small sample of some popular ones.

Table 10-7: Useful Utilities for Palm OS

Application	Address	Information
SilverScreen III	www.pocketsensei.com	Palm OS interface customization
BackupMan	www.bitsnbolts.com	Intuitive backup software for Palm OS
Secure File PDA backup card	www.gomdm.com	Plug 'n' Play data backup card
JackFlash	www.brayder.com	Palm memory expansion application
ZLauncher	www.zztech.com	Palm OS system management tool

Table 10-8: Useful Utilities for Pocket PC

Application	Address	Information
Resco Explorer 2003	www.resco-net.com	Advanced file explorer for Pocket PC, built-in Zip compression and encryption
Space Reclaimer 2.0	www.valksoft.com	Automatic deletion of junk, temp files, dead shortcuts, and obsolete registry keys
eWallet Professional	www.iliumsoft.com	Storage for credit card information, user names, passwords, and personal data—all encrypted for protection
Pocket Controller-Professional	www.soti.net	Pocket PC operation from desktop computer, battery/memory usage viewer, screen capture application, and more

Secret #107: PDA Synchronization Software

Although PDAs come with synchronization software, it is often minimal or inadequate. Tables 10-9 and 10-10 list a number of third-party synchronization and backup applications that are useful and worth your investment.

Table 10-9: Synchronization Software for Palm OS

Application	Address	Information
PocketMirror Professional	www.chapura.com	Synchronization for Palm OS and Microsoft Outlook data
XTNDConnect PC Desktop Synchronization	www.extendsys.com	Synchronization between Palm device and desktop computer
BackupBuddy for Windows	www.bluenomad.com	Complete backup of Palm device at every HotSync
Card Export	www.synclive.com	Access from Windows to SD/MMC inserted in Palm device
Pylon Pro	www.avantgo.com	Access from Palm device to Lotus Notes PIM applications and e-mail on desktop computer

Table 10-10: Synchronization Software for Pocket PC

Application	Address	Information
Sprite Backup Premium Edition	www.spritesoftware.com www.spritesoftware.com	Pocket PC backup to storage card, host computer, or network share
XTNDConnect PC Desktop Synchronization	www.extendsys.com	Synchronization between Pocket PC and desktop PC
Intellisync	www.pumatech.com	Two-way synchronization between desktop computer and Pocket PC
mNotes	www.commontime.com	Lotus Notes mail, contacts, tasks, calendar, and journal support for Pocket PC; wired and wireless devices supported

Secret #108: Security Software

Tables 10-11 and 10-12 list some useful applications for securing and protecting your PDA. There are fewer antivirus applications available for Palm devices than for Pocket PC devices. This isn't an indication that the Palm OS is more secure; it just means that there are more developers targeting the Pocket PC right now. Viruses on PDAs are still rare but antivirus software helps you avoid transferring viruses to your desktop from infected files on your handheld.

Table 10-11: Security Software for Palm OS

Application	Address	Information
VirusGuard	www.mevix.com	Virus protection for Palm OS
SplashID	www.splashdata.com	Secure storage of all personal identification information, including user names, passwords, credit cards, calling cards, bank accounts, and more, in a secure, encrypted format
DataShield	www.ultrasoft.com	Organized, secure storage of information on Palm OS
PDA Defense Professional	www.pdadefense.com	Complete security and encryption for Palm OS

Table 10-12: Security Software for Pocket PC

Application	Address	Information
Airscanner Mobile AntiVirus Pro	www.airscanner.com	Powerful virus scanner for Pocket PC
F-Secure Anti-Virus	www.f-secure.com	Protection against malware (malicious software) for Pocket PC
System Security Monitor Pro v2.2	www.valksoft.com	Event and activity tracking on Pocket PC
MindSoft Pocket VirusShield	www.mindsoftsite.com	Combination of antivirus and firewall technology for fighting malware on Pocket PC

Having Fun with Your Wireless Device

Chapter

11

◆ ◆

Secrets in This Chapter

◆ ◆

obile devices are convenient and helpful, but they can also be fun. For example, most SMS mobile phones play polyphonic ring tones. There are numerous sites that offer cool ring tones free of charge, as well as subscription or pay-per-download sites.

Customizing Your Phone

Many new phones allow you to design and download your own logo screens and graphics. The following sections provide information on customizing your phone for your own entertainment.

Secret #109: Modifying Graphics

The graphics on newer phones can be customized. Generally, the graphics that you can modify include operator logos, *caller line icons* (CLIs), wallpaper, and screen savers. The amount of customization available varies among cell phone manufacturers and models. In general, phones manufactured after 2002 offer more features. Among the newer phones, GSM phones tend to have more graphic features that users can customize. Keep in mind that even though a phone may have the capability, the carrier may not take advantage of it or enable the service on its network.

You can find directions for modifying graphics in a number of places. First, check your carrier's Web site for instructions. You may also find directions on the Web site of your phone's manufacturer or in the user manual that came with your phone. Lastly, some of the Web sites where you can download graphics (see Table 11-1 later in this chapter) provide directions for modifying graphics on many different models of cell phones.

Operator Logos

An operator logo is the logo of your cellular carrier. When you purchased your phone from your carrier, the phone was preprogrammed to display the carrier's logo when you start it up and whenever it makes a connection to the network (see Figure 11-1)

On some newer phones, you can modify the operator logo and display another graphic in its place. When you replace the operator logo with a custom graphic, your phone will display that graphic whenever it would otherwise display the operator logo (see Figure 11-2).

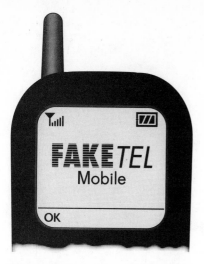

Figure 11-1: A phone displaying an operator logo.

Figure 11-2: A modified operator logo.

Caller Line Icons

Newer phones support a feature called caller line icons (CLIs), essentially a graphical caller-ID feature. Load a graphic on your phone and associate it with a specific number or person in your contact list and your phone will display that graphic whenever that person calls (see Figure 11-3). It's a cool feature; unfortunately, it isn't available on many phones yet, although you will find it on newer Nokia phones.

Figure 11-3: A caller line icon.

On some phones, you can associate CLIs to specific groups of callers, in which case they are referred to as *group graphics*. You create a group (friends, work, and family), load a representative graphic, and then assign individuals to a group. When one of them calls, the graphic for that group is displayed (see Figure 11-4).

Figure 11-4: A group graphic.

Wallpaper and Screen Savers

On some new phones with larger color displays, you can load customized wallpaper and even screen savers. Like operator logos and CLIs, this ability is dependent on the phone you have and your service.

Connectivity

There is a lot of variation in the connectivity features available on cell phones. Some let you download a new graphic from the Web, while others let you connect using an IR port or data cable and download the graphic directly from your computer.

Downloading directly from your computer has its advantages. There are no airtime charges. You can even create cell phone graphics on your computer to your heart's content.

Secret #110: Modifying Ring Tones

Modifying ring tones is the most popular way to individualize your mobile phone. Maybe *individualize* isn't the right word since so many people download and use the same ring tones. Visit any ring tone Web site and you'll see a *Top 10* or *Top 50* list. Often the top five songs have been downloaded tens of thousands of times. So when every other phone you hear plays 50 Cent's "In da Club," it's hard to be exactly an individual.

Understanding Different Types of Ring Tones

You can compose your own ring tones and even share them with friends—if your phone supports it. Many newer Motorola, Nokia, and Sony Ericsson phones have this feature. You can compose right on your phone or use a third-party application on the computer and download your tune to your handset using a data cable or SMS messaging.

There are two types of ring tones that you're likely to see on download sites: mono and polyphonic. Most phones support one of the two, but some newer handsets support *digital music* (MP3) for ring tones.

Mono ring tones are the old one-tone "beep-beep-boop" ringers that sound like old video games. Mono ring tones can only play one note (or beep) at a time. They don't even come close to real music. All phones, even older ones, have mono ring tones, though not all are programmable.

Polyphonic ring tones are ones made up of multiple notes, or phonics, played at the same time. They sound more like real music. The number of notes that a phone can play at one time depends on the chipset and model. Many polyphonic phones are *quadraphonic*, capable of playing four notes at once; but some handsets can play over 24 notes simultaneously.

Another popular choice for ring tones among owners of the newest phones is *real tones*, or ring tones that are clips of real sounds or celebrity voices. Instead of ringing or playing a tune, your phone can play a sound effect, like a dog barking or maybe even Barry White saying, "Pick up the phone, you sexy beast."

A ring tone's file format depends on the phone for which it was recorded. Nokia paved the way for ring tones and graphics; as a result, you'll find a lot of ring tones available in RTTTL or the *Nokring* format. Don't worry if you don't have a Nokia phone. You'll still be able to find ring tones; you just might not be able to create custom tones.

Some carriers use proprietary ring tone formats for their phones, which means you have to get your ring tones from your carrier. This means that, unlike Nokia which made its format available for people to create their own customized sounds, these carriers are missing out on a way to drive demand for their services.

Downloading Ring Tones

There are many sites on the Web where you can download ring tones. Some offer tones for purchase, while others are free. When you purchase a ring tone or download a free one, the site delivers it to your handset either through a WAP portal or using *smart messaging*.

Smart messaging is a protocol designed by Nokia and Intel that allows software upgrades to be sent to handsets as specialized text messages. Smart messages have a special prefix that alerts the phone that the message isn't a standard message for the user; it contains instructions and code for the handset. The instructions could be a new ring tone, a graphic, software update, or the like.

Many carriers and handset manufacturers support smart messaging, or deliver their ring tones and graphics through EMS. Many EMS services use the *iMelody* ring tone format. iMelody has advanced features, such as volume control for varying the volume in a tune and the ability to make a phone light up or vibrate.

Regardless of the delivery method, you should be able to download a ring tone as long as the site supports your carrier and handset.

Secret #111: Ring Tone and Graphics

There are a number of sites on the Internet that have ring tones and graphics available for download. An Internet search will turn up hundreds. Be careful, however, because most of these sites are in Europe or the U.K. If you try to get a ring tone or logo from them, you'll either throw away good money or pay for an overseas phone call.

> **caution**   You can do an Internet search for free ring tones but beware of some sites you visit—you may be in for a nasty surprise. Many of the "top sites" are laden with pornographic advertising, which is how these Webmasters make their money.

Besides your cell carrier's site, try some of the Web sites listed in Table 11-1.

Table 11-1: Sites for Custom Graphics and Ring Tones

Site	Address	Description
Yahoo! Mobile	`http://mobile.yahoo.com/photos`	Create screen savers, slide-shows, and download photos to your phone. A picture phone isn't required. Most U.S. carriers are supported.

Site	Address	Description
Zingy-Zing Up Your Phone	www.zingy.com	Zingy offers graphics, ring tones, and games. You can also upload your own photos and use their online tools to edit them and create screen savers or wallpaper.
MSN Mobile	www.greathealth offers.biz	MSN Mobile has partnered with Zingy to offer Zingy's services to MSN mobile users. If you have an MSN mobile account, you can take advantage of Zingy"s content as well as some additional MSN mobile graphics and ring tones.
AOL Mobile	http://mymobile. aol.com	AOL Mobile offers custom logos, CLIs, and screen savers, as wells as ring tones, IM, alerts, e-mail, and more. Just like MSN, it offers graphics in conjunction with the Zingy service, with some additional AOL content thrown in.
Laiwa	www.laiwa.com	A great site for graphics, games, and ring tones, with a great interface and available downloads sorted by carrier and handset model.
BoltBlue	www.boltblue.com	An international site that offers service in the U.S. to customers of AT&T, Cingular, and VoiceStream GSM services. Logos, ring tones, and more. Make sure you select the proper country.
Musigate	http://musigate. sonnerie.net/us	French site with ring tones, graphics, and more. Some available in the U.S.
2 Thumbz Entertainment	http://2thumbz.com	Ring tones, graphics, games, and more.
Ringtone Jukebox	www.ringtonejukebox. com	Ring tones, graphics, games, and more.
Midiringtones	www.midiringtones.com	Ring tones, graphics, and games.

Secret #112: Cool Accessories and Software

The best place to find accessories for your handset is on your carrier's Web site. Depending on your phone, available accessories may include interchangeable faceplates, custom cases, hands-free kits, or even gaming accessories. Recently, Sprint PCS teamed with Samsung to produce the PCS game pad that attaches to some Sprint PCS–branded Samsung phones (see Figure 11-5).

Figure 11-5: Sprint PCS phone with game pad.

You can also download software that allows you to manage files, graphics, and ring tones on your computer and transfer them to your phone. Most of the available software supports Nokia phones; but as more handsets include advanced features, applications will be released to take advantage of this. Table 11-2 lists some graphics/ring tone editors and where you can download them.

Table 11-2: Mobile Graphics/Ring Tone Editors for Computers

Application	Address	Description
LogoManager	www.logomanager.co.uk	Logo manager for Nokia phones. Manage and edit graphics, ring tones, phonebook, and more.
MobiMB: Mobile Media Browser	www.logomanager.co.uk	Drag-and-drop transfer of logos and ring tones to Nokia phones.
DataPilot	www.datapilot.com	Transfer contacts, edit images, and compose ring tones. Many phones and carriers supported.
Nokring	www.mjimports.com/users/nokring	Nokia ring tone composer. Compose and transfer ring tones to your phone.
Nokia LogoExpress	www.mjimports.com/users/nokring	Send new ring tones, operator logos, and group logos to Nokia phones.

Secret #113: The Truth about Secret Functions

Every phone has some secret functions that can be unlocked—almost none of them are of any interest to the average user. Most unlocked features do such things as display network identification codes, date of manufacture, date of last repair, software versions, and so on.

caution	Messing with your phone and trying to unlock hidden features could render it useless and violate terms of your contract with your cell carrier. It really isn't worth the trouble, especially since any cool customization that you'll want to do (graphics, ring tones) can be done without unlocking anything.

There are one or two handsets that have hidden games, usually hidden within other games installed on the phone. An Internet search will reveal if your model of phone has any hidden games and how to unlock them. These are generally limited to some Ericsson and Nokia handsets.

on the web	For a sample of features that can be unlocked on a number of different phones, visit www.mobileworld.org/tech.html.

Gaming on Your Mobile Device

There are several Web sites that offer game software for your mobile phone. Although gaming capabilities vary from phone to phone, newer models, like the Nokia N-Gage, feature games that rival some Game Boy titles. The trend of gaming on cell phones (dubbed *casual gaming*) is growing quickly as more game developers and better games appear all the time.

Unlike desktop and console games that can be extremely complicated and have a long learning curve, most mobile games are almost intuitive. They may take only a moment to learn and a few minutes to play. The limitations of mobile devices have led developers to be creative and create simple games that are entertaining and addictive.

In most cases, you will only be charged airtime when downloading a game, not when you are playing it. The exception to this is if you are playing a multiplayer game over your carrier's network, or a game that requires you to interact with a game server, like a WAP game.

If you're an avid gamer, remember that gaming can be a drain on your phone's battery. Games utilize the phone's processor and display more than placing a call does; and they are more than a little addictive, so you can quickly find yourself spending hours playing them.

Secret #114: Game Platforms

Because of the number of handsets and competing carriers, game developers have a number of mobile game platforms to choose from. Games available for your phone depend on which platform your carrier and handset support. Here is a list of the major platforms for mobile gaming:

♦ **Java 2, Micro Edition**—The Java 2 Platform, Micro Edition (J2ME) is a mobile version of the Java programming language from Sun Microsystems developed for mobile devices. Devices that support J2ME run the K Virtual Machine (KVM), a specialized virtual machine for mobile devices with limited resources. Applications developed for J2ME platform are called *midlets*, as opposed to *applets* for regular Java programs.

Many carriers support J2ME games, including Sprint PCS in the U.S. and any GSM carriers worldwide. Not all J2ME devices play the same games since J2ME is available in different versions with different capabilities, depending on the device. This means that many carriers offer J2ME games tailored specifically for their devices.

♦ **Brew**—The Binary Runtime Environment for Wireless (BREW) is a wireless application development environment for Qualcomm CDMA phones. Qualcomm developed BREW and it is supported by the chipsets in Qualcomm phones. The advantage to this is that BREW applications are supported no matter what the system software in the cell phone is.

♦ **Mophun**—Synergenix developed the Mophun game engine for use in mobile phones. Mophun is a virtual machine created solely for games, and Synergenix claims it outperforms J2ME by a factor of 100. This remains to be seen; however, Mophun games are impressive, given the limitations of cell phones. Sony Ericsson has begun to incorporate the Mophun game engine into its newer handsets and more manufacturers are likely to follow suit in the near future.

♦ **DoCoMo Java**—DoCoMo Java (DoJa) is a modified, compact version of the Java programming language for cell phones. Japan's NTT DoCoMo developed DoJa for its i-appli system. DoJa is seen mainly in Japanese products; however, as DoCoMo seeks to enter markets like the U.S., it will start appearing in handsets available from U.S. carriers.

♦ **Wireless Application Protocol**—Yes, good old WAP supports gaming, but in a limited form. WAP games are more text-driven and not too visually stunning. Still, some can be addictive. One popular WAP game is called Alien Fish Exchange, available through several U.S. carriers.

---

on the
web   For an example of a WAP game, visit the Alien Fish Exchange at
www.alienfishexchange.com.

Secret #115: Finding Game Sites

The list of sites where you can download mobile games continues to grow. Often these sites also offer ring tones and graphics. Perhaps the best place to look for games is on your carrier's Web site. You'll find games that are compatible with your handset there. Table 11-3 offers a few other Web sites to consider.

Table 11-3: Mobile Gaming Sites

Site	Address	Description
Wireless Gaming Review	www.wgamer.com	"The site for the mobile gamer," Wireless Gaming Review publishes reviews, interviews, game previews, and more for mobile gamers. The site has a comprehensive list of reviews for hundreds of mobile games. You can search by carrier, platform, ratings, and more. Easily the most comprehensive mobile gaming site around.
Gameloft	www.gameloft.com	"Load and play," Gameloft is a mobile phone site that has over 20 games you can purchase and download for your cell phone and your PDA. The site supports five major cell carriers and many newer phones.
eWirelessgames	www.ewirelessgames.com	This site offers the latest games, top ring tones, and graphics. Select your country to purchase and download available games.
JAMDAT Games	www.jamdatgames.com	JAMDAT Games is one of the leading mobile game developers, and offers its own games plus top games from some of the leading game developers.
Fommy (For Me and My Mobile)	www.fommy.com/usa	Fommy offers games, graphics, ring tones and more.

Secret #116: Extending Battery Life

The biggest factor hindering mobile technology is battery life. Any device not plugged into an AC outlet is running on batteries, and that means that it will eventually run out of power. How long it takes depends on the amount of power the device draws and what sort of battery it has.

The more services and features a device has, the more power it demands, and the faster it drains a battery. Big color screens require more power than the small grayscale screens standard on older phones. As we take advantage of more features, we use our phones more and drain the battery even faster.

Battery technology hasn't exactly kept up with other mobile advances. In fact, it crawls along in comparison. Because of this, manufacturers of mobile phones constantly try to maximize energy conservation and extend battery life. Mobile processors use less power than other chips, and integrated circuits built into high-end phones manage battery use and reduce power drain when the phone is idle.

There isn't a whole lot you can do to extend the charge time of your mobile device's batteries. If you find your phone always running out of power, you may want to consider buying a larger, extended battery. Although bulkier, an extended charge battery may offer up to twice the talk time as the battery that came with your phone.

If your phone has an *econo-mode* (economy mode), use it. Usually econo-mode deactivates the screen when the phone has been idle for more than 60 seconds. This can make a big difference, especially if your phone has a large color screen.

You can also get an emergency charger, or battery extender, similar to the type used for PDAs. These devices allow you to run or recharge your phone using AAA or 9V batteries. This can come in handy, and if you use rechargeable batteries, you'll save a lot of money compared to buying a backup battery for your phone.

---

on the web   **For a selection of battery-charging solutions and battery extenders, visit** `www.seidioonline.com`.

There are four types of batteries you are likely to encounter when using a mobile device. Each has its advantages and disadvantages. Usually you have no choice but to use the type that came with your device; occasionally, you may find replacement batteries of a different type. To help you make an educated decision, here's a brief explanation of each of the more common battery designs.

Nickel Cadmium

Nickel cadmium (Ni-Cd or NiCad) batteries are very common and are used in cameras, tools, and many portable electronic devices. NiCad batteries recharge quickly and are durable. Because they use cadmium, they're relatively expensive for the amount of power density contained in an individual battery.

NiCad batteries have their strong points:

- ◆ Quick charge
- ◆ Rugged
- ◆ High number of recharges
- ◆ Long shelf life

NiCad batteries also have their weak points:

- ◆ Memory effect (see below)
- ◆ Toxic
- ◆ Must be recharged after storage
- ◆ Lower power density compared to other batteries
- ◆ Relatively expensive to produce

NiCad batteries are susceptible to the *memory effect*. If a NiCad battery is frequently partially discharged and recharged, it will develop a "memory" and it will hold less power with each successive charge. This is caused by the formation of potassium-hydroxide crystals inside the battery.

As the number of potassium-hydroxide crystals increases, the amount of power that the cell can retain from a charge reduces. Eventually, the battery will be useless. NiCad batteries can be reconditioned, and memory can be reversed (or prevented) by regular deep-discharging and recharging. When a NiCad battery is completely discharged and then recharged a few times, the potassium-hydroxide crystals dissolve and the battery can hold a full charge again.

Nickel Metal Hydride

Battery designers looking for an alternative to NiCad batteries developed Nickel metal hydride (NiMH) cells. NiMH cells last up to 40 percent longer than comparable NiCad cells and are less susceptible to memory effects. NiMH batteries are widely used in wireless devices and mobile computers.

NiMH batteries have their strong points:

- ◆ Up to 40 percent higher power density than NiCads
- ◆ Less susceptible to memory effects than NiCads
- ◆ Not as toxic as NiCads

NiMH batteries also have their weak points:

- ◆ Relatively expensive
- ◆ Not as durable as NiCads
- ◆ Don't hold a charge as long as NiCads when not in use
- ◆ Shorter shelf-life

Lithium-Ion

Sony developed the first commercial Lithium-ion (Li-ion) rechargeable battery in 1991. The power density of Li-ion batteries is almost twice that of NiCad batteries. Many cell phones today use Li-ion cells for power. Compared to NiCad and NiMH cells, Li-ion batteries are low-maintenance.

Li-ion batteries have their strong points:

- ◆ Low-maintenance
- ◆ Long shelf-life
- ◆ High power density
- ◆ Lighter weight

Li-ion batteries also have their weak points. They are:

- Expensive
- Fragile
- Hazardous

---

caution | **Lithium reacts violently with water, producing a lot of hydrogen gas that may ignite or explode!**

Li-ion batteries are not susceptible to the memory effect. Do not let Li-ion cells completely discharge or store them in a discharged state.

Lithium-Polymer

Lithium-polymer batteries are the most recent improvement in battery technology. Lithium-polymer batteries contain a gel rather than a liquid; as a result, they do not need to be contained in a metal casing like Li-ion batteries do. Because of this, lithium-polymer cells can be made into a variety of shapes, with batteries feasibly as thin as a credit card.

Lithium-polymer cells have their strong points:

- Small size
- Lightweight
- Safer than Li-ion cells

Lithium-polymer cells also have their weak points:

- Expensive
- Lower power density than Li-ion

Regardless of the type of battery you have, avoid operating or storing it at extremely high or low temperatures. This will damage the battery and shorten its lifespan.

Part IV

Other Wireless Technologies

Controlling
Your Home
Remotely

Chapter

12

♦ ♦

Secrets in This Chapter

♦ ♦

Have you ever left home and wondered whether you left the lights on? Would you like to go out for the night and be able to check on the babysitter and kids? Now you can use your mobile device to access and control your house remotely. Depending on the peripherals you choose, you can view live video feeds and control the lighting and even the temperature remotely. This chapter discusses wireless home controllers, their use, and potential misuse, as well as security and privacy issues.

Explaining Standards and Technologies

Home control and automation is not new. Products have been around since the 1970s and hobbyists have designed systems around the Z80 microcontroller and personal computers for years. Home control has been a hardware hacker's playground from the beginning.

Thankfully, there are now low-cost, easy-to-use consumer products because not all of us are electronics hobbyists or hardware hackers. Even a technical neophyte can automate control of lighting, heating, and other devices with a minimum of fuss and relatively few headaches. In this chapter, I focus on systems that don't require you to rewire your house. If you're interested in home control and automation, read on. This chapter will get you started on the right foot.

Secret #117: The X10 System

Once you decide to investigate home control and automation, you'll probably start to see X10 systems everywhere. That's because X10 Wireless Technology Inc. is the dominant player in the industry. You can hardly surf the Web without encountering an X10 pop-up (or pop-under) advertisement.

X10 Inc. created the X10 standard for home controllers. X10 is a proprietary standard that uses electrical wiring as its network medium, similar to the HomePlug standard. X10 devices communicate with one another over the existing power lines in your house using low voltage, coded signals. By coded, I'm not suggesting encrypted; in fact, X10 is not a secure standard (more on this later).

There are hundreds of X10 products on the market, produced by X10 Inc. and several other manufacturers. X10 devices are compatible with each other. The large number of products available allow you to create a custom-tailored solution for controlling your home.

X10 devices include transmitters (controls) and receivers (modules), although there are some X10 devices that can communicate both ways (transceivers). You can use X10 transceivers in conjunction with other automated controllers or a desktop computer to control multistep events.

---

cross
ref   You can learn more about the remote options for X10 in "Secret #121: Remote Options."

X10 devices have two codes that you assign when you're setting up your system: a house code and a unit code. House codes are lettered A–P; there are 16 unit codes. In effect, each house code has 16 possible unit codes for a total of 256 available codes. When you install an X10 device you assign a house code and unit code to the device (see Figure 12-1).

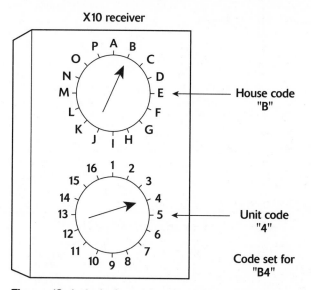

Figure 12-1: Assigning codes to an X10 controller.

Plug an X10 receiver into a wall outlet and plug the device you want to control, for instance a lamp, into the receiver (see Figure 12-2). You can install an X10 controller as a wall switch or as a separate controller that plugs in elsewhere. You have to set the controller's house code to the same house code as the receiver that you wish to control. When you want to turn that lamp on or off, you simply choose the button on the controller that corresponds to the unit code of that lamp.

For example, let's say you have five lamps that you want to be able to control from an X10 controller. You decide on house code A for all five lamps and then assign each one a unit code—in this case, 1–5. That means you now have five X10 receivers with the following codes: A1, A2, A3, A4, and A5. Next you set the house code of the controller that you are going to use to the same house code as the receiver's, which is A.

With the house code set, each numbered button on the controller now corresponds to a unit code associated with house code A. The button labeled "1" controls receiver A1, "2" controls A2, and so on. Now you can turn each of the lamps on and off using the same controller (see Figure 12-3).

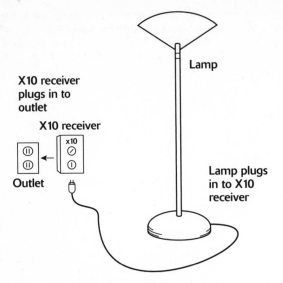

Figure 12-2: Installing an X10 receiver.

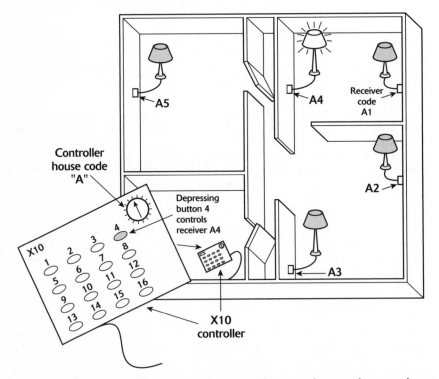

Figure 12-3: Controlling receivers with a controller set to the same house code.

You can control groups of receivers as if they were one unit by assigning them all the same house and unit codes. For instance, if you have a number of lamps in your living room and you want to be able to turn them all off or dim them simultaneously, you can assign all of them an identical code—for instance A1.

Now when you use a controller to command receiver A1 to dim, the lamps respond as a group because they are all receiver A1 (see Figure 12-4).

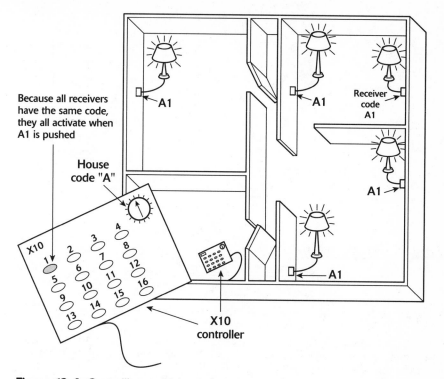

Figure 12-4: Controlling multiple receivers as a group.

This is a very simple method and it has obvious disadvantages. You can no longer control the receivers independently of one another. Advanced controllers and X10-compliant home automation software allow you to control groups while also allowing for independent control of each lamp (see Figure 12-5). Still, this is an effective low-cost option for controlling multiple receivers.

X10 home automation software allows you to use your computer as an X10 controller to create schedules and automate the control of all the X10 devices and controllers in your home. You must have an X10 computer interface that connects to your PC over a serial port and then plugs into an outlet, allowing your computer to send X10 signals over your home's power lines. Home automation software controls the computer interface and uses it to communicate with and control X10 devices.

There are also X10 wireless products, including wireless remotes for controlling X10 devices and X10 wireless security cameras that operate in the same 2.4 GHz frequency band as Wi-Fi devices do. They can (and do) interfere with Wi-Fi networks (and vice versa). X10 wireless devices are not secure because they do not use encryption and hackers can easily intercept their signal.

X10 devices are relatively inexpensive and, in general, they work quite well. The system is easy enough for even a technical neophyte to install and configure. The main drawback with X10 devices is that they lack any sort of security at all. At the end of this chapter, I'll discuss X10 security issues and what you can do about them.

PC with controller
software and X10
interface

Software can
schedule receivers
to go on and off

Receiver
A1

A2

A4

A3

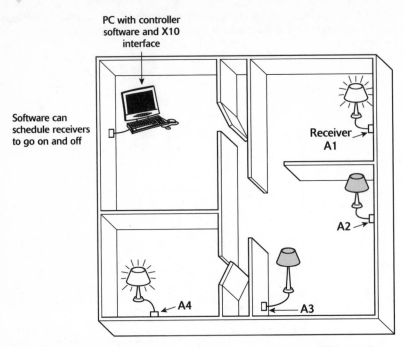

Figure 12-5: Using home automation software to control multiple receivers.

Using third-party software and a computer with an X10 interface and an Internet connection, you can control your X10 devices remotely from any Web browser (see Figure 12-6).

X10
receiver

X10

Remote PC contacts
home PC with X10
software; home PC
turns on light

PC with
Internet connection
and X10 interface

Internet

Remote
PC

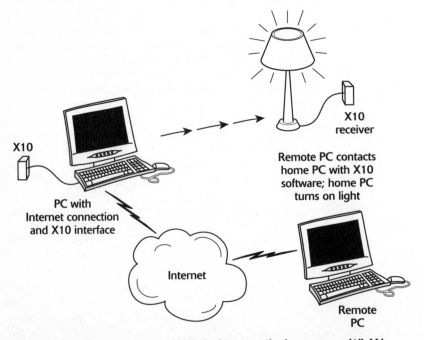

Figure 12-6: Remote control of X10 devices over the Internet or a WLAN.

One of the best applications for remote control of X10 devices is HomeSeer, available from HomeSeer Technologies LLC. HomeSeer allows you to control your X10 devices using your WLAN or the Internet.

---

on the web For more information about X10 devices, visit `www.x10.com`. To learn more about HomeSeer, visit `www.homeseer.com`.

Secret #118: The XANBOO System

An alternative for remote control, automation, and monitoring is the XANBOO system. XANBOO systems use a proprietary protocol called AFMII. Devices using the AFMII protocol communicate with one another using a proprietary 418 MHz transceiver technology. The XANBOO system can bridge to other protocols to allow communication with non-XANBOO devices. These protocols include 802.11, X10, UPNP, RS485, RS232, CEBus, and LonWorks.

XANBOO devices communicate with a XANBOO gateway in your home. The gateway can be a computer, DSL modem, set-top cable box, or XANBOO gateway device. All XANBOO-enabled devices and controllers (see Figure 12-7) communicate with the XANBOO central servers through the gateway.

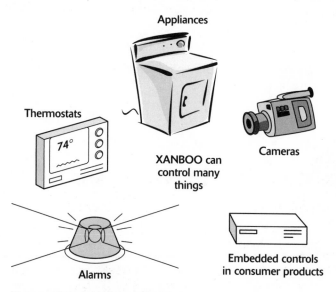

Figure 12-7: XANBOO devices.

In turn, you can connect to the XANBOO servers from any Web browser to monitor and control your XANBOO devices (see Figure 12-8). XANBOO is safe and uses encryption to secure users accounts and device control. Considering XANBOO allows full remote control of devices, it is a good system to consider—and it is relatively inexpensive.

Remote clients communicate
with the XANBOO servers, which
in turn communicate with the
XANBOO gateway PC

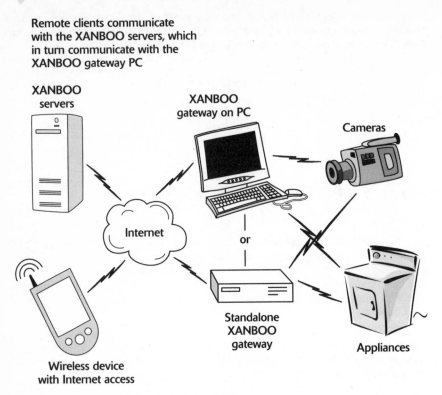

Figure 12-8: Remote control with XANBOO.

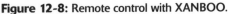

on the
web

For more information about **XANBOO** products and solutions, or to find a
dealer near you, visit `www.xanboo.com`.

Secret #119: Other Automation Systems

There are other standards and systems available for home automation but none
of them begins to approach X10 in manufacturer support and sheer number of
available products. For the do-it-yourself home automation enthusiast, X10
devices are the way to go. As a remote solution, XANBOO is an attractive alternative to X10 but doesn't have as many devices available yet.

Some of the other standards for home automation include the following:

♦   CEBus /Home Plug & Play (HPnP)

♦   LonWorks

♦   Zwave

The CEBus/HPnP standard (we'll call it just HPnP from here on out) was proposed as a next-generation alterative to X10. The CEBus Industry Council, Inc., announced HPnP in 1994 as an open standard that would ensure interoperability between devices using different methods of transmission. Like X10 units, HPnP devices use home power lines to communicate but they can also use RF or CAT5 cabling.

HPnP looks great on paper. The problem is that we're still waiting for products to show up on the market. As of yet I haven't seen any switches or other units for sale to the general consumer. I've heard of proprietary systems installed by professional home or industrial automation companies that were HPnP-compliant, but nothing that you or I could purchase and install ourselves.

There are a number of proprietary systems offered by professional home automation companies. These systems require professional design and installation and can be very expensive. Perhaps one of coolest systems I have seen is from Pluto Corporation. Pluto incorporates home automation, remote control, monitoring, entertainment, and telecommunications in one system. This doesn't come cheap; the cost of the system can range from $15,000 to over $50,000. This is representative of what you pay for a custom home automation system.

Planning for Automation

Just like installing a WLAN, it's important to plan carefully prior to jumping into a home automation project feet first. This saves you money, prevents headaches, and gives you better results.

Secret #120: Deciding What to Control

The first thing you need to decide is exactly what you want to control. Start by making a list of things you want to accomplish with your system. These may include the following:

- Controlling lights
- Controlling or monitoring thermostats
- Video surveillance
- Monitoring water and power systems
- Remote monitoring over the Internet
- Controlling appliances
- Caring for pets and plants

If you want to do something on this list, chances are good that there's a way to do it automatically. Home automation is actually a mature market and companies like X10 have been designing solutions for 20 years. Consider ordering a catalog from any home automation company. You'll come up with great ideas while browsing through it. Table 12-1 lists some companies that sell home automation equipment.

Table 12-1: Home Automation Equipment Suppliers

Company	Address	Description
SmartHome	www.smarthome.com	Huge online retailer of home automation equipment
Smart Home Systems, SmartHome USA	www.smarthomeusa.com	Large online retailer with a large selection of X10 devices
Bass Home Electronics	www.bass-home.com	Home automation retailer
Automated Outlet	www.automatedoutlet.com	Home automation retailer
X10	www.x10.com	Web site of X10 Corporation
X10 Superstore	www.x10-store.com	Large retailer of X10 equipment
RadioShack	www.radioshack.com	Largest consumer electronics specialty retailer in the U.S.

After deciding what you want to automate or control remotely, investigate your hardware and software options. There are many things to choose from but now that you've taken the first step and set your goals, you can plan a system that accomplishes what you want for the least amount of money and hassle.

Secret #121: Remote Options

XANBOO built its system around remote access but you'll still have options for remote control if you choose X10. Controlling X10 devices remotely requires getting an X10 interface for your computer and connecting it to an always-on Internet connection.

You'll need an application that interfaces with the controller and allows you to log in over the Internet. Table 12-2 lists some controllers and compatible software solutions.

Table 12-2: X10 PC Interfaces and Software

Device/Application	Address	Description
Premise Home Control Software	www.premisesystems.com	Fully featured home-control application for Windows 2000/XP or higher; interfaces with X10
Indigo Home Automation Software	www.advancedquonsettech.com	Home-control software for Mac OS X; interfaces with X10 and allows remote control over e-mail

Device/Application	Address	Description
HomeSeer	www.homeseer.com	Remote access and control for X10 devices
JDS Stargate Interactive Intelligent Home Control	www.jdstechnologies.com	X10 device control over the phone, Web, or through remotes and keypads
HomeVision Interactive Intelligent Home Control	www.csi3.com	X10 device control through set-top box or over the Internet
X10 Activehome Computer Interface Kit CM-11A	www.x10.com	X10 computer interface that works well with HomeSeer
CM17A "Firecracker" Interface	www.x10.com	X10 RF computer interface that works well with HomeSeer
HouseLinc-way X10 Controller	www.smarthome.com	X10 computer interface and controller

Secret #122: Choosing Hardware

When you're choosing hardware, you need to make sure that all the devices you buy support the same standard. Some other factors to consider when choosing hardware are as follows:

- **Electrical rating**—Make sure the device is rated for the job that you want it to do. For example, a 500W lighting controller will not be able to handle a large appliance. The excess electrical load will cause the receiver's switch to fuse and destroy the unit.
- **RF or power line**—There are X10 devices available, including remote controls, that communicate using RF. In order for them to control X10 devices you need an X10 RF receiver plugged into an outlet so that it can relay commands onto the line.
- **One-way or two-way**—Using newer two-way devices (transceivers), you can take advantage of advanced features and options in many home automation applications.

If you're installing an X10 system, make sure that all devices you purchase are X10-compliant. X10 devices have the X10 logo on the package or device. Beware of products that don't bear the X10 logo; X10 probably hasn't licensed them and they may not be fully compliant.

Secret #123: Troubleshooting Electrical Interference

Even though X10 units communicate over wires they can still suffer from interference. The power lines that X10 uses as its communication medium are anything but quiet. Normally the interference isn't enough to cause problems but some devices in your home can introduce RF interference onto the line, making it hard if not impossible for your X10 devices to function.

A device doesn't have to introduce noise onto the line; it can actually absorb the X10 signal and weaken it. To many devices, the signal from an X10 controller looks like electrical noise and they treat it as such.

Many consumer electronic devices, especially those with microprocessors, have power supplies designed to stop electrical noise from entering the system. These devices absorb and interfere with the X10 signal if they are close on the same circuit. The following products can cause problems for X10 signals:

◆ Televisions

◆ Computers

◆ Monitors

◆ Cell phone and battery chargers

◆ Cable and satellite boxes

◆ Uninterruptible power supplies

◆ Surge protector

◆ Stereo equipment

Monitors, televisions, and other video systems are especially hard on X10 signals because they need very clean power. Electrical noise that enters a TV or monitor interferes with the video signal and appears as static. Because of this, they have power supplies that absorb a lot of power line noise.

It may seem strange that these devices can absorb the signal from an X10 unit, but that is the nature of an electrical current. The power supplies of these devices absorb noise on the line and draw the current. The X10 signal is just electrical current at a specific frequency. In effect, these devices soak up the signal like a sponge.

To prevent signal loss from these devices you can install filters on the outlets that these devices use. These filters prevent the X10 signal from becoming absorbed by any device plugged into a filter (see Figure 12-9).

Determine which device is causing your problem by unplugging any "suspects" and testing the X10 devices. If they work when the device is unplugged but not when it's plugged in, you've found your culprit.

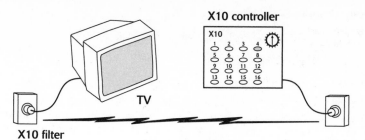

X10 filter

Filter keeps TV
from absorbing X10
from controller so
receiver can get
signal and operate

X10 receiver

Figure 12-9: Using a signal filter to improve X10 performance.

Secret #124: More Interference: X10 Cameras and Wi-Fi Networks

If you install an X10 wireless camera and suddenly start having problems on your WLAN, it's because the camera also uses the 2.4 GHz spectrum. X10 cameras don't play well with Wi-Fi. You can get the two to coexist; you just have to make a few adjustments to your Wi-Fi configuration.

According to X10 Inc., its video equipment uses four channels on the following frequencies:

- ◆ Channel A: 2.411 GHz
- ◆ Channel B: 2.434 GHz
- ◆ Channel C: 2.453 GHz
- ◆ Channel D: 2.473 GHz

802.11b divides the spectrum into the following channels:

- ◆ Channel 1: 2.412 GHz
- ◆ Channel 2: 2.417 GHz
- ◆ Channel 3: 2.422 GHz
- ◆ Channel 4: 2.427 GHz
- ◆ Channel 5: 2.432 GHz
- ◆ Channel 6: 2.437 GHz

- Channel 7: 2.442 GHz
- Channel 8: 2.447 GHz
- Channel 9: 2.452 GHz
- Channel 10: 2.457 GHz
- Channel 11: 2.462 GHz

The easiest thing to do is set the camera's channel as far away from your WLAN's channel frequency as possible. For example, if your WLAN is operating on channel 3 (2.422 GHz), you could reset your camera to channel D (2.473 GHz) to keep the signals from overlapping. You could also change the WLAN's channel but that might be a lot more work, depending on your Wi-Fi setup.

Secret #125: Using an X10 Phase Coupler

When you install your X10 devices, you may notice that your controller has problems communicating with some receivers in your home. You may think this is due to interference and install filters or even signal repeaters in an attempt to strengthen the signal. None of that works; what do you do now?

The problem you are having is that the receivers you can't control are on a different leg of your house's electrical circuit than your controller is. In the U.S., most houses have a 220-volt power supply that enters at the house's circuit breaker panel and then splits into two separate 110-volt phases (see Figure 12-10).

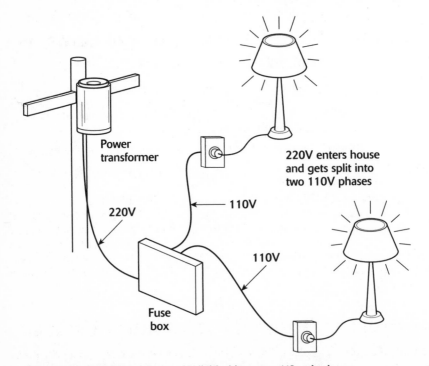

Power transformer

220V enters house and gets split into two 110V phases

110V

220V

110V

Fuse box

Figure 12-10: A 220-volt supply divided into two 110-volt phases.

The signal from your controller is having trouble going from one phase to the other. There are two ways to deal with this; one is to hire an electrician to install a hardwired signal bridge across the breaker for each phase. The other way is to install an X10 phase coupler/repeater (see Figure 12-11).

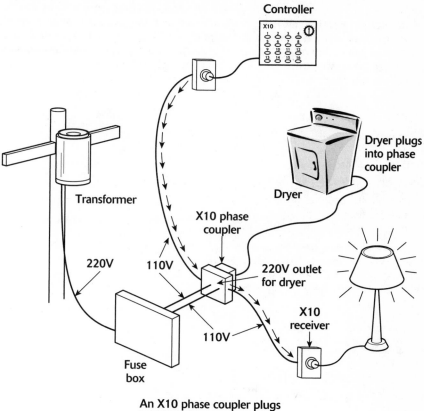

Figure 12-11: Bridging an X10 signal across both phases of your electrical system.

An X10 phase coupler/repeater plugs into a 220-volt outlet like the kind used for electric clothes dryers. The 220-volt outlet is one place where both 110-volt phases meet. The coupler/repeater transmits the X10 signal across both phases and boosts the signal to help ensure reception on the opposite phase. You can also get a phase coupler that doesn't repeat the signal but does bridge it across both phases. (Your dryer plugs back into the 220-volt outlet through the phase coupler.)

Maintaining Your Security and Privacy

Like any wireless technology, home automation has its own set of security problems, whether it involves wireless cameras or power line home control units.

Secret #126: Dangers of Wireless Cameras

Wireless cameras, especially aggressively marketed X10 wireless cameras, are a danger to your privacy. Because X10 cameras broadcast an unencrypted analog signal, all anyone needs to intercept it is an X10 video receiver plugged into a laptop (see Figure 12-12). That's right, someone sitting in a car parked on the street could be watching the video from your X10 nanny-cam.

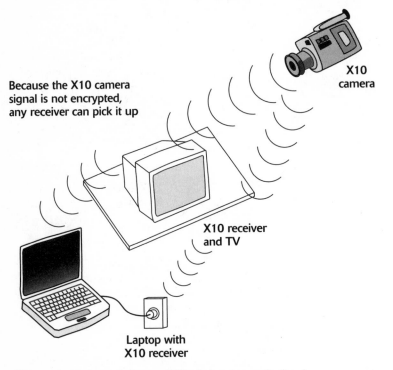

Because the X10 camera signal is not encrypted, any receiver can pick it up

X10 camera

X10 receiver and TV

Laptop with X10 receiver

Figure 12-12: Intercepting an X10 wireless camera's signal.

The worst part about this is that X10 remains silent about the problem and makes no effort to warn consumers. With hundreds of thousands of these cameras sold in the U.S., many people's privacy is in jeopardy and most don't even know it.

If you use an X10 camera, there really isn't anything I can tell you that will protect your privacy. You can't do anything to encrypt the signal because it's analog. The best advice is either to stop using it or at the very least don't point it anywhere you want to ensure your privacy.

insider insight	There are wireless 802.11b cameras available that offer more security. These have a digital signal and use encryption. However, because WEP encryption is flawed and WPA has issues as well, you should assume that if someone really wants access to your camera's signal, they could get it. So don't put it in the bathroom.

Secret #127: Security Precautions

Other X10 devices have security issues as well. You may wonder how anyone can intercept or tamper with the X10 signal that's on your power lines but it's actually a trivial affair. The signal from X10 transmitters travels along power lines and these power lines don't end at your wall. The signal from your transmitters can travel right out of your house, back to the pole or buried cable in the street, and into another home (see Figure 12-13).

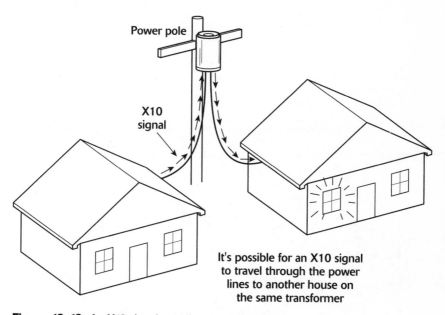

Power pole

X10
signal

It's possible for an X10 signal
to travel through the power
lines to another house on
the same transformer

Figure 12-13: An X10 signal traveling between homes.

As long as two houses are on the same transformer, the signal can travel from one house to another. Obviously, there are factors that affect this, such as signal strength and interference, but it is possible. There have been instances where neighbors were turning off or dimming each other's lights because they had both set their devices to the same house code on their controllers.

There are X10-enabled door locks and garage door openers. Because there are only 256 possible codes, it would be trivial for an intruder to plug a control unit into an external outlet and try all the codes until the door opens! Trying all 256 codes would take only about five or six minutes.

There are shortcuts that an intruder could take to make finding the code even easier. Rather than trying every code, he could simply set his controller for each house code in succession, and send an "all on" signal. When the lights came on he'd know that he was probably in the ballpark.

Rather than crouching in the bushes, he could be less obvious and simply plug an X10 wireless receiver into the external outlet. Then he could sit in his car and try the codes using a remote control (see Figure 12-14). So avoid using X10 locks and garage door openers!

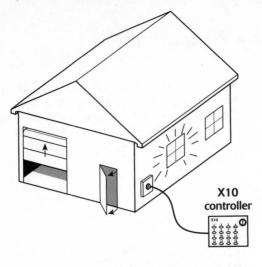

An X10 controller plugged into
an exterior outlet can open
X10-controlled doors

Figure 12-14: Using a controller to break into a home.

Wireless and Multimedia Devices

Chapter

13

◆ ◆

Secrets in This Chapter

◆ ◆

Tired of listening to all of your MP3 files through computer speakers or headphones? Why not add a wireless media hub to your stereo and broadcast all of your music from your computer? You could even watch your digital video and photos on your television or surf the Internet from your couch.

Choosing a Digital Entertainment Hub

Broadcasting digital music, sharing video, and gaming are some of the exciting options that use wireless technology to connect your home entertainment center and your computer, extending the use of both systems. This chapter introduces a few of these new devices and shows you how to select the best media solution.

Secret #128: What Is Digital Convergence?

Digital convergence is the latest and greatest techno-buzzword. It promises us a world where all our disparate consumer electronics and personal computing devices coexist peacefully, communicate, and seamlessly integrate to serve all our entertainment and informational needs. This begs the question: When will it arrive?

Some convergence is so intuitive that it's hard to imagine it not happening. Combining complementary services into a single device, such as a cell phone that can also do messaging and send e-mail, is a prime example. The result is a communications device that provides us with access to the main ways we already communicate.

Other ideas aren't as straightforward; they cater to lifestyle choices rather than marrying similar technologies. Merging a mobile phone and a digital camera is one such example. This isn't a combination that necessarily leads you to question how you ever lived without it; it's more of a "that's so neat" reaction.

The vision of many companies—including Sony, Apple, and Microsoft—is a convergence of our computer and home entertainment system into a do-everything, one-box solution (see Figure 13-1). All of the functions of these now separate devices will be available through one device or system, presumably built around our televisions or home theaters.

Right now these systems inhabit different parts of our homes and lives. Combining the two may not necessarily be as harmonious an arrangement as the technology pundits would have us believe. One major issue seems to elude the pro-convergence crowd: Multiple family members usually simultaneously share home entertainment systems, but a computer is a one-person-at-a-time deal. When was the last time everyone in your house sat down and surfed the Web together or worked on a Word document as a group?

In some form, a desktop PC will remain a standalone personal computing device. We may see smarter consumer electronics that have overlapping abilities or integrate seamlessly with our computer, but the PC still has a lot of life in it.

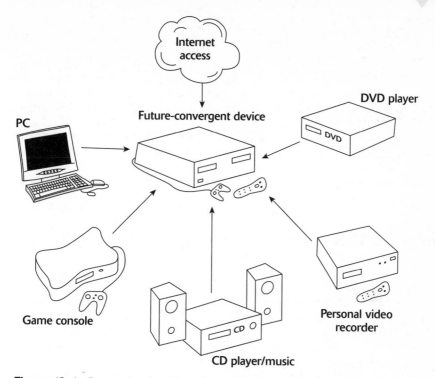

Figure 13-1: Converging functions of multiple devices into one box.

Manufacturers are just starting to take the first steps towards integrating more functions into smart entertainment devices or digital media hubs. In the next few years, we'll see more entertainment options repackaged and improved. This will be an example of the first type of convergence: combining complementary services and features into one device.

One of the first examples of this idea is the combination of a personal video recorder (PVR) and a cable/satellite set-top box. This synergy makes absolute sense, the sort of "why didn't they think of that before" technology we need to see more of. Companies like Sony are looking to build on this success by packing even more features into a PVR.

Sony unveiled its first big step towards digital convergence with the PSX, which combines a PVR, digital music player, DVD player, and game console into one device. The PSX also has a DVD-R drive and accepts Sony Memory Sticks so that you can view photos on your television. The PSX is currently only available in Japan, but it should be available in the United States by the end of 2004.

To meet the lofty goals that manufacturers set for themselves, future-convergent devices, or media hubs, will have to offer an improvement over current systems, particularly in the following areas. Consider this my "convergence manifesto":

◆ Enhanced, "smart" control and management. Future-convergent systems should allow for intuitive scheduling of tasks, efficient management, and ease of use. Current systems don't learn from your actions and can't determine your needs without you programming them.

♦ The ability to learn your viewing habits and record programming that you would most likely record yourself. This way if you forget to record an episode of your favorite show, or if it switches timeslots or channels, your PVR will know you like it, find it, and record it so you don't miss it.

♦ The ability to search connected devices and networks to retrieve relative information for you based on your viewing and listening habits. If you always watch the Los Angeles Lakers, for instance, agent software on future smart devices might collect news reports (video and Web) about the team and save them for you to view when it's convenient for you.

♦ Convenient storage, with larger disk drives to accommodate a wider range and amount of content. A convergent device should have room for all your digital media such as movies, games, photos, and music, and an intuitive interface for storing and backing these files up.

♦ A convenient upgrade path. Something better always comes out a few months down the road. Manufacturers need to make enhanced and new services available to consumers through easy software upgrades or through a simple system of hardware expansions. For example, the Sony PlayStation 2 has an expansion port that allows you to install a plug-and-play hard disk module or a broadband Internet modem. Future devices should offer a similar modular upgrade path.

Undoubtedly, there will be false starts as manufacturers design and produce the first generation of convergent systems. However, if early products are any indication, convergence may actually become a pleasant reality, rather than vaporware.

Secret #129: Finding Wi-Fi Devices

As more consumers install Wi-Fi networks in their homes, we will start to see more Wi-Fi–enabled home entertainment devices. A few products have started to appear from manufacturers like Linksys, Hewlett-Packard, and SMC. There are ways to add Wi-Fi to an existing component as long as it already has some networking connectivity (Ethernet or USB connections). Table 13-1 lists some digital media devices that are Wi-Fi–ready or upgradeable with an adapter.

Table 13-1: Wireless-Ready Entertainment Devices

Device/Site	Wi-Fi–Ready?
PRISMIQ Media Player www.prismiq.com	Yes, but you must purchase a wireless PCMCIA card separately; the device supports several cards from most major manufacturers.
Motorola Simplefi Wireless Digital Audio Receiver www.motorola.com	Wireless, but not Wi-Fi compatible.
HP ew5000 www.hpshopping.com	Yes, Wi-Fi built in.
cd3o c300 Network MP3 Player www.cd3o.com	Yes, Wi-Fi built in.

Device/Site	Wi-Fi–Ready?
Linksys Wireless-B Media Adapter www.linksys.com	Yes, it's a Wi-Fi adapter that allows you to connect non–Wi-Fi A/V components to your WLAN and stream music or view still photos.
Home Director AudioPoint www.homedirector.com/audiopoint	Ethernet port only; a wireless adapter may work.
Roku HD1000 High-Definition Digital Media Player www.rokulabs.com	Ethernet port only; will work with a wireless adapter.
Rio Digital Audio Receiver with Rio Digital Audio Connector www.rioaudio.com	Ethernet port only; a wireless adapter may work.
Turtle Beach AudioTron www.turtlebeach.com	Ethernet port only; a wireless adapter may work.
Sound Blaster Wireless Music http://us.creative.com	Yes, Wi-Fi; built-in 802.11b/g.
US Robotics USR6003 www.usr.com	Wireless, but not Wi-Fi; proprietary 900 MHz system.
RCA Lyra Wireless Transmitter www.rca.com	Wireless, but not Wi-Fi.
SMC SMCWMR-AG www.smc.com	Yes, 802.11a/b/g-supported.
RF LINK WAVECOM-SR www.rflinktech.com	Wireless but not Wi-Fi; proprietary 2.4 GHz; may interfere with Wi-Fi WLAN.
Terk LF-30S www.terk.com	Yes, but not Wi-Fi; 2.4 GHz proprietary; may interfere with a WLAN and 2.4 GHz cordless phones.
HP DMR-EN5000 www.hp.com	Ethernet port only; a wireless adapter may work.
Hauppauge MEDIAMVP 1000 www.hauppauge.com	Ethernet port only; a wireless adapter may work.
Pinnacle ShowCenter www.pinnaclesys.com	Yes, with PCMCIA wireless card.
Acer iRhythm Wireless Remote Tuner www.acer.com	Yes, but not Wi-Fi; uses proprietary 900 MHz wireless.

Most devices that are Ethernet-ready work with one of the Ethernet-to-wireless bridges listed in "Secret #130: Connecting Non–Wi-Fi Devices." The adapter needs to be plug-and-play and not require any drivers, like the Linksys WET11. The Ethernet-ready device will think you plugged it into a LAN, so it should operate just fine.

Before you purchase a device requiring an adapter, check the manufacturer's Web site or online forums to determine whether the device works with an adapter and, if so, which adapters work best. Chances are good that someone has already experimented with the same device and may have solved most of your problems for you.

Secret #130: Connecting Non–Wi-Fi Devices

What do you do if you've found a device that does everything you want, but it doesn't support Wi-Fi? The first step is to write or e-mail the manufacturer and politely suggest that they support Wi-Fi in future versions. After that, it's up to you to correct their oversight and get that thing on your WLAN. Fortunately, you can do this easily in most cases.

Most companies that manufacture Wi-Fi networking equipment also produce adapters that can connect an Ethernet device to a WLAN. There's a good reason for this; these adapters extend the usefulness of their own Ethernet products and drive adoption of Wi-Fi by people who have already made an investment in Ethernet LAN equipment.

Generally, if a device supports Ethernet and it's compatible with Universal Plug 'n' Play (UPnP), you should be able to connect a wireless adapter, like Linksys's wireless Ethernet bridge (WET11), to the device and have it on your WLAN in no time (see Figure 13-2). It's important that any adapter you attempt to use be driver-free and support UPnP.

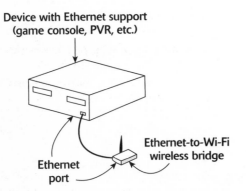

Figure 13-2: Connecting an Ethernet device to a WLAN with a Wi-Fi adapter.

By "driver-free," I mean fully self-contained and not requiring the device plugged into it to have a device driver installed in order to use it. Most adapters made for desktop computers and laptops require you to install a device driver in order for it to function.

I can't guarantee that all of these adapters will work in every situation, so take the time to research your Ethernet product before you invest in an adapter. Manufacturers' Web sites usually have technical support addresses or at least a FAQ section where you may be able to determine whether your Ethernet device and adapter work together. Table 13-2 lists some available Wi-Fi adapters.

Table 13-2: Wi-Fi Adapters for Ethernet Devices

Device/Address	Manufacturer/Standard
WET11 Wireless Ethernet Bridge www.linksys.com	Linksys, 802.11b. Connects most devices with an Ethernet port to an 802.11b WLAN.
WGA11B Wireless-B Game Adapter www.linksys.com	Linksys, 802.11b. Made to connect Ethernet-ready game consoles, but some users report that it also works with other Ethernet devices.
WGA54G Wireless-G Game Adapter www.linksys.com	Linksys, 802.11g. Made to connect Ethernet-ready game consoles, but some users report that it also works with other Ethernet devices.
WET54G Wireless-G Ethernet Bridge www.linksys.com	Linksys, 802.11g. Connects most devices with an Ethernet port to an 802.11g WLAN.
ME101 Wireless Ethernet Bridge www.netgear.com	NETGEAR, 802.11b. Connects most devices with an Ethernet port to an 802.11b WLAN.
WGE101 Wireless Ethernet Bridge www.netgear.com	NETGEAR, 802.11g. Connects most devices with an Ethernet port to an 802.11g WLAN.
Wireless Ethernet Bridge WE800G http://broadband.motorola.com	Motorola, 802.11g. Connects most devices with an Ethernet port to an 802.11g WLAN.
DWL-810+ AirPlus www.dlink.com	D-Link, 802.11b. Connects most devices with an Ethernet port to an 802.11b WLAN.
DWL-G810 AirPlus Xtreme G www.dlink.com	D-Link, 802.11g. Connects most devices with an Ethernet port to an 802.11g WLAN.
DWL-810 Air www.dlink.com	D-Link, 802.11b. Connects most devices with an Ethernet port to an 802.11b WLAN.

Digital Entertainment Devices

There are many digital toys for you to choose from. Some of them integrate into your Wi-Fi network and connect your home entertainment center to the Web and digital music. The list of innovations and features grows monthly, so you're sure to find a device that fits your needs.

Secret #131: Digital Music Players

You have a huge collection of CDs and you wish you could have instant access to all of them without having to sort through stacks of discs. What can you do to avoid this? You can rip your entire CD collection to MP3 audio files. Because MP3 audio is compressed, it takes up much less space on a hard drive than a normal CD audio file does. You can hold hundreds of hours of music on a large hard drive.

You can rip your CDs on your computer using software such as MusicMatch Jukebox, or you can purchase a CD player/audio server and use it to rip your CDs. Many digital media players stream or play back MP3s (see "Secret #133: Digital Media Players"). For more flexibility, get a portable MP3 jukebox or player, and take your music on the road with you.

While most portable MP3 players are not wireless, the next generation of MP3 players, due out in 2004, will most certainly have Bluetooth capability built in. This means that you will be able to use wireless headphones with your player and perhaps upload and download music to your computer wirelessly. Some manufacturers plan to offer adapters that will allow you to stream music to your car stereo.

Secret #132: Personal Video Recorders

Sometimes called digital video recorders (DVR), personal video recorders (PVR) are changing the way we view and interact with television. With a PVR such as TiVo, you can pause, rewind, and play back live television at the same time you are recording a show on another channel. Some PVRs let you record two programs simultaneously while watching a third. Television will never be the same after that!

PVR functions are finding their way into many new devices, including cable and satellite set-top boxes. There are also new PVRs that you can add a Wi-Fi adapter to (not a bridge, a wireless NIC) and get your PVR on the WLAN. Having your PVR on your network allows the device to connect to its service over your Internet connection to get the current TV listings (see Figure 13-3).

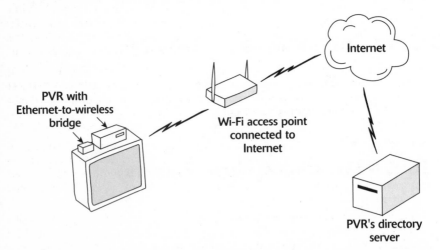

Figure 13-3: A PVR connecting to its directory service over a WLAN.

If your PVR is on your network, you can also send digital video to your computer so that you can burn it on a DVD (see Figure 13-4).

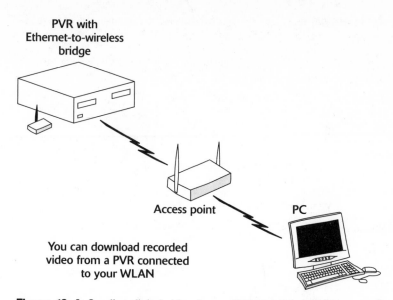

PVR with
Ethernet-to-wireless
bridge

Access point

PC

You can download recorded
video from a PVR connected
to your WLAN

Figure 13-4: Sending digital video from a PVR to a PC via Wi-Fi.

Secret #133: Digital Media Players

Digital media players, media hubs, or media adapters allow you to view or listen to digital media from your computer on your home entertainment center. Functionality and design varies among devices, but there are two basic types. One type connects to your network and allows you to upload all your video and audio files to the unit. You then play back using the media player whenever you like (see Figure 13-5).

The second type interfaces with your home entertainment center and network and allows you to stream media to your entertainment center using the media player. This type of device doesn't store your audio or video files; it just acts as your computer's interface with your entertainment center (see Figure 13-6).

The second type of unit is more flexible: You can have all your music and photos in a central place (your computer), and broadcast it to media players in different rooms. Many media players have a wireless remote, and you can browse and select your music and picture files on your TV screen. Table 13-3 lists some of the more popular media players and hubs.

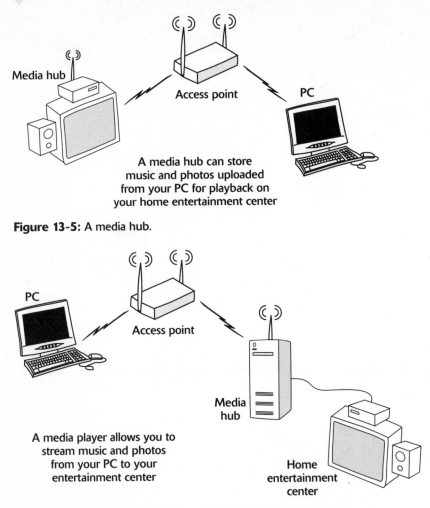

Media hub

Access point

PC

A media hub can store
music and photos uploaded
from your PC for playback on
your home entertainment center

Figure 13-5: A media hub.

PC

Access point

Media
hub

A media player allows you to
stream music and photos
from your PC to your
entertainment center

Home
entertainment
center

Figure 13-6: Streaming media to your home entertainment center.

Table 13-3: Popular Media Players and Hubs

Device/Address	Description
PRISMIQ Media Player www.prismiq.com	Browse the Web, stream audio and video, use instant messaging, view photos, listen to Internet radio, and more.
Motorola Simplefi Wireless Digital Audio Receiver http://broadband.motorola.com/consumers	Listen to your MP3s and WMAs; tag-it feature allows you to learn about artists and buy concert tickets.
HP ew5000 www.hpshopping.com	Play music and view photos stored on networked computers using Wi-Fi.

Device/Address	Description
c300 Network MP3 Player www.cd3o.com	Play MP3s over Wi-Fi; remote control with voice command announces the names of songs and directories so you can find what you're looking for without getting out of your chair and walking across the room to read the player's display.
Linksys Wireless-B Media Adapter www.linksys.com	Listen to MP3 and WMA files, view photos, and browse files using a remote and your T.V.
Home Director AudioPoint www.homedirector.com/ audiopoint	Stream digital audio and Internet radio to your stereo.

Secret #134: Home Theater PCs

One of the coolest toys around is the home theater PC (HTPC). The HTPC is a fully functional computer that's optimized for playing and recording video and music. An HTPC contains all the usual computer components (hard drive, DVD/CD player or recorder, and video card) but may also include a high-definition television tuner (HDTV) card and a TV card for receiving a TV signal. The HTPC is a personal computer turned into a convergence device, a PC that can take over the functions of many of your consumer electronics tasks (see Figure 13-7), including the following:

- Music serving
- High-definition TV tuning
- Gaming
- PVR functions
- Web surfing

Because an HTPC is a fully functional computer, you can add a wireless network adapter and hook it up to your WLAN. Then you can access all your video and music files from any other computer.

The best part about an HTPC is that you don't have to buy one; you can build one yourself. The Internet has an active community of HTPC enthusiasts. You can find everything you need to design and build your own system, from hardware and cases to HTPC software applications. Of course, you could just buy an HTPC system, but half the fun is the do-it-yourself aspect of the HTPC. This also allows you to customize the system so that it's just the way you want.

Designing and building your own HTPC is not difficult, and there are plenty of resources on the Internet to help you get the job done (see Table 13-4).

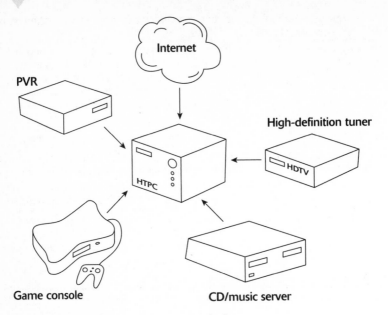

Figure 13-7: HTPC as a convergence device.

Table 13-4: HTPC Resources

Name/Address	Description
HTPC forums www.htpcforums.com	Great forums for HTPC enthusiasts; lots of good information.
HTPC News www.htpcnews.com	"The online source for the HTPC enthusiast".
AVS forum www.avsforum.com	HTPC forum.
Lurgen.com www.lurgen.com/toys/htpc	Matt Duggan's personal HTPC site.
MyHTPC http://myhtpc.net	A customizable, menu-driven front end for HTPCs with free download for personal use.

Secret #135: Windows XP Media Center Edition

Media Center PCs are Windows XP computers designed for home entertainment. Similar to HTPCs, manufacturers optimize Media Center PCs for entertainment. Like an HTPC, a Windows XP Media Center PC can be connected to your WLAN with the addition of a wireless adapter. When connected to your WLAN, a Windows XP Media Center PC serves as the digital entertainment hub for your family. Depending on the manufacturer and model, they may include the following features:

- ◆ TV tuner
- ◆ Remote control
- ◆ TV recorder on your hard disk
- ◆ Digital audio output
- ◆ Output to your TV

Unlike HTPCs, Media Center PCs have some limitations for recording video. They record video in a proprietary format called DVR-MS. Only Media Center PCs can play this format and you can't burn recorded shows to a DVD for playback on a DVD player. Copy protection on some broadcasts limits the viewing and copying of recorded files to the Media Center PC that they were recorded on.

Media Center PCs run an enhanced version of Windows XP. You can't purchase Windows XP Media Center Edition separately; it's only available preinstalled on Media Center PCs. A number of manufacturers have started producing Media Center PCs (see Table 13-5).

Table 13-5: Windows XP Media Center PC Manufacturers

Name	Address
Dell	www.dell.com
Gateway	www.gateway.com
ABS	www.abspc.com
Cyber Power	www.cyberpowersystem.com
Hewlett-Packard	www.hp.com
Howard Computers	www.howardcomputers.com
IbuyPower	www.ibuypower.com
Mind	www.mind.ca
Northgate Innovations	www.northgate.com
Sony	www.sony.com
Systemax	www.systemaxpc.com
Tagar Systems	www.tagarsystems.com
Toshiba	http://csd.toshiba.com
Touch Systems	www.touch-systems.ca
Viewsonic	www.viewsonic.com
ZT Group	www.ztgroup.com

Windows XP Media Center PCs provide an alternative to HTPCs for those of us who don't like the idea of building one ourselves. However, with its limited PVR functions and lack of an HDTV tuner, an HTPC is still the best way to go for any serious home theater fan.

on the
web For more information about Media Center PCs from owners and enthusiasts, visit www.thegreenbutton.com.

Secret #136: Surfing on Your TV

In every family there's at least one of them: relatives who refuse to have anything to do with the Internet. They think the Internet is a passing fad and that there's nothing on it for them to enjoy or make use of. Many people think the Web will go the way of the hula hoop or the Pet Rock.

Sometimes the real problem isn't the Internet; it's how people get to it: the PC. Internetphobia is often just computerphobia. Some people, especially seniors, just aren't comfortable with computers. The learning curve can seem steep and intimidating.

This is unfortunate because, especially for seniors, the Internet is a great way to stay in touch with the family, see pictures of the grandchildren, and meet people with similar interests. Fortunately, some products help them go on the Web quickly and easily, without having to go near a computer.

Set-top Internet boxes connect to your television set and a phone line (and in some cases Ethernet) and allow you to surf the Web on your television (see Figure 13-8). The dominant product in this area is MSN TV from Microsoft (formerly WebTV). MSN TV provides access to Web browsing, instant messaging, and e-mail. Some of the positive aspects of surfing the Web on your TV include the following:

- ♦ It's easy to use and set up
- ♦ You don't have to buy a computer to get on the Web
- ♦ To some family members it's less threatening than a computer

caution AOL used to have a TV-based service called AOL TV, but AOL shut it down in November 2003. Unfortunately, unscrupulous dealers on some online auction sites are still selling the boxes, which are now useless paperweights. Don't purchase any AOL TV device, and report anyone selling them (it's fraud) to the auction site's moderators.

Two other companies have started providing devices that allow users to access the Internet using a television. CompuCable produces an Internet-ready television called the iTV. The iTV doesn't require a set-top box; it's built into the television. Like MSN TV, users can surf the Web and enjoy e-mail access as well.

TVPC produces a small, powerful media computer that runs Windows XP and hooks up to any television, home theater, and stereo system. The TVPC plays DVDs and MP3 music files, as well as all PC games and software. You can also surf the Web over your Internet connection and view it all on your TV.

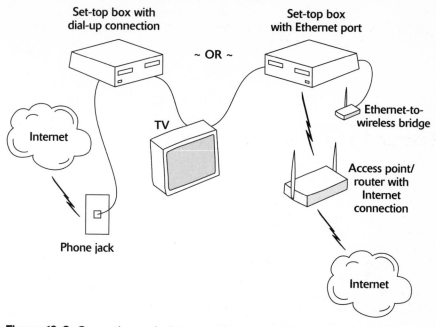

Figure 13-8: Connecting to the Internet using a set-top box.

on the web For information about MSN TV, visit www.msntv.com. To learn about iTV, visit www.itv.com. To see what PCTV is all about, visit www.pctv.com.

Browsing the Web on a TV does have its drawbacks. People create Web pages for high-resolution computer monitors, so most regular Web pages won't appear well on a low-resolution TV screen. Services like MSN TV (and the old AOL TV) try to remedy this by designing content to fit TV screens, but general Web surfing on the TV is not a comparable experience to using a computer. Still, it may be the best way to get Internet-wary relatives online so you can keep in touch with them.

Part V

Safe and Secure Wireless Computing

Exposing Crackers, Hackers, and Their Tools

Chapter

14

◆ ◆

Secrets in This Chapter

◆ ◆

Y
ou may ask why you should worry about understanding hackers. After all, what you really want to know is what they can do and how you can stop them, right? There's more to it than that. Taking the time to understand the mindset of hackers, their subculture, and their motivations will help you to determine whether you are a likely target and avoid becoming a victim.

The media's representation of hackers is a mixed bag of sensationalism and misinformation. Understandably, sensationalism sells papers and commercial spots, whereas plain facts probably wouldn't. When reporting a new virus or worm (Blaster comes to mind), it's not uncommon for a reporter to drag a crew down to the nearest home electronics or computer store and interview an "authority" about the worm.

The authority in question may be a salesperson, a repairperson, or perhaps even a manager, all of whom I'm sure are world-class authorities on computer security and malicious software. Unfortunately, what you usually don't see is the same news crew taking the time to interview a computer scientist or certified information security professional. I refer to this as "assumed authority syndrome" when Bob in aisle five decides that because he sells computers, he must be an expert. Guess what, he isn't.

Assumed authority syndrome leads to misinformation, panicked computer users, and wasted time. Threats often aren't dealt with effectively, or the resulting confusion delays users from taking necessary and often simple steps to protect their computers. The first step in undoing this sensationalism is examining who hackers are and what they can or cannot actually do.

Hackers and crackers have their own language and subculture. Different groups have different goals, slang, and modus operandi.

Secret #137: How to Tell Hackers from Crackers

The term *hacker* hasn't always been the negative title that it is today. A hacker originally described a person with a desire to learn about technology and to experiment and who was technically proficient with whatever systems they hacked. The word predates personal computers; some of the first hackers were members of the Massachusetts Institute of Technology (MIT) Tech Model Railroading Club (TMRC) in the late 1950s. Students at MIT traditionally used the word *hack* to describe elaborate pranks that they played. Thus a hack came to mean something truly original, elegant, and ingenious. (To view a gallery of some of the most ingenious hacks at MIT visit `http://hacks.mit.edu`.)

---

cross
ref

You can find a more detailed description of the birth of hackers and hacking in *Hackers, Heroes of the Computer Revolution* by Steven Levy (Penguin USA, 2001).

There once was a time when being called a hacker was a sincere compliment of your technical abilities and problem solving skills. These days, largely due to the popular media, when people hear *hacker,* they wrongly think *criminal.* The tech community now distinguishes between hackers, who identify security flaws in order to improve computer systems, and *crackers*, who attempt to exploit those flaws to their own advantage.

> **note** Throughout the rest of this chapter, I use the term *cracker* to refer to computer criminals or people unethically exploiting systems.

Hackers: The White Hats

Just like in the old Hollywood westerns, the good guys wear the white hats, at least metaphorically. *White hat* is a term often used to describe ethical hackers that stay entirely within the law. They never access a system or network illegally, and they work tirelessly to expose holes in systems with the ultimate goal of fixing flaws and improving security. Upon finding a flaw, a white hat will usually notify the software vendor and give the company a chance to patch the flaw before making the bug public knowledge.

White hats may be security professionals, hired by companies to audit network security or test software. Using the same software tools that crackers use, a white hat seeks to improve the security of his own network by proactively attacking it as a cracker would. White hats may even create software aimed at thwarting tools available to crackers. White hats can use tools such as the Fake AP, mentioned later in this chapter, to thwart wireless sniffers that crackers might use to discover wireless networks.

Knowing how a cracker operates enables a white hat to take steps to secure a network against likely avenues of attack. Although some ex-crackers work as security consultants, simply knowing how to crack a system doesn't translate into being able to secure it. White hats don't acquire their skills illegally. By demonstrating sound judgment and admirable ethics, they make a much better choice for companies looking to hire a security consultant.

Crackers: The Black Hats

Hackers refer to the computer world's outlaws as *black hats*. The opposite of the white hat, a black hat or cracker breaks into systems illegally for personal gain, vandalism, or bragging rights. A cracker doesn't need to be particularly knowledgeable or skillful; in fact, most of them aren't. Few crackers are skilled enough to create their own software tools, so most rely on automated programs that they download from disreputable Web sites.

Because crackers know they are breaking the law, they do everything they can to cover their tracks. Fortunately, security professionals catch quite a few of them because the majority of crackers lack real skill. When the authorities do catch them, their skill with a computer is often greatly exaggerated to promote the agency making the arrest (and to sell newspapers and commercials). Still, it's important to acknowledge that crackers present a serious threat: Many are technically proficient and can cause a lot of damage, and many systems are so woefully insecure that even technically inept crackers can wreak havoc on them.

The most dangerous crackers

Although the majority of crackers are relatively unskilled, not all are inept. Some crackers have extensive training and advanced skills. Often these crackers work as programmers or IT consultants and learn the ins and outs of networks by administering them. They have in-depth knowledge of network programming and can create tools to exploit the weaknesses they discover.

This programming skill is what separates them from less-skilled computer criminals. It also makes them more dangerous and harder to catch. Often these crackers create tools that enable less-skilled criminals to subvert security and exploit weaknesses in computer systems.

While skilled crackers are in the minority, they can't be ignored. By creating tools and malicious software (viruses, worms) they act as a force-multiplier and create a greater problem than their numbers may indicate. When planning for security it is wise to take the more dangerous crackers into account and plan for a worst-case scenario.

Script kiddies, packet monkeys, and s'kiddiots

The most common type of cracker goes by many names: *script kiddies, packet monkeys, s'kiddiots, lamers, warez d00dz* (dudes), and *wannabes*. They lack any real technical ability and, for the most part, cannot even program. To thwart the security of systems, they rely on software tools created by others. They often use these tools without any real understanding of what the actual program does.

A common pastime for script kiddies is Web page defacement. They break into an insecure Web server and replace the home page of a site with a page of their own design (see Figure 14-1 for an example of a defaced Web site). Due to their ineptitude and clumsiness, they are actually far less of a threat than the media (and government) claims. However, because script kiddies make great headlines, they are acknowledged by the press as hacker-geniuses.

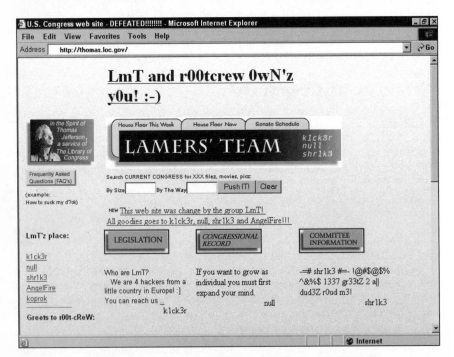

Figure 14-1: The Library of Congress Web site defaced by a script kiddy.

One recent example of a script kiddy is the case of 18-year-old high school student Jeffrey Lee Parson. Authorities arrested Parson in August 2003 for creating a variant of the Blaster worm, dubbed Blaster.B. Parson, who went by the handle t33kid (teekid), created the variant by editing the code of the original Blaster worm without any understanding of what that code did. Luckily, due to his ineptitude, his version of the worm was less virulent than the original Blaster and did little damage in comparison. It's amazing that it took the FBI as long as it did to catch him (two weeks). Parson modified the worm to connect to his personal Web site, where he openly provided other malicious software for download. Tracking Parson through registration information for his Web site was simple.

Laughingly, the press and prosecutors dubbed him a computer genius, further illustrating the problem of sensationalism in computer crime reporting. (In fact, his mother went out of her way to tell the press he "is not brilliant, he's not a genius.") You can't defend against a threat that you don't understand, and promoting novice crackers as dire threats to national security doesn't further the cause of public education on computer security.

insider insight   Besides the ethical difference between the two, the major factor that separates hackers from the vast majority of crackers is an understanding of computer systems and the ability to create software. A real hacker can write code in one or more languages (C, C++, assembly, Java) and understands what that code does and why it works (or doesn't). The majority of crackers have little programming ability, or none at all, and usually don't understand how the tools they use work. If a machine gets hacked by a script kiddy, it's usually because the administrator didn't maintain the machine and apply patches for known vulnerabilities.

Many crackers use aliases online and hang out on Internet Relay Chat (IRC). Crackers like to brag about their exploits, share software, and organize on IRC and Usenet newsgroups. Often an alias can give you a good idea about whom you're dealing with. If the alias is L0rd Death, Terminator, or CyberGod, then you're probably not dealing with a secure, mature adult.

Script kiddies have their own language. Called l33t (*leet*, short for *elite*), it has nothing to do with real hackers or the way they write and speak. l33t evolved separately from writing conventions in legitimate hackerdom, which usually were influenced by the way users were required to write in older Unix text editors, or from system commands. l33t evolved on the old BBS systems and later IRC and Usenet. The following are some examples of l33t from *The Jargon File* (version 4.4.7), Chapter 9, by Eric S. Raymond, located online at www.catb.org/~esr/jargon/html/index.html:

- Purposeful misspellings, such as *fone* (phone) and *phreak* (freak)
- Substitution of z for s, as in *passwordz, gamez, sitez*; the use of z has evolved to denote something illegal, such as copied software and stolen passwords
- Random emphasis characters: *Hey doodz!#!$#$*
- Use of emphatic *k* prefix: *k-kool, k-awesome*
- Compulsive abbreviation: *I got lotsa warez w/docs*
- Type in all caps SO IT APPEARS LIKE THE SPEAKER IS YELLING ALL THE TIME

Some letter/number substitutions are common:

- ◆ 4 substituted for *A*
- ◆ 3 substituted for *E*, as in *l33t*
- ◆ ph substituted for *F*, as in *phreak*
- ◆ 1 or | substituted for *I* or *L*
- ◆ |V| substituted for *M*
- ◆ |\| substituted for *N*
- ◆ The digit 0 substituted for the letter *O*
- ◆ 5 substituted for *S*
- ◆ 7 or + substituted for *T*

Using these substitutions, you would write *elite* as *31337*. Other less common character substitutions include:

- ◆ 8 substituted for *B*
- ◆ (, k, |<, , or /< substituted for *C*
- ◆ <| substituted for *D*
- ◆ 6 or 9 substituted for *G*
- ◆ |-| substituted for *H*
- ◆ |< or /< substituted for *K*
- ◆ |2 substituted for *P*
- ◆ |_| substituted for *U*
- ◆ / or \/ substituted for *V*
- ◆ // or \/\/ substituted for *W*
- ◆ >< substituted for *X*
- ◆ `/ substituted for *Y*

Crackers use the suffixes 0r and x0r to mark words as l33t, as in:

```
DUDEZ!#!#  I am an 31337 hax0r
```

As you can see, l33t has its own unique conventions for spelling and grammar. Here is an example of l33t, followed by a rough translation:

```
1337d00d: A code monkey wedge his st00pid's gonkulator and
the st00pid is MAD!#!#$$ Lamer can't rel0ad wind0$e - st00pitude
```

Translation:

```
A low-level programmer broke his boss's expensive and pretentious
new computer and the boss is mad. He doesn't know how to reload
Microsoft Windows on his computer.
```

---

on the web   For a laugh, visit the English-to-h@x0r translator at
www.eskimo.com/~mvargas/hax0r.htm.

Gray Hats

Nothing is ever as black and white as we would like it to be—least of all human behavior. A gray hat is a name given to an otherwise ethical hacker who walks a fine line between legal and illegal hacking. Like white hats, gray hats find security holes and report them; but unlike white hats, they often publicize the flaw before giving the software developers a chance to fix the problem. Gray hats maintain that they are improving security by compelling companies to fix software.

Gray hats may also access computer systems without permission, with the intent to find and report flaws. While it's better to have a gray hat finding holes in your network rather than a black hat, when you're under attack you have no way of distinguishing between the two. In addition, in an attempt to thwart network security, a gray hat that means well may inadvertently cause damage.

Skilled gray hats may produce software that exploits known flaws in systems, intending for network administrators and security professionals to use the program for network security testing. Unfortunately, even though this software can be very constructive, crackers can use it for less noble purposes.

Occasionally you may hear the term *samurai hacker* or *Ronin*. This refers to an independent white hat (or gray hat) security consultant hired to audit and improve security. Most samurai hackers claim to be loyal to their employers and to engage only in ethical cracking. The name samurai hacker derives from the fierce loyalty and high ethics associated with Japan's samurai warriors.

Phreaks

A *phreak* is a hacker who specializes in phone systems. These days, however, phreaking is more of a cracker activity. At one time, phreaks were enthusiastic about telephone networks and simply wanted to understand how they worked and explore them. Ethical phreaks didn't steal services or cause damage; they just used their technical skill to play with the system.

Phone systems have changed and are less susceptible to technological hacks. As a result, modern phreaks intent on cracking the telecommunications systems often rely on criminal acts such as stealing phone cards and cloning cell phones.

Hacktivists

The *hacktivist* is a gray hat or cracker who defaces Web pages to bring attention to a political agenda or social cause. Companies, organizations, and governments that engage in controversial practices or that have unpopular policies are likely targets of hacktivists. How ethical this behavior is depends on whether or not you support the hactivist's agenda or believe in his cause.

Being a hacktivist is not an indication of technical prowess. Often Web sites are hosted on servers with known security holes and can be defaced with automated tools. In the United Kingdom, a hacktivist with the alias Herbless went on a hacktivism spree in 2000, hacking the HSBC bank and government Web sites to protest fuel prices and the government's stance on smoking. His defacement of the Web pages included an activist statement, as well as instructions for other hacktivists. On one site, he left the following message for the administrator:

Note to the administrator: You should really enforce stronger passwords. I cracked 75% of your NT accounts in 16 seconds on my SMP Linux box. Please note the only thing changed on this server is your index page, which has been backed up. Nothing else has been altered.

Cyberwars between hacktivists on opposite sides of a political debate are becoming more common. Israeli hacktivists deface Arab sites, particularly Palestinian, and Arab hacktivists return fire. Indian and Pakistani hacktivists routinely hack Web pages from each other's countries. While hacktivism and

Web page defacement may seem harmless when compared to other cyber-crime, such as online credit card fraud, the damage done to the reputation of a company or agency can be considerable.

Secret #138: What Makes Hackers and Crackers Tick?

There are as many reasons for hacking as there are hackers. It's hard to pin down just a few personality traits that define a hacker. A typical hacker profile is a male, age 14 to 40, with above-average intelligence, obsessively inquisitive with regards to technology, anticonformist, introverted, and broad intellectual interests.

A hacker is driven to learn everything he can about any subject that interests him. In fact, most hackers that excel with technology also have proficiency in nontechnological hobbies or interests. Hackers tend to devour information, hoarding it away for some future time when a random bit of technical trivia may help them solve an intriguing problem. Hackers seem especially fond of complex intellectual challenges and will move on to a new project once the challenge and novelty wears off. Contrast this with the following cracker/script kiddy profile and you start to get an idea of why hackers resent being lumped in with crackers.

The average cracker or script kiddy (in the United States) is a 14- to 28-year old white male, usually intelligent but academically underachieving, who lives in his parents' basement and collects comic books (OK, I added those last two). Cultural and behavioral distinctions between groups can help identify a cracker because they often leave clues when they deface a Web site or break into a computer.

Crackers and script kiddies differ from ethical hackers. They often lack social skills, are loners (most hackers I know love company), and show poor judgment and impulse control. Where a hacker may work for days or weeks to solve a particularly difficult problem, a script kiddy lacks the discipline to even begin to become a competent programmer and so depends on code written by real hackers.

Financial gain motivates some crackers. Credit card and bank fraud present opportunities to use cracking to increase personal wealth. Cracker/script kiddy culture sees stealing from large corporations as a kind of Robin Hood game. While major financial crimes involving crackers are not commonplace, there have been instances of theft on a grand scale by the more talented among them. In 1994, a Russian computer programmer stole millions of dollars from Citibank accounts. The cracker, Vladimir Levin, was part of a group that created a complicated scheme of wire transfers and pickup all over the world.

Secret #139: Finding Hacker Conventions, Gatherings, and Publications

A kid with blue hair, a guy with a pocket protector, and a federal agent walk into a casino hotel. No, this isn't the start of an off-color joke. It's what you might see if you were to hang around the entrance of a hacking convention. Some of these conventions started out as semiformal gatherings of hacking pioneers or offline meetings of online hacking groups. Other events, like 2600 meetings (mentioned later), grew up around publications.

Some conventions have grown into huge events with people flying in from all over the world. The biggest hacker conventions attract white hats, crackers, script kiddies, and even businesspeople and federal agents. Have you ever wanted to play a game of "spot-the-fed"? Go to a convention. Want to learn advanced hacks, programming, and buy some "kewl" T-shirts? Go to a convention. The following subsections list some of the top spots for hackers.

DefCon

This event started in 1993 and has gotten bigger every year. Held in Las Vegas and billed as the largest underground hacking event in the world, DefCon is huge and, being in Las Vegas, a lot of fun. The lectures and contests are the highlight of DefCon. Lectures are separated into different tracks, each one geared toward a particular skill level.

Attendees can compete in events like capture-the-flag (the hacker version, not the schoolyard version), spot-the-fed, and hacker Jeopardy. The convention is attended by famous hackers as well as crackers and, of course, plenty of script kiddies. DefCon has become a place where serious debate takes place between security experts, hackers, companies, and even government agencies. It has become a must-attend event for people interested in information security.

on the web For more DefCon information, visit www.defcon.org.

ToorCon

Held in sunny San Diego since 1999, ToorCon (that's "toor," as in *root* spelled backwards) is becoming another worthwhile event attended by hackers and security professionals. Like Defcon, ToorCon offers several lectures during the convention, divided into two categories: "attack and defense" and "policy and compliance." Crackers, hackers, and industry professionals conduct the lectures.

on the web For ToorCon information, visit www.toorcon.org.

Hackers on Planet Earth

Sponsored by *2600: The Hacker Quarterly* magazine (see the related section in this chapter) and held in New York City roughly every two or three years, HOPE is a great convention, attended by many of the same groups and individuals that haunt DefCon every year. Information on upcoming HOPE conventions is posted on *2600* magazine's Web site.

Worldwide Wardrive

While not a convention, this is a noteworthy event, especially in a book about wireless technology. The Worldwide Wardrive (WWWD), now in its fourth year, is a coordinated effort to collect statistical data on the security of Wi-Fi access points. Put simply, a lot of people *wardrive* (drive around looking for unsecured wireless networks) and then compile the data and present the results.

on the
web For information about the WWWD, visit www.worldwidewardrive.org.

2600 Magazine

First published in 1984, and named for an early phreaking exploit (2600 Hz was the frequency used to unlock some phones), *2600: The Hacker Quarterly* contains articles about computer security and telecommunications. *2600* sponsors the HOPE convention and, through its Web site and print versions, disseminates information related to cracking different systems. The quality of the articles varies, with some articles written by script kiddies and other crackers as well as hackers. Overall, the majority of the content is of a respectable technical level.

In cities around the world, *2600* readers meet on the first Friday of every month to discuss, learn, and teach one another about technology. All are welcome to attend; a list of meetings is maintained on the *2600* Web site.

on the
web Visit *2600* magazine on the Web at www.2600.com.

There are more conventions, meetings, and publications than these, but these are the largest and most well-known. More conventions spring up every year, some continuing from year to year while others make a one-time appearance. The DefCon Web site hosts a list of other events, updated regularly.

Examining the Hacker/Cracker Toolkit

There are hundreds, perhaps even thousands, of tools available online for hackers and crackers. The toolkit used depends on the type of hacking/cracking, the skill level, and the motivations of the individual. The toolkit of a proficient hacker may consist of programming tools (editors, compilers) and software that he has written himself. At the other end of the spectrum is the inept script kiddy with a computer full of software exploits written by someone else. He may not know how they work but as long as he has them, he's an "31337 hax0r" (elite hacker).

insider
insight An *exploit* is a program or script that a cracker runs on a computer to "exploit" known vulnerabilities in the system. The existence of automated or canned exploits is one of the reasons why it is important to stay aware of vulnerabilities in your system and apply patches in a timely manner. The Security Focus site at www.securityfocus.com maintains a database of vulnerabilities, as well as patches and exploits. Check there often to keep your system up-to-date and safe.

Because this is a wireless book, I concentrate on tools and exploits for wireless. That doesn't mean you don't have to worry about other vulnerabilities. A weakness in Windows is a weakness regardless of whether you network your PCs with Ethernet cables or Wi-Fi cards. You have to keep your systems up to date and patched, or you run the risk of a disgruntled 14-year-old, with no dating prospects in his future, finding and cracking your computer. If you have an "always-on" broadband Internet connection and you don't patch vulnerabilities in the operating system, it is very possible that a script kiddy using automated scanning software may locate and crack your computer.

Secret #140: The First Layer of Defense

Let's go out on a limb and guess that you're running some flavor of Windows on your home computer. On the Security Focus site, there are over 85 vulnerabilities listed that affect Windows XP Home Edition. That is a lot for a cracker to work with, especially if you don't apply the patches that Microsoft has released to correct these problems.

Crackers look for easy targets: systems that haven't been patched to correct known vulnerabilities, misconfigured software, and hardware and access points that have been left unsecured or that were deployed with the manufacturer's default settings still in place. Crackers usually aren't going to expend a lot of effort on a target, especially since there are so many unsecured systems available.

Always stay aware of the vulnerabilities that affect your operating system, applications, and hardware. Apply patches as they are made available to ensure that you don't remain vulnerable to an exploit that capitalizes on a known vulnerability.

> **insider insight** Many of the recent Internet worms that did so much damage and caused so many headaches took advantage of a known vulnerability in Windows operating systems. Microsoft released a patch to correct the problem, but, unfortunately, many people did not use it to secure their computers (especially at home). If more people patched their computers, the problem would not have been so widespread.

Most access points and other wireless hardware come configured to make it as easy as possible for you to set up your network. Unfortunately, this usually means they are also configured to be insecure. Manufacturers often leave features enabled that make it easy for crackers to locate and access your WLAN. It is always wise to study your hardware manuals and change the manufacturer's default passwords and network names. These defaults are well known to crackers and your failing to change them is like giving a burglar a key and an invitation to rob your house.

802.11b networks use Wired Equivalent Privacy (WEP) encryption to secure data. WEP has recently been defeated by crackers, and tools are available that automate discovery of WEP encryption keys for crackers (see the "Software for Wardriving" section). This doesn't mean that you shouldn't enable WEP on your WLAN; by all means do it. Not every cracker or script kiddy will know how to use the cracking utility or even have the right NIC and software to run it. Would you leave your front door unlocked just because a burglar might be strong enough to kick it in anyway? Of course you wouldn't. Don't make it any easier for the crackers. Use WEP on your WLAN unless you have a better option.

cross
ref

Chapter 15 covers more exploits and threats in greater depth as well as steps to take to secure your WLAN. Please consult Chapter 15 and follow the steps contained there to defend yourself against wardriving and other common threats.

Secret #141: Identity Theft Scams

Recently crackers have turned to rigging independent ATM machines (those found in groceries, gas stations, restaurants, and other small establishments) to defraud customers. Usually, the owner of the establishment gets a small fee on every transaction as rent for having the machine in his or her store. Some crackers, as well as organized crime groups, have been modifying machines so that the machine scans the customer's ATM card and stores the account data along with the personal identification number (PIN). The criminals then take that data, create forged ATM cards, and clean out the victim's account. To date this has only occurred with independent ATMs, not bank-owned machines.

Perhaps the most common type of fraud committed by crackers is identity theft. Crackers steal personal data, either by cracking computers or through scams, referred to as *social engineering*, designed to trick people into revealing personal data. A cracker may pose as an employee of an Internet service provider (such as AOL) and attempt to get your password. Other scams include setting up fake Internet storefronts to collect credit card data. When the crackers collect enough data, they steal the identity of the victims and get credit issued under the victims' names.

caution

Guard your personal information both online and offline; never divulge it to anyone—least of all to strangers who e-mail you and claim to be from your bank, credit card company, or ISP. Vigilance can help protect you from crackers and script kiddies intent on defrauding you.

Secret #142: Wardriving

Wardriving is the act of driving around with Wi-Fi equipment to detect and map Wi-Fi access points (see Figure 14-2). Because many access points are not secure, it's possible to locate many open access points, especially within urban areas. A cracker wardrives to find vulnerable networks that can be broken into. Once inside a WLAN, a cracker can connect to the Internet and attack other computers without being caught. The cracker effectively covers his tracks because his activity will be tracked back to the WLAN he compromised, not back to him. Of course, connecting to someone else's network isn't just unethical, it's illegal.

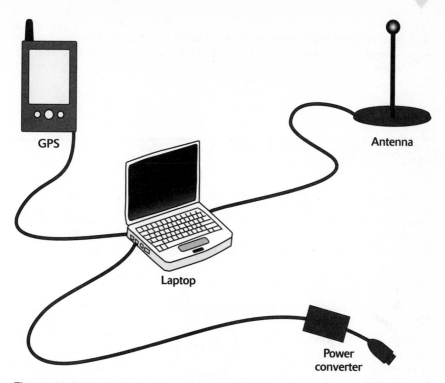

Figure 14-2: The basic elements of a wardriving setup.

Wardriving isn't exclusively a cracker activity. Many wireless user groups (WUGs) wardrive to map networks in their area, just for fun and to improve the technology. In this case, WUG members will notify network administrators if their WLAN is visible and unsecured. Wardrivers also collect data to compile statistics about the number of public Wi-Fi networks and their security.

Later in this chapter I discuss the hardware and software you need for wardriving. If you decide to try wardriving, you must be careful to set up your sniffing software to prevent automatic connection to discovered networks (see your sniffer's documentation). Even accidentally connecting to a private network is illegal.

Why is this called "wardriving"? In the days of dial-up bulletin board systems (BBSs), before the Internet was widely available and before the spread of the World Wide Web, a hacker (or cracker) would use a piece of software called a wardialer to discover computers attached to phone lines over modems. The wardialer would dial a huge range of numbers, one after the other, and listen for a computer to answer at the other end. It would then log the number and attempt to connect and identify the computer and service at the other end of the line. Because of its resemblance to wardialing, wardriving got its name.

Wardriving in itself may not be illegal (at this time), as long as you do not trespass on the discovered networks. In 2002 FBI special agent Bill Shore addressed this in an e-mail to the Pittsburgh business community. You can read this memo and follow up information on Declan McCullagh's Web site.

on the web   Read the FBI memo on Declan McCullagh's site: `www.politechbot.com/p-03884.html`.

Secret#143: Warchalking

Warchalking is inspired by the old hobo language that the railriders used to alert each other to danger or the location of food and shelter. Warchalking occurs when a wardriver (or walker) uses chalk to mark symbols on walls or pavement to indicate the location of a wireless access point. Wardrivers see the symbol and know that there is wireless access nearby (see Figure 14-3).

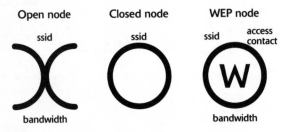

Figure 14-3: Warchalking symbols.

Recent polls of the wardriving community indicate that few people actually engage in warchalking. A poll on netstumbler.com had no respondents indicating that they warchalked. So far, it looks like warchalking is the domain of taggers and script kiddies rather than serious wardrivers.

on the web   For more information on warchalking, visit `www.warchalking.org`.

Secret #144: Hardware for Wardriving

Wardriving (or warwalking) doesn't require much in the way of specialized equipment. All a wardriver needs to get started is a computer with a wireless NIC (a laptop is best), an antenna, a power converter for the computer, and sniffer software (described in the following section). A global positioning system (GPS) unit can be used to automatically record the map coordinates for each discovered access point, as explained later in this chapter.

For decent performance, any Pentium computer with a PCMCIA slot for the wireless NIC will do. A desktop computer will also work, as long as it has a wireless card. For portability, a laptop or notebook is ideal—the smaller the better. A desktop computer will also require a power converter to run off of a car's electrical system. (You can run a laptop off of batteries, but you can stay on the road longer with a power converter.) An antenna, either readymade or home-grown, that works with the wireless NIC completes the setup.

Secret #145: Software for Wardriving

Software for wardriving consists of scanners and sniffers, along with tools to crack encryption on WLANs (although such activity is illegal). Tools are available online for most operating systems. Wireless sniffers and scanners are software tools that facilitate finding Wi-Fi access points. In conjunction with a wireless network interface card (NIC), wireless sniffers and scanners scan the airwaves and analyze Wi-Fi network traffic. Sniffers and scanners can detect and identify most access points and wireless devices. These tools can also report information about the security of each device.

There are a number of free scanners and sniffers available on the Internet, as well as some associated utilities for mapping and cracking security. In this section I list several freeware and open source tools. I have excluded commercial and shareware sniffers. The software appropriate for a system depends on its operating system and NIC. I have listed the operating system with each tool below; the Web sites for each utility list the compatible NICs.

note
: This is not a complete list of sniffers and cracking utilities. There are many more freeware tools available on the Internet. Use Google to search for "wireless sniffers," and you will find tools for just about every operating system. I have chosen to limit the utilities here to the more popular and easier-to-install programs that are available for free. I've listed Windows, Mac OS, Pocket PC, and some Linux software, just to give you an idea of what is available.

- **Netstumbler**—An 802.11b sniffer that runs on Windows 9x, Windows 2000, and Windows XP (it will work with 802.11a cards in XP). It lets you discover Wi-Fi networks and integrates with GPS to facilitate mapping of access points while wardriving. You can download Netstumbler at www.netstumbler.com or www.stumbler.net.
- **ApSniff**—A sniffer program for Windows 2000. I recommend ApSniff only for more advanced Windows users because it is a work in progress and may take some tweaking to run properly on your system. ApSniff works with some Lynksys hardware; check the Web site for full compatibility lists. You can download ApSniff at www.bretmounet.com/ApSniff/index.asp.
- **AirSnort**—A tool that recovers encryption keys and can crack the Wireless Equivalent Privacy (WEP) encryption scheme used in 802.11b WLANs. AirSnort passively gathers network traffic; once it has gathered a sufficient amount of traffic, AirSnort can guess the key in under a second. AirSnort works on Linux and Windows 2000 and can be downloaded from http://airsnort.shmoo.com.

◆ **Ministumbler**—A version of Netstumbler that works on Pocket PC 3.0 and Pocket PC 2002. It is available for download at the Netstumbler site at `www.netstumbler.com`.

◆ **Airscanner**—A sniffer/analyzer that runs on Pocket PC operating systems and is free for noncommercial use. Airscanner is a product of Airscanner Corp., which produces antivirus software for the Pocket PC. It's available for download at `www.airscanner.com`.

◆ **Pocket Warrior**—A free scanner for the Pocket PC. Pocket Warrior supports GPS and is available for download at `www.pocketwarrior.org`.

◆ **Prismstumbler**—A sniffing utility for Linux that identifies WLANs. Prismstumbler works by detecting beacon frames from Wi-Fi access points. (An access point broadcasts beacon frames to announce its presence and relay identification to NICs in the area.) Prismstumbler is available at `http://prismstumbler.sourceforge.net`.

◆ **Kismet**—An 802.11b sniffer for Linux and Mac OS X. With certain card chipsets, it will support 802.11a sniffing. Kismet is well documented and is continually improving. You can download Kismet from `www.kismetwireless.net`.

◆ **KisMac**—A free sniffer application for Mac OS X, with full documentation including hardware compatibility lists available online. Mac users can download KisMac at `www.binaervarianz.de/projekte/programmieren/kismac`.

◆ **Fake AP**—A utility that generates thousands of fake access points to confuse sniffers and scanners. The idea is to allow your real access point to get lost in the noise signals from fake WLANs, in effect hiding it from wardrivers. Fake AP runs on Linux and is available for download at `www.blackalchemy.to/project/fakeap`. Developers of sniffing software are working on filters that would allow scanners to thwart Fake AP by recognizing and ignoring its broadcasts. But until sniffers can defeat it, Fake AP is a worthwhile download for Linux users.

---

cross
ref

Now that you're familiar with the threat posed by wardrivers, follow the steps in Chapter 15 to defend your network against discovery and trespassing.

Secret #146: Using the Global Positioning System for Wardriving

The Global Positioning System is a network of 24 satellites used for navigation. The U.S. Dept of Defense launched the first GPS satellite into orbit in 1978. By 1994, the network as we know it now was complete. Although the GPS system functioned prior to all 24 satellites being operational, it's far more accurate with the full complement of satellites in orbit. There are occasionally more than 24 satellites in operation because the DoD continually launches replacements for older satellites. In the 1980s, the government made the GPS system available for civilian use.

GPS satellites circle the earth in a very precise orbit and transmit signals to earth. GPS receivers receive this signal and, by calculating the time it takes to receive a signal from at least three satellites, triangulates the receiver's location anywhere on earth. If the GPS device receives a signal from at least four satellites, it can determine the user's altitude in addition to latitude and longitude.

With a GPS device, you can usually determine your position to within a few meters. Using a GPS device in conjunction with a wardriving setup, you can map the location of discovered networks as your sniffer discovers them. Your best bet is to use a National Maritime Electronics Association (NMEA) compliant unit, with a serial connector. Many popular GPS units are NMEA-compliant, including some Garmin units, although they require you to enable that option (by default Garmin units use their own proprietary format).

Depending on the sniffing software you use, the GPS data recorded by the sniffer usually corresponds to the location of the strongest signal. You can export location data from your sniffer into mapping programs, such as Microsoft Map Point 2004, and create location maps from your wardrive.

Secret #147: Interesting Hacking/Cracking Resources

There are many interesting online resources devoted to hacking and cracking. You can locate and download the same tools used by crackers and script kiddies and read tutorials about exploits and security. Many cracking and hacking groups have home pages where members post kewl war3z and m4d hax0r 3xpl0its. Some are clever and entertaining; others are just st00pid.

If you decide to visit some of these sites, be prepared. They are not intended for minors, and many of them contain vulgar language, nudity, porn, and adult themes. Others are just bizarre. It's common practice for script kiddies to have banner ads for porn sites on their home pages; it helps pay for the bandwidth used by all of their friends downloading illegal software.

♦ **The Cult of the Dead Cow** (www.cultdeadcow.com)—La vaca es muerto. The cow is dead. The cDc has been around since 1984 and is one of the more respected groups of crackers (depending on whom you talk to). Some members are talented programmers and have created popular tools that script kiddies hoard like gold. Most script kiddies probably worship these guys. The site is humorous if not outright bizarre.

♦ **Phone Losers of America** (www.phonelosers.org)—The PLA was originally an electronic magazine devoted to phreaking and computer hacking. The site contains many of its projects, archives, and a lot of stuff dedicated to crank calls.

♦ **Chaos Computer Club** (www.ccc.de)—The CCC is a German organization that began as semiregular meetings of hackers in 1981. It was founded as a club in 1986 and is one of the most respected computer clubs in Europe. The CCC Web site is informative, but most of it is in German. It's worth a look, even if you aren't fluent in German.

◆ **Attrition.org** (www.attrition.org)—This is a computer security Web site that collects and disseminates information about hacking and security issues in general. This is a site worth visiting if you're really interested in hacking and security.

◆ **DoC** (www.dis.org)—"Dis Org Crew" is an eclectic group of talented hackers in northern California.

◆ **Security Focus** (www.securityfocus.com)—This is one of the most comprehensive security sites on the Web. It maintains the security focus vulnerability database and the Bugtraq security mailing list. Check this site often to keep abreast of vulnerabilities that affect your systems.

These are just a few sites for you to sample. Do a search online for the words *hax0r* (hacker) or *war3z* (warez) and you'll find hundreds of sites run by script kiddies and crackers. Most of these sites will be incomprehensible mazes of porn ads, dead links, and poorly implemented cut-and-paste JavaScript effects. Don't say I didn't warn you.

Easy Steps
to Securing
Your WLAN

Chapter

15

♦ ♦

Secrets in This Chapter

♦ ♦

Throughout this book, I've mentioned that Wi-Fi is vulnerable in a number of ways that a wired network isn't. I've dropped many cautionary notes throughout these chapters. I'm not intending to alarm you, I'm just encouraging vigilance. The truth is that all systems are vulnerable in some way. A system that is 100 percent secure hasn't been invented and probably never will be. Anyone who tells you differently is mistaken or probably trying to sell you something.

Even though no system is—or ever will be—unbreakable, you can lock down most networks to a point where it is extremely unlikely that anyone can compromise them. Taking the proper steps to secure your network and computers reduces the number of people who will have the necessary skills to break in and steal data. If you leave your WLAN unsecured, then it is accessible to every script kiddy with the necessary wardriving gear. Taking steps to lock down your WLAN significantly reduces the number of feasible threats you face.

WLANs have their own particular security issues partially because of how Wi-Fi works—broadcasting in all directions—and partially because of how many people install and maintain their own wireless networks without considering any security at all. You can make a home WLAN reasonably secure. This chapter shows you how.

Secret #148: Assessing the Risk to Your WLAN

The first step toward safe wireless networking is assessing the situation and determining just how vulnerable you are. I'm not just talking about your Wi-Fi hardware. You have to consider and examine all the elements of your network. That includes client computers, software, network hardware, and even users. Risk analysis is always a good place to start. After all, you can't defend yourself against something if you don't even know that it's threatened. A simplified risk analysis for a small network consists of the following steps:

1. Identify hardware and software assets.
2. Determine the value of each asset and cost of replacement.
3. Identify the threats to each asset.
4. Determine the vulnerability to threats.

> **note** Remember to keep this analysis simple. The goal is to get a handle on where you actually stand with regards to WLAN security.

For your first task, you need to identify all the assets on the WLAN. Make a list of your hardware, operating systems, and software. The hardware should include computers, access points, routers, wireless NICs, and anything else that connects to your WLAN. Note the manufacturer and model for all your hardware and firmware version (if known) along with a rough cost estimate for each asset.

Next, make a list of software. This might include operating systems, personal firewalls, and antivirus software. For your purposes, you don't need to check every application on all your computers even though it is good to keep your software patched and up-to-date. You just need to know the operating system and any network software you might be running, along with the approximate cost of each piece.

Using this chapter, you will learn about the threats that are particular to a WLAN. With this information, you will be able to determine your vulnerability to those threats. Once you have a realistic picture of how vulnerable you are, I'll show you how to take the information you have compiled about your hardware and software and use it to secure your network.

This chapter focuses on wireless threats, but that doesn't mean you should ignore threats to any wired equipment that you may have. You can use these steps to assess and secure those, too.

Secret #149: How Crackers Attack a WLAN

Just as there are many ways to attack a wired network, there are numerous ways to attack a WLAN. If a WLAN isn't secured properly, an attacker may be simply able to connect to the network without having to make any sort of elaborate effort and without using any specific exploit.

When the situation warrants, crackers have a number of techniques for cracking a WLAN. A basic understanding of these attacks will give you a better idea of the threats you face and how you should deal with them. Crackers are continually locating new avenues for intrusion and updating their tools to take advantage of them. Many types of exploits are very technical and require significant knowledge of networking to understand. Because highly technical material is beyond the scope of this book, I will present simplified explanations of some exploits that threaten Wi-Fi networks.

cross ref	Chapter 14 discusses wardriving. It's important to point out that some of these attacks may result from that activity. Wardrivers can attack a WLAN as well as locate one.

Man-in-the-Middle Attack

A man-in-the-middle-attack involves an attacker intercepting and monitoring network traffic or client authorization information and using it to authenticate with a server. In the first attack, an attacker intercepts authentication data from a legitimate user's computer by configuring his computer to pose as an access point and then uses that data to authenticate his own computer with the network server. The attacker can then gain access to additional network resources (see Figure 15-1).

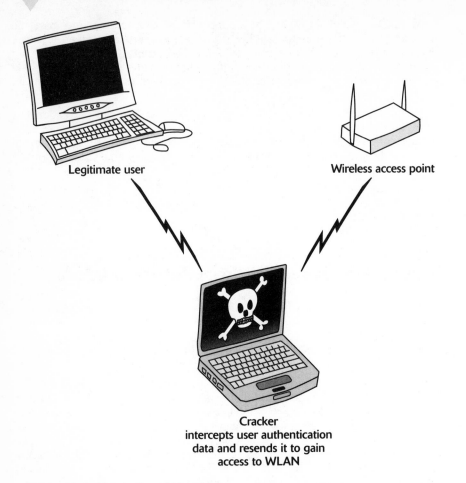

Legitimate user

Wireless access point

Cracker
intercepts user authentication
data and resends it to gain
access to WLAN

Figure 15-1: Man-in-the-middle attack.

The attacker listens for a reply to the ARP request and then either "spoofs" the MAC address (see Figure 15-2) by posing as a legitimate computer or sends an unsolicited ARP reply by transmitting his own MAC address to the WLAN. Computers on the network receive the unsolicited ARP reply and update their list (cache) of MAC addresses with the attacker's MAC address. Legitimate computers may then associate the attacker's MAC address with that of a legitimate one by routing traffic to the attacker's machine.

In the second method (Figure 15-2), an attacker listens for and intercepts an address resolution protocol (ARP) request sent from one legitimate user's computer to another. ARP is a network protocol used to determine a computer's physical network address, which is also known as the media access control layer address (MAC address). Every NIC and access point has a unique MAC address assigned at the factory where it is manufactured.

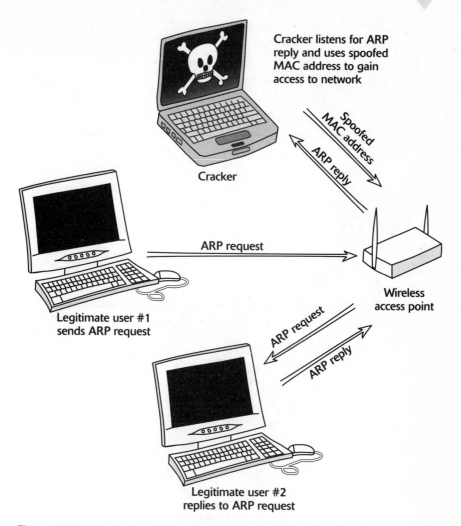

Cracker listens for ARP reply and uses spoofed MAC address to gain access to network

Spoofed MAC address

ARP reply

Cracker

ARP request

Wireless access point

Legitimate user #1 sends ARP request

ARP request

ARP reply

Legitimate user #2 replies to ARP request

Figure 15-2: Man-in-the-middle attack: ARP spoofing/cache poisoning.

MAC Address Spoofing Attack

An attacker monitoring traffic on a WLAN can listen for replies to ARP requests and intercept MAC addresses of legitimate computers on a network. The attacker then configures his computer to transmit and receive data on the network using a stolen MAC address to gain access to network resources and information (see Figure 15-3).

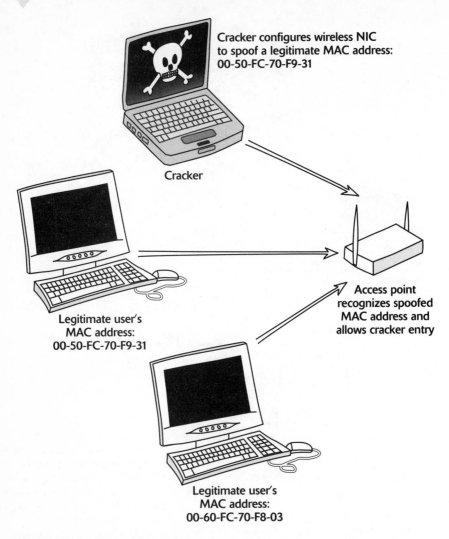

Figure 15-3: MAC spoofing attack.

Internet Protocol Address Spoofing Attack

To gain access to a WLAN, an attacker can acquire an Internet protocol address. Using a sniffer, the attacker monitors the WLAN to see what IP addresses the WLAN uses (this range of addresses is called the subnet). After the attacker determines the IP subnet, he assigns himself an unused address and connects to the WLAN.

If a network uses the dynamic host configuration protocol (DHCP), it's even simpler. DHCP software automatically assigns IP addresses to computers logging onto the network. If an attacker knows the service set identifier (SSID) for the network (which can also be sniffed), he can connect, and the access point or router with DHCP software will assign him an IP address (see Figure 15-4). Manufacturers have included DHCP service in most routers and access points.

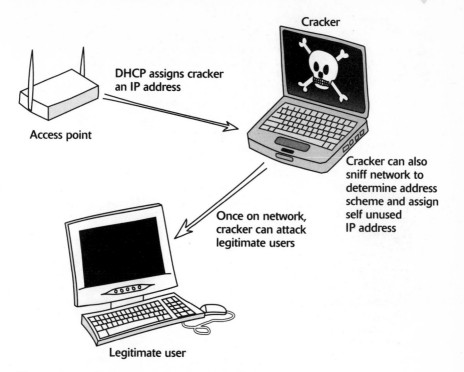

Figure 15-4: IP spoofing DHCP-related attack.

Denial of Service Attack

An attacker doesn't use a *denial of service* (DoS) attack to gain access to a WLAN. Instead, DoS attacks are used to deny legitimate users access to the network and its services. WLANs are vulnerable to DoS attacks in a number of ways. First, using a *brute-force attack*, an attacker can "flood" an access point with network traffic, which effectively shuts it down for other users. Users attempting to use that AP are unable to connect, which is much like receiving a busy signal when calling someone on the telephone (see Figure 15-5).

An attacker can also use a high-power radio source on the same frequency to interfere with the WLAN and drown out its signal. The resulting radio noise prevents devices on the network from talking to and hearing one another, which brings network operation to a halt. This sort of attack is risky for an attacker. Getting close enough to the WLAN with a high-powered transmitter can make him easy to locate using sniffers and scanners.

A denial of service resulting from a high-powered signal may not always be an intentional attack. RF interference from other devices that share the same spectrum could result in essentially the same network conditions as a DoS attack. However, this sort of accidental "attack" is rare if you take care in designing your network.

---

note I discuss sources of RF interference and ways of dealing with them in Chapter 4.

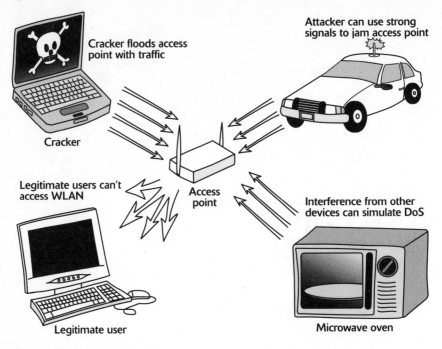

Figure 15-5: Denial of service attack.

DoS attacks are nothing new. They've been a problem on wired networks and the Internet for years. Certain applications and devices are susceptible to different forms of DoS attacks. Crackers may exploit design flaws that can trigger shutdown or crashing of devices. The best way to become aware of these DoS threats is to be knowledgeable about vulnerabilities that affect your equipment and deal with them as they arise (more on that later in this chapter).

Secret #150: Understanding Encryption

Encryption takes data in its original (plaintext) form and uses a mathematical algorithm (cipher) and an encryption key to transform it into an unreadable form (ciphertext). *Decryption* takes ciphertext and transforms it back into plaintext, which once again uses the cipher in conjunction with a key (see Figure 15-6).

What do you think of when you hear the word encryption? Is it spies sending their superiors information in secret code? Perhaps you visualize windowless rooms in some secret government facility where pale, bespectacled code-breakers pour over pages of secret messages and try to decipher them.

This might happen in the movies, but the code-breaker today is just as likely to be a 14-year-old script kiddy, and the secret facility his bedroom. He enjoys a slice of pizza and listens to his pirated music collection while he uses tools written by a real hacker to crack the encryption on your network.

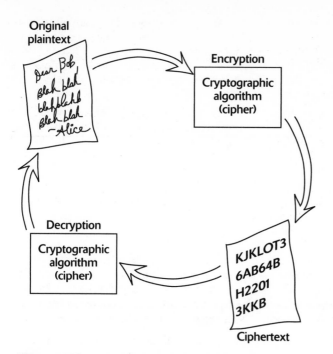

Figure 15-6: A basic encryption system.

Encryption is an incredibly useful security tool. It can prevent crackers from sniffing information on your WLAN, it secures authentication of computers and users, and it can protect data on hard drives. However, not all encryption is created equal. Some methods are stronger than others, and even strong encryption can be undermined by poor implementation or improper use.

Secret #151: Using Encryption to Secure Your WLAN

Encryption has been in use for a long time. The ancient Greeks and Romans used early encryption techniques to secure their communications, and governments and individuals have used encryption ever since. Many early types of encryption are still in use in some form today, including steganography, restrictive algorithms, and proprietary encryption schemes. These older encryption techniques often suffer from numerous design and implementation flaws, and, when companies integrate them into networking products, security suffers.

Modern encryption techniques utilizing computers and advanced mathematical science are far more secure than those that preceded them. They use unrestricted algorithms in conjunction with numeric keys to secure information. Because unrestricted algorithms are public, and have been tested and withstood scrutiny and attack by the world's best cryptanalysts, they are more secure than the older restrictive algorithms. These techniques, even though they are not foolproof, have proven to be robust and reasonably secure.

Wired Equivalent Privacy (WEP) is the encryption standard developed for wireless networking. WEP encrypts data traveling between access points and computers on the network. It's a nice name, but the technology hasn't lived up to its promise. WEP suffers from a number of flaws that allow attackers to discover keys by analyzing network traffic. Attackers can then decrypt all data in real time and continue to compromise the network.

The IEEE is working on a new security standard for 802.11x networks. This standard, which is called 802.11i, promises to improve security considerably. However, the 802.11i standard won't be finalized until late 2004 at the earliest. In the meantime, to improve security, the Wi-Fi Alliance has used a subset of the upcoming standard to produce Wi-Fi Protected Access (WPA).

WPA will help secure WLANs until 802.11i becomes available. However, some older devices may not be upgradeable to WPA, and mobile devices (Pocket PC and Palm) may not have enough processing power to take advantage of WPA.

---

insider insight   **Although it is better, WPA is vulnerable to simple DoS attack. If an attacker sends two forged data packets to a WPA-enabled access point in under one second, he can trick WPA into thinking it's under attack and force it to shut down for over a minute. This effectively locks all users out of the access point. If the attacker does this repeatedly, he can cause real headaches.**

All protocols are susceptible to DoS attacks in some form, so this is a trivial vulnerability. I say don't worry about it; if your system allows you to do so, upgrade to WPA as soon as you can.

If WPA is compatible with your network, then enable it. You can enable WPA (and WEP) using the configuration utility for your device or through its Web interface. If you can't use WPA, then use WEP. Even if WEP can be broken, it takes some effort, and you can deter all but the most determined crackers. Faced with having to crack WEP or simply moving on to the next open WLAN, most crackers will just move along.

If you telecommute or work from home and need extra protection, use a virtual private network (VPN). A VPN acts as a "tunnel" to protect data traveling between your workplace and home (or laptop). Chances are good that your company already has one installed so all you need to do is contact your IT dept and (very nicely!) ask for a VPN client. This allows you to check and send e-mail and other data through an encrypted link with the company mail server.

Dealing with Default Settings

Failing to change the default settings on WLAN equipment can facilitate attacks and allow unskilled script kiddies to access your network with little effort. Each manufacturer has default settings for all the equipment they produce. These settings facilitate installing the equipment; unfortunately, many users never change them. They just take the equipment out of the box, hook it up, and start using it.

Default settings are public knowledge to crackers, who post them all over the Internet. There are default settings for passwords, SSIDs, broadcast strength, and IP addresses. Failing to change any of these can leave your network vulnerable to attack.

Secret #152: Locking the Door to Your Network

The following security measures are relatively easy to implement—provided you read the manuals that came with your wireless devices. "The manual?" you ask. Yes, the manual. You know, it's the thing propping up the short leg on your computer desk. Take it out for now; you'll only have to deal with the wobble until we're done. None of the measures described here are particularly dramatic, and there are ways to get around them. But, doing so requires some skill and understanding of networking. In this case, they serve as a sort of "intellectual firewall" that prevents script kiddies from cracking your network.

These steps include the following:

1. Change the default SSID.
2. Disable SSID broadcast.
3. Change the default IP subnet.
4. Consider disabling DHCP.
5. Enable MAC address filtering.
6. Change default administrative passwords.
7. Change default user names.
8. Enable WEP or WPA encryption.
9. Adjust broadcast power.
10. Set minimum connection speeds.
11. Set access times.

The first step toward making a WLAN reasonably secure is changing the default SSID. This is important because anyone using a wireless sniffer can determine what sort of access point you use by looking at the default SSID. Knowing your access point model allows the cracker to guess the rest of the default settings and attack your WLAN that much easier.

Don't change the name to something obvious like your street address (I have actually seen this done) or your name. Consider using random numbers or even changing it to something like "NOTPUBLIC" or "NOTRESSPASSING" just to make a point.

> **note** If you have any MS-DOS clients, the SSID must be in all caps.

Wireless access points are set to broadcast the SSID by default. Turn this feature off to make it harder for casual wardrivers to discover your network's name. It won't stop a determined cracker from discovering it, though, because wireless NICs always broadcast the SSID when communicating with the access point.

The procedure for disabling SSID broadcast is different for each manufacturer, so consult your access point's manual. Once you turn off SSID broadcast, you have to configure each NIC manually and input the new SSID.

The next thing you should consider doing is changing the default subnet IP addresses. Each manufacturer has a default IP subnet, and this can make it easy for an attacker to discover the IP address of your access point (see "Secret #153: Protecting Your Access Points"). Consider also disabling DHCP and assigning static IP addresses.

Most access points support built-in DHCP service. This allows the access point to assign IP addresses dynamically to new computers as they connect to the network and to computers that are reconnecting after a shutdown or reboot. This also allows an intruder to connect to the WLAN and have the access point assign him an IP address, which makes the intruder's computer a legitimate member of the WLAN. By disabling DHCP, you make this far more difficult. You have to assign permanent (static) IP addresses to each computer on your WLAN and manually configure them. Once again, this is an extra step, but it is well worth the effort.

insider insight
Without DHCP enabled, an intruder has to monitor and analyze network traffic in an attempt to determine the IP subnet and addresses in use. He can then assign himself an IP address and attempt to establish a connection. This makes it difficult for casual sniffers and neophyte intruders to access your WLAN.

Another step that you can—and should—take is to enable MAC address filtering. Remember that each network device has a unique MAC address assigned by the manufacturer. Many access points have an option that allows you to restrict access to specific MAC addresses. This should block any MAC addresses that are not on the "allow" list from connecting to the network.

This is effective, but it is not perfect. As I pointed out when discussing attacks earlier in the chapter, an intruder can monitor network traffic and discover the MAC addresses of legitimate computers on the WLAN. He can then change the MAC address of his NIC, which allows him to masquerade as a member of the network and connect even when filtering is turned on.

Change the default administrative passwords on all access points. Once again, these are public knowledge, and, if a cracker knows what type of access point you use, he'll know the default password. This will aid him in attacking your access point (see "Secret #153: Protecting Your Access Points").

caution
Write down the new settings and passwords, and store the list in a secure place. This will be helpful if you forget this information and need it at a later date.

As I mentioned earlier, even though WEP encryption is flawed and vulnerable, you should use it. Enable 128-bit WEP on your WLAN, and use it. With the relatively low traffic on a WLAN in a home, it could take a cracker several hours to collect enough packets to crack your WEP key. Again, each step you perform just adds another piece to the intellectual firewall you're building. As a whole, these measures will discourage most script kiddies and casual wardrivers.

On some access points, you can adjust the broadcast power of the unit. I recommend that you experiment and turn this down as low as you can while still maintaining decent connection speeds between computers on your WLAN. The idea is to keep the signal within the confines of your house rather than having it reach across the street (see Figure 15-7). This makes the signal more difficult to receive for outsiders. Wardrivers can use directional antennas to pick up weak signals at a greater distance, but doing this will at least make it harder for them.

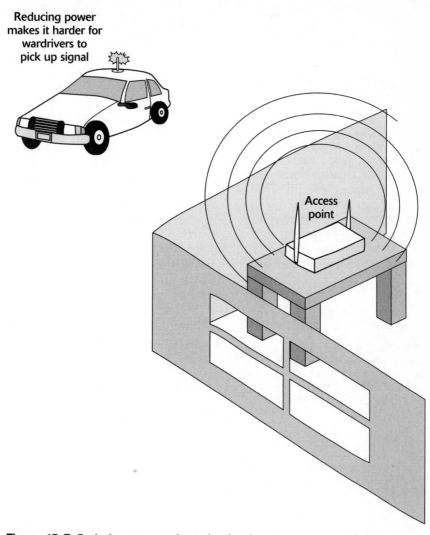

Reducing power makes it harder for wardrivers to pick up signal

Access point

Figure 15-7: Reducing power reduces the signal range.

On many access points, you can set a minimum access connection speed. The further away from an access point an intruder is, the weaker the signal will be (both ways). Therefore, if you set the minimum connection speed higher, computers will have to be closer to the access point to connect and stay connected. Once again, this makes it harder for an intruder to access your WLAN because he will have to be closer to connect.

> **note**   Anyone standing on your lawn with a wireless laptop is probably up to no good unless he's the water meter reader.

Lastly, some access points allow you to configure the times of day to allow access. If it supports this, consider using it. If no one is home during the day, consider configuring it to block all access between 8:00 a.m. and 5:00 p.m.

Secret #153: Protecting Your Access Points

While discussing default settings, I mentioned changing default administrative passwords and IP addresses. These two steps are important to help protect your access point. If you fail to do these things, it can be easy for an intruder to take control of it. Once he does that, he grants himself legitimate access and circumvents all your security precautions.

If an attacker knows what kind of access point you have, maybe because you're still using the default SSID, he will know what the default IP address range is. If you're still running DHCP, once he connects to your WLAN, he can look at the IP address your access point assigned him and, voilà, he knows the address scheme. From there, he can guess the IP address of the access point.

For example, if you have a Linksys wireless access point, the default address range is usually 192.168.x.x. The default IP address for the access point itself is probably 192.168.1.1. If it isn't 192.168.1.1, then it's probably another number close to that (192.168.1.2, 192.168.1.3, and so on).

Almost all wireless access points have a Web interface that allows you to configure the access point using a Web browser. If the attacker knows the access point's IP address, all he has to do is enter it into his browser to connect to the Web interface. Provided that you haven't changed the default username/password, he can enter those as well because he will know what they are, and he will be in control.

Take the time to change the defaults in order to protect your access point. If you don't do this, you will undermine all of your other security measures.

Using a Layered Approach

Besides changing default settings to secure your access points, there are some other tools in your arsenal that you can use to protect your data. By using all of these tools, you can take a layered approach to security, with each tool addressing a different threat. The first layer of defense is changing all the default settings and using encryption to secure the network against intrusion to the best of your ability.

Using firewalls and antivirus software, you can extend the protection to individual computers and protect your data if your first line of defense ever falls. Even though no security is totally invulnerable, each layer adds to the robustness of your defense and makes it more of a headache for any cracker trying to get to your data. We're adding more bricks in the intellectual firewall.

Secret #154: Building a Personal Firewall

Firewalls are software applications or hardware devices that filter unwanted traffic on a network and prevent unauthorized users from getting through. Many routers have built-in hardware firewalls, but, for the scope of this book and a small wireless network, I'm going to concentrate on software applications called personal firewalls.

Personal firewall software resides on your computer and prevents unauthorized traffic from getting through. A personal firewall can also prevent unauthorized outbound connections from leaving your computer. This is effective when trying to keep a worm or Trojan (see "Secret #155: Protecting Against Viruses and Worms") from spreading to other computers or "dialing home" to give an attacker a back door into your system.

> **note** Windows XP comes with a basic firewall, but you should still consider upgrading to a more complete firewall package.

Personal firewalls are configurable to suit the level of security that you feel you need on your network. I recommend installing a firewall on every computer connected to a network (wired or wireless) or with an Internet connection. Firewalls will help prevent an intruder from accessing your PC even if he gets on to the WLAN.

> **on the web** ZoneAlarm is an excellent personal firewall. For information about ZoneAlarm or to download a trial, visit www.zonelabs.com.

Secret #155: Protecting Against Viruses and Worms

In November 1988, Robert Morris released a self-replicating program called a *worm*. His worm exploited various UNIX vulnerabilities to gain access to machines, replicate, and then seek out other machines to infect. His worm brought the fledgling Internet to its knees, and he soon found himself in court.

Since then, the number of viruses, worms, and other malicious software has grown almost exponentially. Worse than the number itself is the fact that they are getting more sophisticated and have the potential to do a lot more damage than Morris's worm ever did.

As with crackers, the media loves to sensationalize the threat of viruses and worms. Every time a new one appears, they run right back down to interview Bob working in aisle five of the computer store. Of course, because he sells computers, he's not only an expert on hackers and crackers, he knows all about viruses, too.

Protecting yourself against computer viruses (and hoaxes) is easy. You just need to understand exactly what they are and install up-to-date antivirus software.

Computer Viruses

A *virus* is a potentially destructive program that attaches itself to a file or program, creates copies of itself, and infects more files and programs. Note that I said "potentially destructive." Not all viruses cause damage. Some do damage files or delete data, whereas others cause problems with their out-of-control replication.

Destructive viruses have a routine or payload that is triggered, perhaps by a date, and then proceed to wreak havoc. Viruses replicate and remain undetected until they are triggered (see Figure 15-8).

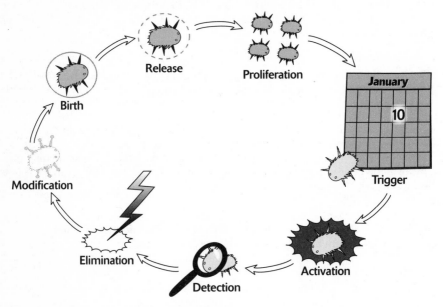

Figure 15-8: A computer virus life cycle.

Worms

Worms spread over network connections and e-mail. They are self-contained and can function and spread without infecting another program or file. Many worms have been appearing on the Internet lately. Most recently, the Blaster worm and its variants infected thousands of computers by using an exploit to spread among Microsoft Windows machines.

Blaster exploited a flaw in the operating system's Remote Procedural Call (RPC) function. This flaw allowed Blaster to gain access to a machine and install itself. Once it infected a PC, Blaster then used any active network connections (including WLANs) to scan for and infect other vulnerable computers.

This ability to replicate and spread without infecting another program or file differentiates a worm from a virus. A worm is an autonomous program capable of performing its malicious function without user intervention.

Antivirus Software and Security Patches

Antivirus software is one way to protect yourself against worms and viruses. A good antivirus software package detects and eliminates known viruses before they can do any damage. The problem is that not all viruses are known, and you have to be quick to update your antivirus software when a new threat surfaces.

Applying security patches, particularly operating system patches, in a timely manner is as important as the antivirus software itself. The Blaster worm exploited a known security vulnerability in Microsoft Windows to infect computers and spread. Microsoft had issued a patch to this vulnerability before the worm appeared. If more people had patched their systems, the worm would not have spread so fast and caused so much damage.

Using the Windows Update feature on Windows XP/2000, you can automate patching your operating system. Windows Update notifies you when a critical update becomes available so that you can download it and update your system right away. Windows Update is enabled by default on most new Windows XP computers.

Also, use common sense regarding e-mail attachments. If an attachment seems suspicious, don't open it. Delete it. If you open an e-mail attachment containing a worm, that worm will then be able to infect your computer. Common sense combined with proper system maintenance and antivirus software will protect your computer from malicious software.

There are many antivirus software packages available for home use, including Norton AntiVirus from Symantec, VirusScan Home from McAfee, and eTrust EZ Antivirus from Computer Associates. Any of these antivirus products will protect your computer from viruses, worms, and other malicious code. The developers of these antivirus software packages also post virus updates for their software as new viruses are discovered.

---

on the
web

For more information about antivirus products, visit Norton AntiVirus at `www.symantec.com`, **VirusScan Home** at `www.mcafee.com`, and eTrust EZ Antivirus at `www.my-etrust.com`.

Secret #156: Password and Security Best Practices

Passwords are one of the weakest links in computer security. Improper use of passwords is worse than no password at all. If crackers can get a user's password, they don't have to worry about using exploits to get past security. Worst of all, you can make it easy for them by not following best practices for password selection and security.

There are many ways for crackers to get passwords. Some are technical hacks that involve sniffing a network or cracking a password file. Others are as simple as guessing the password or tricking a user into giving it to them.

Good management can thwart many attacks aimed at cracking passwords. The following best practices can help secure your passwords:

- ◆ Don't write down your passwords. You would be surprised to find out how many networks have been compromised because of passwords that were written down. If you must write your passwords down, either because they are difficult to remember or change frequently, make sure you keep the list in a very secure place.

- ◆ Don't use plain words for passwords. If it's in the dictionary, it's not a password. Crackers can use software that automatically tries every word in a dictionary file. If you use a plain word, such as *horse*, they can easily crack it.

- ◆ Don't use personal information as passwords. Crackers can easily guess the names of friends, kids, pets, and other personal information. That includes birth dates and phone numbers, too.

- ◆ Consider using computer-generated passwords that consist of random strings of letters and numbers. These are harder to remember, but they are more secure. Randomly mix upper- and lowercase letters within your passwords.

- ◆ Don't reuse a password; select a new one for each account. If you use the same password across several accounts, they could all be compromised.

- ◆ Never tell someone your password over the phone. Companies never contact their customers and ask for passwords over the phone. Crackers pose as tech support personnel from an ISP and obtain passwords from unwitting customers.

- ◆ Change your passwords periodically, every few weeks or so.

- ◆ Make passwords sufficiently long so that they will be difficult to crack. A minimum of six characters, preferably eight, should be a rule of thumb.

Secret #157: Being Proactive About Security

Perhaps the most important defense is to be proactive in securing your WLAN. Don't wait for threats to emerge before taking action. Do you remember the risk assessment list we did at the beginning of this chapter? Now that you know the threats to your WLAN and some ways to deal with them, we can take that list and put it to work.

Each vendor maintains patches and updates on its Web site. You could go to every Web site and search for all the vulnerabilities that affect your devices. You may even find most of what you're looking for after quite a while.

The best place to start is the Security Focus Web site (www.securityfocus.com). Security Focus maintains an exhaustive list of vulnerabilities for hardware and software from every vendor. If it's vulnerable, it's listed on their site. Often vulnerabilities are listed on Security Focus even before the developers of an application or device know about the problem. In those rare cases when a company refuses to acknowledge an issue, this Web site may be the only place where you'll find it listed.

Make it a habit to check the site regularly for new threats. Many vendors will send you an e-mail warning you of vulnerabilities—if you took the time to register your product. For the 90 percent of users that use a Microsoft operating system, the Windows Update feature will help you keep the operating system patched and save you from becoming a casualty when the next worm surfaces.

Most cracker tools exploit holes that have not been patched. If you don't maintain your systems, you are remaining vulnerable when you should be safe. Taking the time to patch software and update the firmware on devices will minimize your risk and reduce your headaches.

Secrets to Safe and Secure Mobile Computing

Chapter 16

Secrets in This Chapter

Mobile devices are everywhere. They have become an integral part of many people's lives. Whether they are fully functional notebook computers, cell phones, or PDAs, they make our lives easier, allowing us to access personal financial data, shop, and stay connected when we are on the road.

Sales of portable computing devices—including notebooks, PDAs, and smart phones—continue to rise and will eventually outpace sales of desktop computers. We are becoming a more mobile society and expect the same from our computers. Manufacturers are stepping up to the challenge and producing smaller, cheaper, and more powerful computing devices every year.

As mobile devices increase in functionality and decrease in size and price, we will become more dependent on them. The more we use and depend on a device, the more likely we are to store important personal information on it. In addition, as we become dependent on mobile computing devices, we are more likely to suffer when we lose one.

Mobile devices are vulnerable in a number of ways. Damage is the number-one cause for the loss of a computer, phone, or PDA. You are far more likely to accidentally damage your device than you are to have it stolen from you (see Figure 16-1). Damage can occur anywhere: home, office, or while you're traveling, although travel presents the biggest opportunity for it to occur.

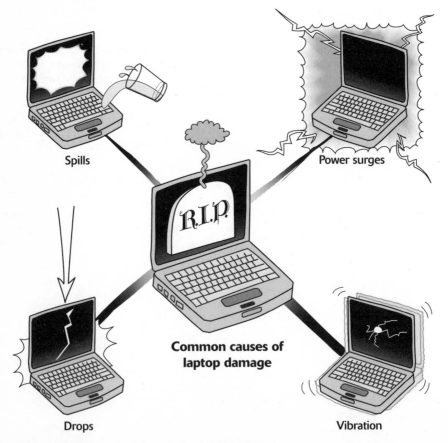

Spills

Power surges

Common causes of
laptop damage

Drops

Vibration

Figure 16-1: Sources of damage to mobile computers.

Recently, with the heightening of security in airports, there has been a reported rise in the number of laptops damaged in X-ray machines at security checkpoints. Security screeners require you to take a laptop out of its case, turn it on, and run it through the X-ray machine.

The X-ray machine can physically damage the computer with its rollers or by banging it into the sides of the machine. Sliding down the slope at the end of the machine may damage a computer as well if it strikes the metal sides or end of the chute. However, the X-rays themselves will not damage the computer.

insider
insight

There are steps you can take to protect your laptop from damage when you run it through an airport X-ray machine:

1. Take care to place your computer in the center of the X-ray machine's belt or rollers. This will help prevent it from being damaged against the inside of the machine.

2. Make sure there are no loose or dangling parts or accessories on your laptop. Remove dongles and place them into your laptop case so they won't get caught in the rollers and torn off.

3. Remove wireless NICs and place them in your case. If you fail to do this, the machine may damage the antenna or external portion of the card.

4. When you place your laptop in the X-ray machine, place it in an open laptop case if possible. If security personnel don't allow that, place your case directly in front of your computer to cushion it when it slides out of the X-ray machine.

5. Pay attention to who handles your computer. If it is damaged while going through the X-ray machine or by the careless handling of security personnel, you can file a claim with the Transportation Security Administration.

There are a number of ways you can minimize the risk of damage to your laptop or recover from it more quickly and at less expense than you would otherwise. These include buying specially designed "rugged" computers, protective cases, insurance, and warranties. Carefully consider all of these options, covered in the following subsections, before deciding which is best for you.

Secret #158: Rugged Devices

Rugged computers are special laptops designed to withstand things that would otherwise damage or destroy a standard laptop. Originally designed for field use by the military, rugged computers are available from a number of manufacturers and are now styled to be more attractive to the average consumer. That's right, no more big, blocky, camouflage laptops.

Many things separate rugged laptops from ordinary ones. Manufacturers design them to withstand harsh environments and accidents, so they put them through severe tests. Most rugged laptops are designed with the following criteria in mind.

Impact Resistance

Rugged computers must be impact-resistant. An all-too-common occurrence for laptop owners is dropping it, knocking it off a desk, or dropping something onto it. Such a fall or impact usually results in the following unfortunate situations:

- ◆ Broken components, including case, ports, and internal electrical components
- ◆ Crashed hard drives, making information irretrievable
- ◆ Cracked LCD screens

Rugged computers are designed with impact-resistant cases, often made of a strong, lightweight alloy such as magnesium. Manufacturers design the internal frame to provide shock resistance and avoid damage to electrical components. Many manufacturers design cases to withstand drops of over three feet onto hard surfaces.

Vibration Resistance

Because of the requirements of the original military and industrial market, rugged laptops resist vibration levels exceeding that which you might encounter in a moving vehicle. Vibration damage to laptops might result in the following:

- ◆ Internal component failure
- ◆ Keyboard failure
- ◆ Crashed hard drives

Moisture and Humidity Resistance

Moisture and humidity do not get along well with computers. Other than drops and falls, spills cause more damage to computers than any other accident. How many times have you accidentally spilled coffee or some other beverage next to, or onto, your laptop only to frantically attempt to clean it up with a paper towel? Most rugged laptop designs prevent liquids from entering the case when they're spilled onto the keyboard or through other openings. They also resist humidity, keeping moisture away from fragile electrical components. Moisture can cause the following damage to computers:

- ◆ Damage to display
- ◆ Damage to hard drive
- ◆ Damage to internal components

Drawbacks to Rugged Laptops

While they are especially durable, and can survive many accidents that would destroy the average laptop, there are some things to consider before running out and buying a rugged laptop:

♦ **Price**—all that durability isn't free and rugged laptops can cost significantly more than comparable computers

♦ **Weight**—the most rugged computers usually weigh more than comparable notebooks

If these factors aren't a deterrent to your wallet (or lower back), and you travel often, seriously consider using a rugged laptop. Many major computer manufacturers produce rugged laptops. Usually these are special-order items, direct from the manufacturer, but many are available from online retailers.

---

on the web

For more information on rugged laptops, visit the following Web sites: www.panasonic.com/computer/toughbook, www.sony.com, www.groupmobile.com, **and** www.ruggednotebooks.com

---

Secret #159: Protective Cases

An alternative to purchasing a rugged laptop is purchasing a protective case for your computer or PDA. While a case won't do anything to protect your laptop when it's out and in use, it can significantly reduce the chance of damage the remainder of the time that you are traveling when your laptop is safely tucked away inside.

When I talk about protective cases, I'm not referring to the small, soft, carry cases that often come with a laptop. These do little to protect a laptop; other than preventing scratches, they don't prevent serious damage. Many aren't even water-resistant and won't prevent water damage if you are caught in a downpour while waiting for a cab or airport shuttle.

The sort of case I recommend provides adequate protection against impact, moisture, and vibration. There are dozens of manufacturers of high-quality protective cases for laptops; shop around and find one that best suits your needs. When doing so, consider the following:

♦ Choose a case made of sufficiently strong material to resist damage from impact or crushing. Ballistic PVC or even metal are desirable. Avoid soft cases with hard metal or plastic sheets sewn into the case, as they do not protect against crushing and will not absorb shock.

♦ The case should offer some sort or shock absorption. Fitted compartments of high-density foam with a strong internal frame that holds the laptop away from the sides of the case and provides shock absorption are best.

♦ A case should also provide some degree of water resistance. I'm not talking waterproof, just water-resistant. The ability to repel rain and spilled liquids is sufficient. Your case doesn't have to be watertight when submerged unless you foresee that happening to your laptop (in which case I don't ever plan on being on the same flight as you are).

♦ The case should have sufficient space for your peripherals and disks.

♦ It should not look like an obvious computer case (see the section "Protecting Your Device from Theft" later in this chapter)

on the web For more information about protective cases for laptops, visit the following Web sites: www.targus.com, www.yourmobiledesk.com, **and** http://us.samsonite.com

Laptops aren't the only things that need protection. Your PDA is just as susceptible to physical damage as your laptop, perhaps even more so. Because they are small and lightweight, PDAs are more likely to be knocked off a desk, dropped, or even crushed than laptops are.

There are a number of cases available for PDAs, most of which are designed to protect your device while still being small enough to slip into a pocket. Since these cases are slim and small, they can't necessarily provide the same degree of protection as a larger case might, but look for these features:

◆ A case should provide sufficient protection for the LCD screen. This is the part of a PDA most often damaged by impact and crushing. A metal or ballistic PVC exterior is best.

◆ The case should afford some degree of moisture resistance.

◆ You should be able to work out of the case and, if possible, synchronize your PDA without removing it. Having to constantly remove it from the case will create more opportunities for damage.

◆ A nonslip exterior is a plus. The fewer times you drop it, the better.

on the web For more information on protective cases for PDAs, visit the following sites: www.kensington.com, www.yourmobiledesk.com, **and** www.targus.com

There are wallet-style cases available for PDAs, although many of these are made of leather and won't provide as much protection as a hard-shell case. Since wallet cases provide spaces for business cards, as well as your money and PDA, the presence of a business card with your contact information may facilitate the return of your PDA if you lose it.

insider insight Many manufacturers of PDA cases and wallets also offer insurance against theft and damage as an option when you purchase their products. Read the fine print and consider taking this step.

Secret #160: Protecting Your Screen

The screen is the most frequently damaged part of a PDA and often a laptop. Accidents can result in all sorts of damage, including crushing, cracking, scratches, and electrical component failure. A good case protects your screen from crushing and other damage, but to prevent scratches you should consider a removable protective film (see Figure 16-2).

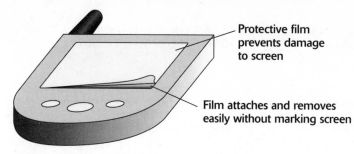

Protective film
prevents damage
to screen

Film attaches and removes
easily without marking screen

Figure 16-2: Removable protective film for screens.

Protective films cling to your display and protect your screen from scratches. They are particularly useful with PDAs because many PDAs require you to touch or tap the screen with a stylus. Protective films are inexpensive, removable, and can extend the life of your screen. If you decide to use protective film, look for the following features:

- Use film that is at least 0.25mm thick. Thinner film does not last as long or provide as much protection.
- Look for antiglare film. This makes your screen easier to see in bright light.
- Film with an anti-ultraviolet light coating protects your screen from damage by direct sunlight.
- Many films are also dust-repellant, a nice feature because LCDs invariably attract dust like a magnet.

on the web Protective films are available at some major computer retailers. For more information about protective films, visit http://ecfilm.com.hk and www.fellowes.com

Using a protective film helps extend the life of your LCD screen. Other steps that you can take to protect your screen are the following:

- Don't point at, poke, or tap a laptop screen with a pen or sharp, pointed object. I have watched an individual furiously tapping at an LCD to point out a mistake in a document, puncture his screen, and ruin it. Now this isn't easy, but it can happen—and if it's your boss, don't laugh (trust me on this). Of course, you can tap a PDA with a stylus, but don't use any thing hard or metallic—and be gentle.
- Keep the LCD screen out of direct sunlight. LCD displays deteriorate when exposed to UV light. This shortens the life of the screen and reduces picture quality.
- Don't place heavy objects on top of your screen, or your PDA for that matter. Doing so may crack the screen. Don't place heavy objects on top of a closed laptop either, as this may also damage it.

Secret #161: Surge Protection

This may seem like a no-brainer, but you should always use a surge protector to protect your laptop from sudden spikes in electrical power when it is plugged into an outlet. These spikes often result from lightning strikes and can ruin the internal circuitry of a computer. Damage from electrical power surges is another common reason for loss of a computer, with only accidental damage and theft causing more inconvenience to owners.

There are a number of small surge protectors ideal for traveling and adequate for providing protection while you are on the road. Consider a surge protector that also has a place to connect to a phone line so that you can protect your computer against power surges that might come through the phone line if you have a dial-up modem. Surge protectors are available at all computer and electronics retailers.

Secret #162: Insuring Your Device

If your mobile device is lost or stolen, what will you do? Insuring your device helps you replace it if it is lost or stolen. You may not even have to buy supplemental insurance; many renters and homeowners policies cover loss of computers and home electronics. Carefully check your policy to determine if your laptop or PDA is covered and, if so, the details and extent of that coverage.

If you aren't covered, you may be able to purchase supplemental coverage from your primary insurance provider. If not, purchase coverage from a third party. Be sure your policy covers theft and accidental damage, as well as damage that occurs while traveling.

Some credit cards provide coverage for loss or damage, usually within 60–90 days of purchase. It may be possible to purchase a policy against damage when you purchase your PC; check with the retailer.

Secret #163: Warranties

A warranty isn't going to cover you if your device is stolen, but you can purchase extended warranties that cover accidental damage and manufacturing defects. Consider buying an extended warranty or repair plan when you purchase your device. A good plan simply replaces a device outright and may include data transfer or recovery from an old hard drive to the new one.

Protecting Your Device from Theft

Mobile devices are popular because they are portable and powerful. Unfortunately, this and the fact that they are relatively expensive make them prime targets for thieves. In the 1980s and early '90s, thieves targeted camcorders for the same reasons (they still do, actually), but now a stolen laptop or PDA can offer more return for the risk taken.

Smart thieves prefer snatching these high-tech, high-value devices instead of picking pockets or robbery because the penalty in most states is usually much less severe. Snatching a laptop or PDA is a crime against property and that usually carries a significantly lighter penalty than picking a pocket, which is a crime against a person.

The amount of cash that a thief can get for a stolen laptop is significant. With some high-end laptops costing as much as $3,000, a thief can expect to collect as much as 50 percent of the laptop's value when he sells it. That's a lot of money for grabbing one unattended laptop and slipping away unnoticed.

Criminals look for an easy score; they don't want to take unnecessary risk. They look for unattended computers that they can grab and then disappear into the crowd. They don't want to spend a lot of time committing the theft because the longer they linger, the more likely they will be caught.

Thieves often target travelers because they are in a hurry and distracted, and because busy airports, convention centers, and other places that travelers congregate make the theft easier because of the confusion created by noise and crowds. Like magicians, thieves and con men rely on misdirection to accomplish their intended goals, directing the victim's attention elsewhere while they slip in and commit a crime.

One popular scam involves stealing laptops while the owners are passing through security. Two thieves wait until they spot a traveler carrying a laptop bag. Then they move into position in line directly ahead of the victim. The first thief goes through the metal detector and the second one creates a delay by setting off the detector, usually with coins or keys located on their person.

At this point, the victim has placed his laptop in the X-ray machine and patiently waits to get through the metal detector. The first thief grabs the victim's laptop as it exits the X-ray machine and then moves on. When the victim finally gets through security, the laptop is gone.

Even with the recently heightened security in airports, this scam still occurs. While security is only supposed to allow ticketed passengers through checkpoints, a thief who can collect thousands of dollars for a few laptops has no problem buying a cheap ticket, often for less than $100, just to get through security. Screeners seldom pay attention to which bag belongs to whom, so there isn't much of a deterrent for career thieves.

Things aren't all hopeless, however. There are things you can do to protect your laptop and your data. The best defense is vigilance. Never leave your laptop unattended and pay close attention to it whenever circumstances force you to part with it, such as when you go through a checkpoint. Thankfully, it doesn't take much to deter thieves who want a quick and easy snatch, and your vigilance, along with the following measures, will reduce the likelihood of you becoming a target.

Secret #164: Locks, Cables, and Alarms

Securing your laptop is the simplest way to deter theft. Thieves want to pick up a laptop and walk away. They don't have time to fight with a cable and lock, and don't want to be seen doing so. I've heard the argument that any thief with a set of bolt cutters can cut the cable and run with the computer. That's ridiculous: How often do you see someone walking around an airport, hotel, or convention center with a set of bolt cutters?

Most of these places, especially airports, have security screening. I can't get nail clippers past the checkpoint; good luck getting bolt cutters through. Even if thieves have them, pulling out bolt cutters and cutting a cable with people around will draw attention, and they don't want that.

A laptop security cable works like a bike lock. It allows you to secure a laptop to a fixed object like a desk or chair and prevents a thief from simply walking away with it (see Figure 16-3). People might not notice a thief walking through an airport with a laptop, but they will notice him if he's dragging a chair behind.

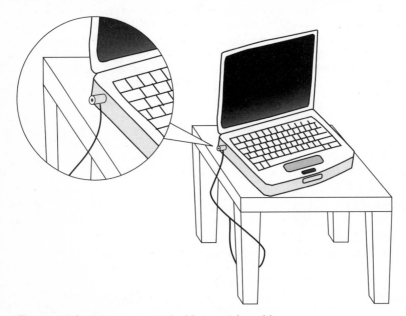

Figure 16-3: A laptop secured with a security cable.

A good security cable costs less than $50 and most new laptops have a channel built in specifically for use with a locking cable. These cables are handy anywhere and it's good practice to use one even in the office, not just when you travel.

If you are worried that a thief might actually be savvy enough to get bolt cutters past security and cut your laptop cable, then consider a cable combined with an alarm. There are cables that have censor circuits built in that detect if a thief has cut the cable. If a thief cuts the cable, the circuit is broken and a high-pitched alarm sounds.

A similar model works with fiber optics. These devices work by creating a circuit through repeatedly sending a pulse of light down a fiber optic cable. When the cable is cut, the circuit is interrupted and the alarm sounds.

Motion and tamper-detecting alarms sound if a thief moves a laptop or tampers with the keyboard. The thief can't disable these alarms; only the laptop owner can do that with a special key. Because thieves have learned to ignore car alarms (along with the rest of us), you might think that these laptop alarms would do little to deter them.

These alarms work, however, because in the setting I am talking about, people take notice. If a high-pitched alarm goes off in a crowded room like an airport terminal, people notice and pay attention. A thief isn't likely to get away once he's caused that much commotion.

Another alarm is the proximity alarm. These go off and alert you if your laptop case moves away from you, beyond a set distance. The laptop owner carries a small transmitter resembling an electronic alarm key ring that comes with many automobiles. The alarm unit consists of a receiver that goes inside the laptop case. The receiver listens for the radio signal from the transmitter carried by the owner. If the laptop case gets too far from the transmitter, or if the signal is blocked, the alarm sounds (see Figure 16-4). A thief isn't likely to walk, or run, through a crowd with an alarm going off under his arm; he's more likely to ditch the laptop and try to disappear.

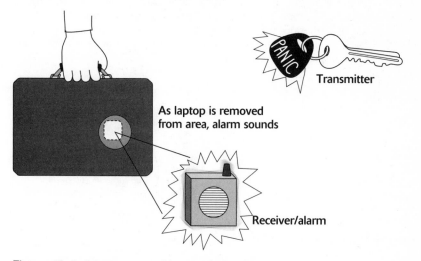

As laptop is removed
from area, alarm sounds

Transmitter

Receiver/alarm

Figure 16-4: A laptop case with a proximity alarm.

By locking down your laptop or adding an alarm, you're making your property a less attractive target. Combine that with vigilance and awareness, and you've found a winning combination for deterring theft. However, should this not be enough, there are things you can do to aid in the recovery of your equipment.

Secret #165: Identification and Recovery Labels

Clearly labeling your device can reduce its resale value for criminals and aid its return. Manufacturers label laptops with stickers or plates with serial numbers. Thieves can remove these, often without much difficulty, making it easier to sell them and more difficult for you to prove ownership.

There are ways to mark your device and make it worthless to casual thieves. There are special identity plates on the market that you can attach to your laptop. These plates use a special adhesive that makes them extremely difficult to remove without noticeably damaging the laptop.

If a thief should succeed in removing the identity plate, they will expose an indelible "tattoo" that will usually say something like "Stolen Property." This makes your laptop virtually impossible to pawn or sell. Thieves aren't interested in the laptops themselves, only in how much money they can get for them. If they can't sell it, they don't want it.

A microdot is another method of marking your device. This is a technology from the Cold War that was once used by intelligence services. Microdots are smaller than a grain of sand and have writing on them that is too small to see with the naked eye. During the Cold War, spies would use microdots to carry messages by pasting microdots over the periods in books. The microdot, appearing to be punctuation, would go unnoticed and could be read when it arrived at its destination.

You can affix a microdot carrying a unique serial number to a portable device. The microdot goes unnoticed and isn't removed by the thieves. The adhesive used to attach the microdot fluoresces under UV light so that police can find it. Police can then read the serial number with a magnifying glass and verify ownership of the device (see Figure 16-5).

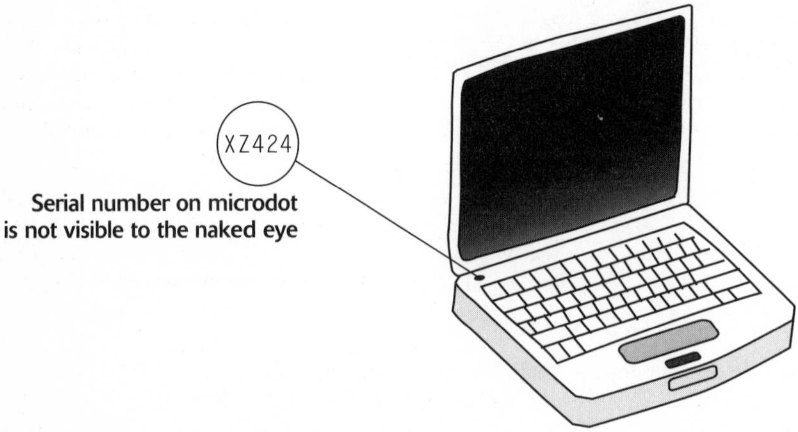

Serial number on microdot
is not visible to the naked eye

XZ424

Figure 16-5: A laptop labeled with a microdot.

Not all missing devices are stolen; many of them are forgotten or lost. Airports and transit authorities collect hundreds of items each day, usually with no way of finding the owner. Your device may have your contact information on the hard drive, but if you have secured your data properly through passwords and encryption this will prevent people from accessing it.

A company called StuffBak has created a unique solution to this problem. They manufacture identification stickers (see Figure 16-6). These stickers carry the message "Reward for Return!" along with a unique ID number, a toll-free phone number, and StuffBak's Web address.

Figure 16-6: Examples of StuffBak stickers.

When a good Samaritan calls the StuffBak number, StuffBak uses the ID number to identify you through your registration. The finder then has a choice of bringing the item to a UPS store or calling Airborne Express for a pickup. As a reward, StuffBak provides the person with free StuffBak stickers for their own use, in addition to whatever monetary reward you may offer. You pay a shipping fee and a small service fee when items are returned.

The surprising thing is that StuffBak's method really works. We may be jaded and believe that people are just not as honest as they used to be. That isn't the case—when given an easy way to return a lost item, most people will do so. Independent tests have been done by CNBC and Asurion Insurance that prove this is the case.

---

on the
web

For more information about StuffBak or to order labels, visit www.
stuffbak.com

Secret #166: Tracking Stolen Devices

In addition to labels, there is special software available to actively track stolen or lost computers and recover them. Often thieves will be unaware that this software is running, and will be unable to delete or disable it even if they notice it.

The tracking software connects to the software company's server whenever the laptop is connected to the Internet. If the owner reports the laptop stolen, the company activates the software and it begins to continually notify them of its whereabouts. The software "phones home" either through an Internet connection or over a dedicated dial-up server. The company then notifies the police, who can work with the thief's Internet service provider or telephone company to locate him and recover the laptop (see Figure 16-7).

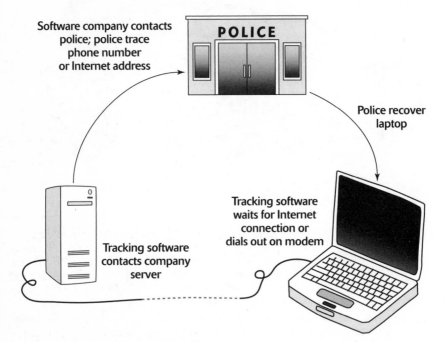

Software company contacts
police; police trace
phone number
or Internet address

POLICE

Police recover
laptop

Tracking software
waits for Internet
connection or
dials out on modem

Tracking software
contacts company
server

Figure 16-7: Tracking software in operation.

A more advanced system of tracking requires the user to have a special piece of hardware installed in the laptop. This device uses a GPS receiver and cellular connection to locate the laptop and report its location to a central server that then notifies police (see Figure 16-8). The GPS system also works with an active Internet connection, reporting its location over the Internet.

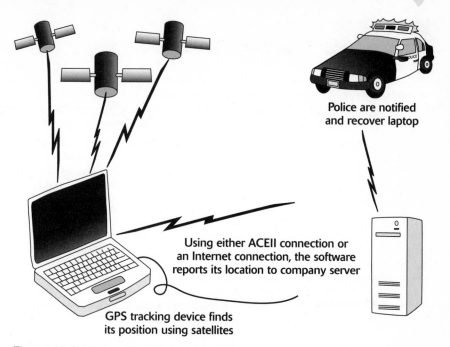

Police are notified
and recover laptop

Using either ACEII connection or
an Internet connection, the software
reports its location to company server

GPS tracking device finds
its position using satellites

Figure 16-8: GPS tracking device in operation.

Secret #167: Secure Docking Stations

Unfortunately, many thefts around the office are performed by either visitors or coworkers. You may use a docking station with your laptop, but did you know that there are secure docking stations designed to prevent someone from stealing your computer? These secure docking stations lock your laptop in place and sound an alarm if someone attempts to remove it. Like other alarms, this is an effective deterrent for a thief who is looking for any easy job.

Secret #168: Reporting Stolen Laptops

Unfortunately, not many people bother to report stolen laptops. In the event that your device is stolen, take the time to file a police report and contact the manufacturer. Your manufacturer may be able to locate the device in the future if someone attempts to register the product or obtain service and support. The police can also check the serial number against recovered stolen property, which may result in your laptop being returned to you at some point.

Threats to Privacy

One potential drawback to ubiquitous mobile devices is the threat to personal privacy that they can represent. Most of us store personal data, including financial data and e-mail, on our portables. This information can be compromised if it's lost or stolen.

Even more threatening is the current trend of including GPS and tracking services with mobile devices. Often targeted at parents and business, these tracking services, if abused, can be used to conduct surveillance on unsuspecting users and track their movements.

Cell phone service providers have always been able to do this to some extent by noting which call came from what phone and through which tower. Police have subpoenaed these records in the past and used them to convict criminals.

In recent years the accuracy of tracking a mobile phone has increased. By using the signal received by three or more towers, cell phone companies can triangulate the position of a cell phone more accurately (see Figure 16-9). This technology was pushed by legislation that required cell phone service providers to locate the origin of a 911 call. The upside of this is that if you are ever in an emergency and you don't know where you are, 911 can triangulate your position with the help of the telephone company and then send help.

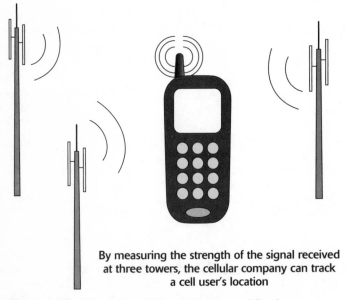

By measuring the strength of the signal received
at three towers, the cellular company can track
a cell user's location

Figure 16-9: Using triangulation to locate a mobile phone.

GPS services are even more accurate, often to within a few feet. Many new phones have GPS functionality built in so that the phone can be located at any time (see Figure 16-10). Once again, this is great if you have an emergency, but the potential for abuse of the system is scary.

Already services are appearing that allow people to check the location of a mobile phone at any time. Although tracking a mobile phone requires the user's prior consent, the potential for abuse still exists, especially in countries that do not have strong privacy laws or that do not value the privacy of their citizens.

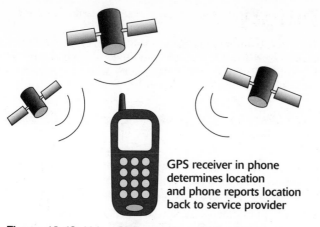

Figure 16-10: Using GPS to track a mobile phone.

GPS receiver in phone determines location and phone reports location back to service provider

Even with privacy laws and regulations in place, the potential threat to privacy is great. Any time data is collected and stored in a database, it can potentially be accessed by unauthorized persons or abused by the database owner for marketing and research purposes. The possibility of data mining through interconnected databases increases the risk to privacy, allowing companies and governments to compile complete profiles of individuals' habits and movements.

Pay careful attention to the privacy policies of your ISP and mobile phone provider. The best way to protect your privacy is not to opt-in unknowingly, and to know how to opt-out should you want to. Carefully weigh the pros and cons of each service.

For example, as a parent you may want to be able to track the location of your child's cell phone. This could provide peace of mind in a scary world. On the other hand, do you want your employer to have a record of your movements? If they pay for your cell service, they may be entitled to track the phone and in the near future that will be an easy thing for them to do.

Secret #169: Location-Based Services

The future of wireless is location-based (or location-aware) technologies. At least that's what all the companies developing the technology and services want us to think. These services work with a phone or handheld that uses GPS to know its position and the cell network, Bluetooth, or Wi-Fi to communicate with the world.

The potential selling points for these services are street-level directions to services and locations, interactive "pushed" advertising, and instant locating of friends, family, and objects: "Where did I park my car?" Using these services, you'll be able to search for the nearest bookstore, push a button, and get a location with directions: "You are 500 ft. from a bookstore. Go south 100 ft. and turn left on Main Street." Pushed advertising means that service providers will track where you are and offer advertising based on your present location (think "phone spam").

For example, if I am walking down the street I might receive an advertisement that says "Today only at Wiffle-Mart, socks half price, only 100 ft. away." Now, do I need socks? Maybe I do. Do I want my phone reminding me to buy new socks? Not any more than I want my e-mail to constantly offer me weight-loss advice or beauty tips. Location-based services promise to open a whole new avenue with which junk advertisers can invade our lives (see Figure 16-11).

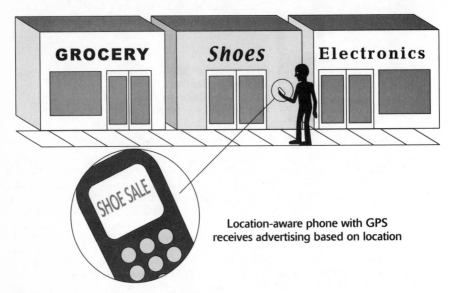

Figure 16-11: Location-aware advertising.

Once again, the downside is the potential misuse of the huge databases that will be created by service providers, plus the potential for a deluge of junk advertising. I'm not sure if I want corporate America knowing where I drive, that I drink too much Diet Coke, and which drive-through joints I frequent. As these services begin to roll out, pay close attention to privacy policies and opt-out if you don't feel your privacy is adequately protected.

Protecting Your Data

Because of the portability of mobile devices and the threat of damage and loss, it's important that you protect your data. While hardware may be replaceable, the data that you lose may be of greater value and result in more damage if lost. Criminals can use personal data to commit identity theft and they can sell business or trade secrets to your competition. You can protect your data from prying eyes and make it easier to recover if your device is severely damaged or destroyed.

cross ref

For information about backing up data in case of loss, theft, or damage, see Chapter 17.

Secret #170: Protecting Data with Encryption or Lockout Software

In Chapter 15, I introduced encryption as a way to secure communications on your WLAN. You can also use encryption to secure at-rest data or data that is located on a hard drive or similar storage medium (CD, DVD, and tape). There are several software solutions available to encrypt your data, whether you choose to encrypt the entire contents of your hard drive or just specific folders.

> **note** An easy-to-use, effective utility for encrypting your files and folders is File Warden, available for download from the utilities section of the *PC Magazine* Web site: www.pcmag.com

One thing to consider before using encryption is that it takes a lot of CPU horsepower. If you encrypt your entire hard drive you will notice significant slowing when you use your computer. You might consider only encrypting the contents of a couple of folders and storing all sensitive files in those.

Smaller devices like PDAs and smart phones lack the horsepower to use significant encryption. There is effective security software for locking a PDA after it's turned off or after it spends a certain amount of time idle. This software locks all unauthorized persons out of the device and prevents wireless connections, synchronizing, or beaming of information.

Whichever device you use, install either encryption or security software to lock down your data if your computer ever falls into the wrong hands. Always set up your device so that it asks for a password and use a security screen saver with a strong password to make it harder for criminals to get to your data.

Secret #171: Using Biometrics

You can install security software that utilizes biometric technology to authenticate you and prevent unauthorized persons from viewing your data. Unlike a password-only system, which crackers can sometimes defeat, a biometric system requires unique biological identification (usually a fingerprint) to authenticate a user.

Biometric software combined with a hardware device, usually a fingerprint scanner, authenticates users who attempt to log on to the computer. Your fingerprint is stored as a unique encrypted digital signature that, in theory, crackers can't forge. To log on to the laptop you must have a password, and the scanner checks your fingerprint and compares it against the print on file (see Figure 16-12). If the prints match, you are authenticated and can access the data.

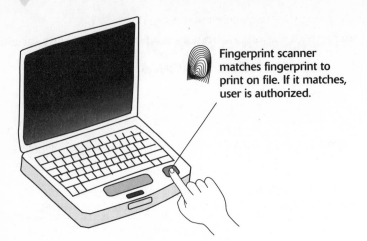

Figure 16-12: A biometric-protected laptop.

Biometrics offers another way to secure sensitive data. Fingerprint scanners are available as an option for computers and PDAs. You will start to see this technology in more places in the next few years, as credit card companies and even grocery stores test the technology as a means of identification. Perhaps soon you won't even have to carry your credit card; you'll just provide your fingerprint when you go shopping.

> **note**   There are relatively inexpensive fingerprint scanners available as add-ons for computers and PDAs. Often these devices connect to your computer with a USB or serial port connection. Some are even built into PCMCIA cards for laptops. Even some computer mice have built-in fingerprint readers. These devices cost $70 to $300 and are available through all major computer hardware retailers.

Secret #172: Threats to Overseas Travelers

If you travel internationally on business there are unique threats that you should be aware of (other than the threat of terrorism, which I do not discuss here). Business travelers are often specifically targeted—not just by criminals but by the governments of certain nations.

There are certain countries that target U.S. businesspeople for corporate espionage. Often these governments seek to acquire trade secrets and financial data that can give their own industry an advantage in the world market. In many countries, particularly China, there is little regard for intellectual property and if your trade secrets are stolen, your competitors will use them.

Consider the following when traveling internationally:

◆ Consider all overseas communications insecure. Often phone networks are owned by the government or are under government control. Intelligence agencies in many countries have the authority to tap phone lines whenever they see fit.

◆ Take all the usual steps to safeguard your portable devices and be extra vigilant. Customs officers in some countries can make copies of files or hard drives while inspecting computers.

◆ Do not use devices like printers, scanners, and shredders that hotels provide for your convenience for transferring or copying sensitive information. Some hotels alter these devices so that they record information and copy it. Printers, scanners, fax machines, and shredders have all been discovered doing this (see Figure 16-13).

◆ Some hotels, particularly in Asia, use cell phone jamming equipment to force guests to use the hotel's landline phone system. Usually this is done to make a profit by charging for calls, but it can also make conversations easier to intercept.

◆ If you use a foreign ISP or broadband provided by a hotel to connect to the Internet, make sure you use a VPN client to secure your communication; otherwise thieves may intercept your data.

◆ Never leave your laptop or PDA unattended or in the open, even in your hotel room. Hide computers or lock them away if you must leave them for a short time. Do not leave computers in plain sight through a window as this may encourage theft.

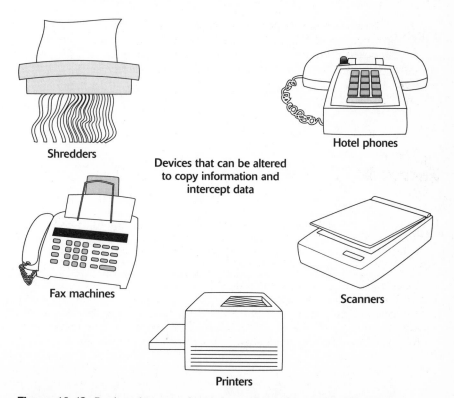

Shredders

Hotel phones

Devices that can be altered to copy information and intercept data

Fax machines

Scanners

Printers

Figure 16-13: Devices that some hotels have altered for stealing information.

Take care to protect yourself and your data and follow the suggestions for deterring theft and recovering lost or stolen devices. Secure your data so that if your device is ever lost or stolen, it won't be compromised.

Simple Steps
for Protecting
Data

Chapter
17

◆ ◆

Secrets in This Chapter

◆ ◆

How much information stored on your computers or mobile devices can you afford to lose? How much data is replaceable, and what would it take to re-create data that you haven't backed up? Data loss can cripple a business or an individual working from home.

The best way to recover from data loss is to maintain a separate backup copy of important data. A backup is a copy of data stored on a different disk drive (on a different computer) or stored on removable media, such as tape, CD-R, or DVD-R. This chapter provides information and best practices for backing up and protecting data on WLANs and mobile devices.

Secret #173: Most Common Reasons for Data Loss

With all the media coverage that computer crime gets, you might think it was the number-one cause of data loss. It isn't, but many people and organizations focus their energy on securing their systems against crackers and script kiddies and often ignore the more likely threats to data (see Figure 17-1).

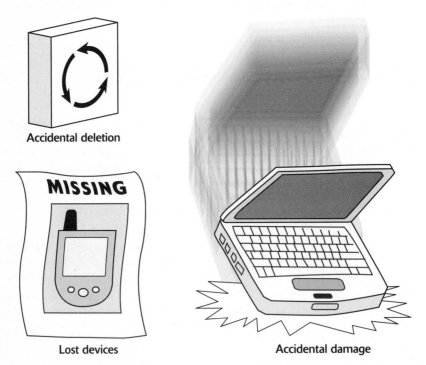

Accidental deletion

Lost devices

Accidental damage

Figure 17-1: Threats to data.

Do you want to know what the most common cause of lost and destroyed data is? It's computer users. That's right, you and I are the most likely ones to lose or destroy our own information, usually through accidental deletion. If you've ever accidentally overwritten a file, or hit Delete, only to recognize your mistake one second too late, then you're in good company.

Mobile devices increase the risk of data loss because they are so easy to lose. Airlines, transit departments, rental car companies, and hotels recover thousands of PDAs, phones, and even laptops every year. Many of these items make it back to their owners, especially if they have taken steps to facilitate this. What do you do if you never get a lost device back?

> cross
> ref
>
> For information on tracking and recovering lost devices using software and labels, see Chapter 16.

Accidental damage to devices is another common cause for data loss and another way that users threaten data. Portable devices are easy to drop, crush, and spill upon—actions that could damage hard drives and memory cards, erasing data in the process. Now that we have established that you are a danger to your own devices and data, we can move on to less common, but equally devastating threats.

Secret #174: Outside Threats to Data

The most publicized threats to data come from outside. Crackers, script kiddies, and cyber terrorists make great headlines but data loss from a malicious attack is less likely to occur than loss caused by user error. However, if you fail to secure your WLAN, you may increase the likelihood of this happening.

> cross
> ref
>
> Refer to Chapter 15 for instructions on locking down your WLAN.

Related to crackers are viruses, worms, and Trojans. This malicious software can delete or compromise data. Some worms facilitate intrusion by a cracker because the worm creates a "back door" or place for a cracker to access a system.

Other external threats include natural disasters such as fire, earthquake, flood, and storms, or, less likely, man-made disasters such as wars and terrorist attacks. While you are unlikely to lose your data due to war or terrorist attack (I hope), adequate planning for data recovery will address even these horrific threats (see Figure 17-2).

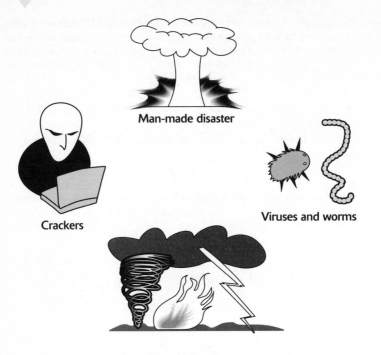

Figure 17-2: External threats to data.

Secret #175: Hardware, Software, and Media Failure

Even though newer hard drives and memory cards are more robust and have a longer working life than they ever used to have, they aren't invulnerable to damage, wear, or material failure. Eventually, equipment wears out and you must replace drives.

Software can also fail, producing errors that corrupt data. Applications can crash, taking data in memory with them. Like hardware, new operating systems and applications are more robust and less likely to fail but they aren't error-proof; problems will arise that can damage or erase your data.

Choosing Data Backup Systems

The best way to defend your data against all of the preceding threats is to start and maintain a regular backup schedule. Having a current backup on hand allows you to be up and running sooner than later after any scenario. Although backing up data is possibly the most important thing you can do, you would be surprised at how many people fail to back up any of their data, especially the files on their home computers.

Backing up data, whether from a mobile device or a desktop PC, doesn't have to be an annoying chore. There are systems that automate backups as well as options for backing up over the Internet or removable media. Careful consideration of the following criteria will help you decide which sort of system suits your needs.

Secret #176: What Type of Data Should You Back Up?

What you decide to back up depends on the level of importance you place on each type of data. Some data may be easily recovered, while considerable time and effort may go into reproducing other data. Consider the following types of data and decide what level of effort would be required to recover from the loss of each, as well as the impact to your daily life or job:

- Operating system and application software. Many operating systems have the ability to back up to a second hard drive for easy recovery, but this won't always include applications and documents. Keep a backup copy of your operating system and application software, in addition to your original disks.
- Personal data, including e-mail and documents.
- Video, photos, and music files.
- Internet favorites, passwords, and settings for regularly visited Web sites.

If you have a small business or work from home, you should also consider the following data:

- Employee data, including e-mail and documents
- Customer data, including databases, orders, and related files
- Accounting data

After considering these lists, you should have an idea of what you might need to back up. At the very least, you should make regular backups of the most important data on your devices. With the cost per megabyte of hard drives and backup media falling, there is no reason why you shouldn't back up all of your data.

Secret #177: How Often Should You Back Up?

After you've decided *what* you want to back up, you need to determine *how often* to back up. The type and frequency of your backup helps determine what sort of solution to consider.

If you modify data frequently, and if you regularly produce a large amount of new data, then you have to back up more often to ensure that you have the latest and greatest copies of your work. On the other hand, if you do not modify or produce data frequently, you don't have to back up nearly as often.

You may also back up *incrementally*, saving only new or modified files daily and backing up all your data less frequently. Incremental backups save storage space and time. You may use a *differential* backup when only the newest version of a file is necessary. A differential backup saves the newest version of a file to backup media, unlike an incremental, which saves all versions of a file.

A *bare-metal* backup is a complete restoration of a device back to its original state before an error occurred. Often this is the quickest way to get back up and running. Many IT departments prefer to do this rather than troubleshoot operating system problems.

Remember, the shorter the amount of time between backups, the quicker and less painful recovering your data will be, should you need to do so. Set a backup schedule for yourself, perhaps doing a full backup once a week with differential or incremental backups interspersed between full backups. Try to do backups when they will cause the least disruption to others, perhaps in the evening or early morning. Remember to back up after any significant event, for instance when you finish writing the chapter of a book.

Secret #178: Determining the Value of Your Data

You determine the value of your data in part by the amount of work it would take to reproduce it and by how important you feel it is. Determining the value of your data aids you in deciding how often to back up and whether you should back up offsite.

For example, I have manuscripts (including this one) on disk, each of which took perhaps hundreds of hours to produce. In many cases, my contracts require me to maintain copies of the manuscripts for a certain number of years. This work is invaluable to me. I plan my backups accordingly and store copies of the files offsite. If anything happens to my home, copies of the files stored offsite will survive.

Storing offsite can be as simple as renting space on an Internet storage site or copying data to a CD-R or DVD-R and placing it in a safe deposit box (see Figure 17-3). The value I assign my data determines whether this is cost-effective. The same goes for personal files, such as photos, videos, or audio files.

Now that you've determined what you need to back up, how often you should back up, and the value of your data, you can take a look at different types of backups and determine which fits your intended application best. Whether you are backing up at home or for a small business, you can consider several approaches.

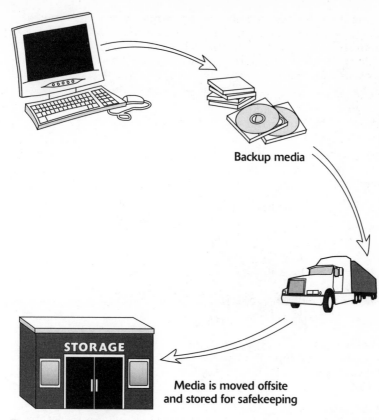

Backup media

STORAGE

Media is moved offsite
and stored for safekeeping

Figure 17-3: Offsite storage options.

Secret #179: Deciding What Type of Storage Is Right for You

Online Storage

When I say online, I'm not referring to the Internet. Here online refers to a backup that is readily accessible by users on the network. For a home WLAN, online storage could consist of a hard disk (or disks) on one of the computers on the network or an external hard drive attached to a PC or with its own Wi-Fi NIC. The idea is that the stored data is instantly accessible by anyone on the network who needs it (see Figure 17-4).

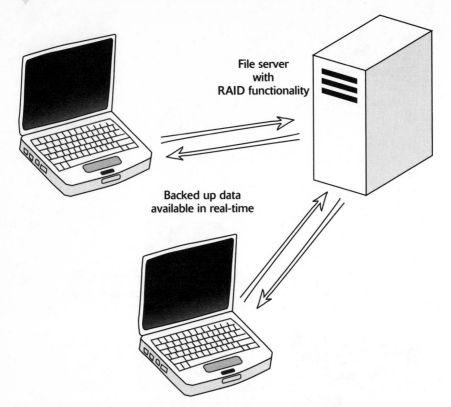

Figure 17-4: Online storage options.

Online storage should offer some sort of redundancy. For a small business the best solution is disk-mirroring using RAID systems. At one time RAID stood for Redundant Array of Inexpensive Disks. Now that all hard disks are relatively inexpensive it stands for Redundant Array of Independent Disks. A RAID system *mirrors*, or writes, data across several hard drives at once. It makes two or more copies of all your data so that if one hard drive should fail, the duplicate(s) can take its place without the users even knowing about it (see Figure 17-5).

There are several different types, or levels, of RAID system. These are numbered and you may hear people talk about RAID 0, RAID 3, RAID 5, and so on. A discussion of the different levels is beyond the scope of this book. Just be aware that it is an option for online storage, using a small server if you should decide that it's the way you want to go.

---

note   For more information on configuring and using RAID systems, consult *Highly Available Storage for Windows Servers* (VERITAS Series) by Paul Massiglia (John Wiley & Sons, 2001).

Online storage isn't a replacement for offline storage because it is still susceptible to a number of threats. It has the advantage of being convenient, both when conducting backups and for retrieving data, but for security's sake combine it with periodic offline backups.

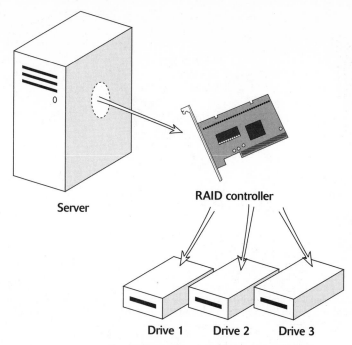

Server

RAID controller

Drive 1 Drive 2 Drive 3

Controller writes data across several drives at once

Figure 17-5: A basic RAID system.

---

insider insight   When using online storage on a WLAN, consider the bandwidth you will require when backing up over the WLAN and plan large backups at off-peak times. While backing up or retrieving data on a WLAN, the bandwidth available to other users will drop significantly and affect network operation.

Nearline Storage

Nearline storage means backing up data to removable media and storing the media onsite. The data can be on CD-R, DVD-R, optical disk, or tape. When you need it, it's available quickly. Often nearline storage systems use some sort of tape changer or "jukebox" with storage media preloaded and ready to go when needed (see Figure 17-6).

Like online storage, you can access data on a nearline storage system relatively quickly. However, because data is stored on removable media, it is a little more secure. Still, the ultimate insurance is offline and offsite storage.

---

note   Norton Ghost is a useful application for creating images of hard disks and burning them to CD-R for data storage and recovery purposes. Norton Ghost is available from Symantec at www.symantec.com/sabu/ghost/ghost_personal.

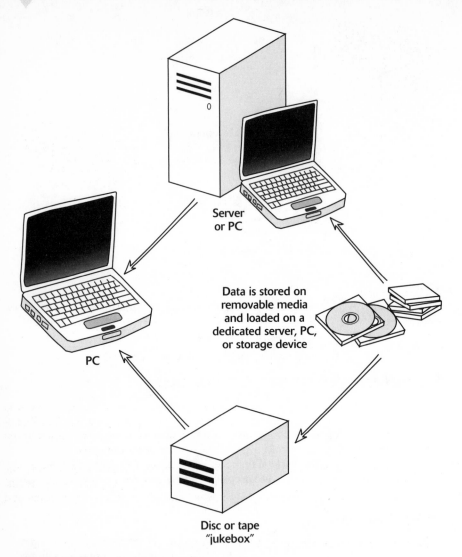

Server
or PC

Data is stored on
removable media
and loaded on a
dedicated server, PC,
or storage device

PC

Disc or tape
"jukebox"

Figure 17-6: Nearline storage option.

Offline Storage

Offline storage consists of copying data to removable media that can be stored
away from the network (see Figure 17-7). Typical media include magnetic tape,
CD-R, or DVD-R. This is especially useful for mission-critical data or personal
data that would be hard or impossible to replace. Even if data is needed in real
time, offline storage is a safe way to secure copies of it in case of disaster. Store
discs in a secure place, such as a safe, and consider keeping an additional copy
at a site in a different geographical location (offsite storage).

Figure 17-7: Offline storage scenario.

Data is stored on removable media and loaded as needed

---

insider insight   Always store your backup media in a secure place. It makes no sense to take care in securing your WLAN, only to leave copies of data lying around where an individual could easily copy or swipe them.

Selecting Media for Backups

The type of storage media you select affects the cost of your backup system as well as the speed of access and space required to store backups. Media reliability is also important. It must be able to maintain the integrity of data without failing due to degradation from age or mechanical wear and tear.

Different media are available for backing up data. They vary in capabilities (see "Secret #181: Synching Your PDA") and each has its strong and weak points. For my purposes, I present only the most commonly used media in home and small office settings.

Internal/External Hard Drives

Every computer has at least one hard drive because it's the primary storage medium in computing. Hard drives work by writing and reading blocks of data magnetically to a rigid disk made of one or more platters. They are fast, reliable, and relatively inexpensive. You can install a hard drive within a computer (internally) or it can be a separate device that interfaces with your computer over a USB, serial, or FireWire port.

Hard drives are ideal for online storage but because data on them is susceptible to user error, malicious attack, and occasionally device failure, they should not be the sole form of backup for important data.

CD-R, DVD-R, CD-RW, and DVD-RW Discs

Unlike standard CD and DVD discs, you can write to a CD-R or DVD-R disc. They can hold a significant amount of data. A DVD-R disc holds up to 4.5GB. Individual discs are inexpensive and easy to store securely. A CD-R or DVD-R drive "burns" a disc by using a laser to alter the reflectivity of a dye layer, creating pits that a CD or DVD drive can read. The different capacity is achieved by narrowing the pitch or distance between tracks on the disc.

You can rewrite and reuse CD-RW and DVD-RW discs. The "RW" stands for rewritable and requires a CD-R drive to write. Older CD-ROM drives cannot read CD-RW discs because the reflectivity is lower than CD and CD-R discs. Theoretically, you can rewrite a CD-RW disc up to 1,000 times.

Magnetic Tapes

There are many different magnetic tape solutions available today. Computers have utilized magnetic tape for storage for over 50 years, starting with big half-inch open reels and now with small removable cartridges. The tape is made of flexible plastic with a magnetic material one side and comes in many different sizes.

Magnetic tapes store data sequentially along the length of the tape. This means that to access different bits of data, a tape drive must rewind or advance the tape to find the requested files. Because of this, magnetic tapes are extremely slow compared to all other storage media. Magnetic tape is also susceptible to damage from head crashes and magnetic fields.

Secret #180: Four Things You Must Consider

When selecting the type of backup solution and media that you will use, there are four main factors to consider. The importance of each varies from situation to situation. You may be most concerned with speed and reliability, while another person may be more concerned with cost.

Speed

Backup or recovery speed varies among systems. Online backup is the quickest because hard drives are faster when writing or reading data. You can retrieve data stored on media such as CD-R or DVD-R quickly but it takes far longer to write to them than to a hard drive. Tape drives take the longest to write and even longer to retrieve data.

If speed is your chief criterion for backups, consider installing additional hard drives in one or more of your systems and use them to perform online backups. An external hard drive works equally well and has the advantage of being removable for storage or transport.

Capacity

If you have a high volume of data to back up regularly, consider a large hard drive (internal or external) or a tape drive. Both of these have capacities of several gigabytes. DVD-R discs have a capacity of around 4.5GB, while CD-R discs have a capacity of 800MB.

For quick incremental backups, either a hard drive or CD-R/DVD-R discs would be ideal. Tape drives, depending on the system, can hold over 100GB, depending on the type of tape system. Tape cartridges cost more than CD-R/DVD-R media, but because of their large capacity they may be more convenient when backing many gigabytes of data.

Reliability

Reliability varies from device to device and among brands. Generally, a hard drive is less susceptible to degradation than tapes and some CD-R/DVD-R discs. At the same time, a hard drive has moving parts and can suffer mechanical failure.

The reliability of CD-R/DVD-R varies among manufacturers. I have had some discs fail after a year, while others are fine after several years. Rewritable discs are more susceptible to degradation than write-once CD-R/DVD-R discs, but again this varies among manufacturers, and from disc to disc.

Tapes seem to be the most sensitive to environmental changes, degradation, and mechanical damage. On several occasions, I have lost gigabytes of data when a tape drive "ate" a tape or when after a few months of use a tape degraded. The quality varies but in my opinion for the most reliable offline storage use write-once CD-R/DVD-R discs.

Cost

In the last few years, the price of storage media and devices has plummeted. CD-R drives are available for less than $70 and external CD-R/DVD-R combination drives can be found for less than $250. You can buy blank CD-R discs for 19 cents apiece and DVD-R discs for as little as 80 cents each.

At the same time, the cost of large external hard drives has dropped and you can outfit a computer with an internal hard drive as large as 200GB for under $130.

Tape drives are by far the most expensive, largely due to the amount of automation they offer to the backup process. A tape drive that uses 10GB tapes can cost more than $700, with tapes as much as $20 each.

For the average user, the most cost-effective route is probably a CD-R/DVD-R combo drive, combined with online backup to a hard drive on the WLAN. Backup software is available to automate backing up over your network, and you can manually create offline backups to discs at regular intervals.

Backing Up Mobile Devices

It is especially important to back up your mobile device regularly to avoid losing data. The battery life of PDAs can vary from a few hours to a month or more, depending on the model and how much you use it. PDAs can also be lost or damaged, resulting in data loss. There are a number of methods available that you can use to back up data from your mobile device.

Secret #181: Synching Your PDA

You should synchronize your PDA with your computer daily to back up files and applications (see Figure 17-8). Depending on your platform (Palm OS or Pocket PC) you may want to consider third-party software that improves and streamlines the backup process and automates synching. You can also synch a Palm OS or Windows Mobile cell phone and save your files, phone numbers, and contacts.

With a Palm OS handheld, this can be especially important because the HotSync feature does not always back up all data for third-party applications. A good solution for Palm users is BackupBuddy by Blue Nomad Software.

---

on the web   For more information about BackupBuddy, visit www.bluenomad.com.

Many new PDAs are available with integrated Bluetooth wireless capability. You can use the Bluetooth connection to sync with your computer and back up your PDA without having to leave it in its cradle. If your PDA has Wi-Fi capabilities, you can synchronize that way also.

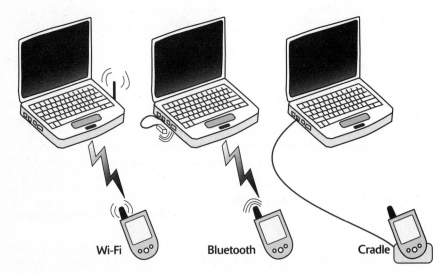

Wi-Fi   Bluetooth   Cradle

Figure 17-8: Different ways to sync handhelds.

Secret #182: Using Portable Storage

There are a number of options for backing up your mobile device on portable media or devices. Most PDAs support removable storage cards. If not, you can add this capability with a hardware accessory. Using Compact Flash (CF) cards, or similar removable media, you can back up your data and keep it handy while you travel.

Some handhelds with USB ports support portable USB flash drives. These small drives plug into the USB port on your PDA so you can store data on them. These devices are very small; some of them are incorporated into key chains, so they are always handy (see Figure 17-9). Not all PDAs support USB drives, however, and some that do may require the installation of third-party drivers. Research this carefully before buying a USB drive for your PDA.

USB flash drive

USB drive with removable media

Figure 17-9: USB flash drives.

For GSM phones that use a Subscriber Identify Module (SIM) card, there are a few devices available that can store data directly from the SIM. One of these is the SIMKey Keyring Databank, available from several online retailers. Simply pop the SIM out of your phone and into the device, which then reads the SIM and stores all of its data. Restoring lost contacts and phone numbers is then as easy as popping the SIM back into the device and copying the stored data back onto the card.

Secret #183: Backing Up on the Internet

In addition to regular synchronizing with your laptop or desktop computer, you can back up your PDA over a wireless Internet connection. The advantage of this technique is that you can access the data anywhere you go, as long as you have Internet access (see Figure 17-10). The best Internet backup site is IBackup.com, which supports Palm OS and Pocket PC handhelds in addition to Windows operating systems found on desktop and laptop computers (95/98/ME/2000/XP).

Once you open your account at IBackup and download the appropriate client software, you can back up your data to the site and even share files and collaborate with coworkers. Once again, Internet access is required so you will need a Wi-Fi card or a PDA with cell phone built in to access the Web.

on the web   **For easy backing up over the Internet, visit** www.Ibackup.com.

If your home computer has an always-on broadband connection, you can also connect to it over the Internet and back up your data that way. Combined with an automated backup solution, this gives you a convenient way to ensure that you and your coworkers can access your data from the road, while backing it up to the same offline media (see Figure 17-11).

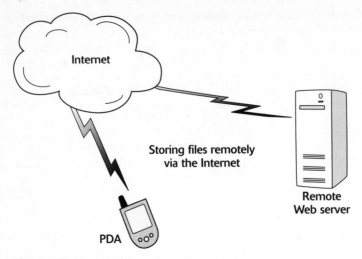

Figure 17-10: Backing up via the Internet.

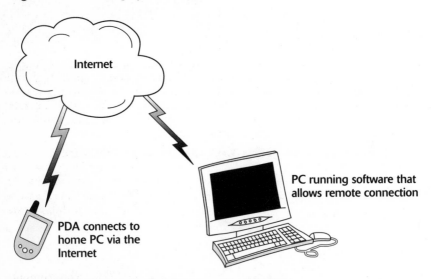

Figure 17-11: Remote backup to your own computer.

To securely access your home computer and perform backups, you need a third-party software solution like GoToMyPC, LoudPC, or a similar application loaded on the computer you wish to access remotely.

---

on the
web

For more information on remote-access software, visit www.gotomypc.com or www.loudpc.com.

Maintaining Hardware

Protecting and maintaining your hardware is another way to prevent data loss from hardware failure. In Chapter 16, I discuss ways to protect your devices from physical and electrical damage, as well as from theft. These are not the only causes for hardware failure and corrupt data.

Secret #184: Top Reasons for Hardware Failure and Data Loss

Aside from impact damage and electrical spikes, there are sources of hardware failure that can arise from lack of maintenance or through improper maintenance. Different sources rank these threats differently, at some point touting each of them as the number-one threat or cause of hardware failure. I haven't ranked them in any particular order, preferring that you consider each and protect yourself from all of them.

Electrostatic Discharge

Electrostatic discharge (ESD) can destroy components within your computer. A common way for ESD damage to occur is when you open your computer case to install new hardware (drives, RAM, and so on). If you don't properly ground yourself, any electrical charge that your body carries will jump from your fingers to conductors in the computer, such as chips.

The same thing happens when you rub your feet on a carpet, generating an electrostatic charge. When you reach out to touch another person or a metal object, sparks fly. Unfortunately, when the sparks fly from your fingers to a computer component, you may destroy the component. You may not think there's enough power to do any damage, but there is. A static discharge from your hand can be very high power indeed—in the kilowatt range.

The best way to prevent ESD from occurring is to use a grounding wrist strap or stand on a grounding mat if you have to open the computer's case (see Figure 17-12). You can also make sure that you are at "zero potential" by constantly touching a bare metal surface. Damage from ESD only occurs if you are working inside a computer or handling a component like a RAM chip or video board, not when you are touching the case.

Dust

Accumulation of dust can damage some components and cause your computer to overheat. It doesn't take a thick layer; even a thin layer that you can barely see can raise the temperature in your computer a few percent, enough to shorten the life of its components. Heavy dust buildup can also short out components and damage hard drives.

Heat

Overheating damages many computers. Excessive heat increases resistance in semiconductor materials, which in turn produces more heat. This heat buildup and increase in resistance causes logic circuits to behave erratically and ultimately fail to function.

Heat can also destroy data on hard drives by causing the metallic layer to expand, potentially putting data tracks out of alignment. Repeated heating and cooling can compound the problem until the drive fails completely. It doesn't take a lot of heat to do this, either.

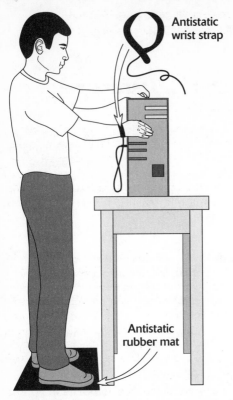

Figure 17-12: Grounding wrist strap and mat.

The CPU of your computer is especially susceptible to heat damage. Because of the number of circuits on the CPU, it generates a lot of heat. CPUs have a heat sink that helps radiate heat away from the CPU, and most computers have one or more fans that cool the CPU and other components.

Bad Hard Disk Sectors

Occasionally, sectors on a hard disk fail due to physical problems on the disk. These problems can result from dust infiltration, heat, or degradation over time. Your computer cannot write or read data from a sector that has failed, and any data already written to that sector is lost. Through proper maintenance, however, you can prevent hard disk damage and detect failing sectors before they fail completely.

Secret #185: Engage in Proper Cleaning and Maintenance

You can help prevent failure of your hardware by performing periodic maintenance on it. This involves routine cleaning inside the case and maintaining the hard drive with special utilities. You will need the following equipment:

- A grounding wrist strap to prevent damage from ESD
- A grounding mat, if possible, as added ESD protection
- Cans of compressed air
- A Phillips screwdriver
- A computer vacuum (would be nice)

---

insider insight   If you have never worked inside a computer, or you are uncomfortable doing so, then take it to a computer store or repair shop to have it cleaned professionally. Never take apart a PDA or mobile phone; you probably will never need to anyway. Cleaning inside a laptop is tricky and they can be difficult to put back together. Consider having a laptop cleaned professionally. You may void your computer's warranty by opening it. Read it carefully and, if this is the case, let a professional do the maintenance.

Discharge any static electricity in your body by touching a metal surface. Then open the case, attach the antistatic wrist strap to your wrist, and clip the end of the grounding wire from the strap to the computer's chassis (metal frame). Do not attach the ground wire to components because this may cause ESD damage.

Using the compressed air, blast dust from all surfaces, in cracks, and from inside connectors. Follow the directions on the compressed air can exactly. Holding the can too close to components or spraying for too long damages electrical components by freezing them and through condensation of water vapor present in the air. If the can gets very cold, you're spraying too long.

If you have a computer vacuum, use it to suck up the dust you've knocked loose. Only use an approved microvacuum; don't use your house vacuum or you could damage your PC. Never touch components with the microvacuum because this may damage them. Hold the vacuum away from components and suction-dust without touching them.

Clean around fans and vents and blast any dust away from the heat sink. If your computer has a filter over the vents, clean it with warm water and blot it dry with a lint-free cloth. Allow it to air-dry before you replace it.

To maintain your hard drive, use a disk utility like Scandisk to scan regularly for errors in the disk media and repair any problems. Often you can catch problems before they reach the point of total failure and data loss. If you experience intermittent problems with your hard drive, back it up immediately. Often people ignore problems in the early stages, only to have the drive fail during continuous use.

Part VI

Appendixes

Wi-Fi Networking Resources

This appendix is a collection of Web resources pertaining to Wi-Fi networking. The Web is full of useful information; here are just a few Web sites to get you started. While many of these sites do not focus exclusively on wireless technology, they all have relevant information for wireless users.

General Networking and News Sites

The following sites are good sources of general information, including news, reviews, and tutorials.

Practically Networked (www.practicallynetworked.com)

A great informational site about networking that includes "how-to" articles, reviews, and troubleshooting information.

Tom's Hardware Guide (www.tomshardware.com)

This is a great hardware site that includes reviews, benchmarking, and bug reports.

ExtremeTech (www.extremetech.com)

This site is billed as a "one-stop shop for serious technological needs." Full of great, hard-to-find information and connected to an active "technocrat" community, this is one of Ziff-Davis Media's best sites.

Wi-Fi Networking News (www.wifinetnews.com)

A source for Wi-Fi networking news and developments.

TechTV (www.techtv.com)

The Web site of the popular TV network, this site is full of useful technology information geared toward the average computer user who wants answers in plain English.

PC Magazine (www.pcmag.com)

The Web site of one of the largest and most useful computer magazines in the world. Read the reviews and buying guides before you invest in any equipment.

Wi-Fi Planet (www.wi-fiplanet.com)

The largest portal for wireless, this site features news, reviews, tutorials, and forums where users can participate in discussions about Wi-Fi technology and products.

Broadband Wireless Exchange Magazine (www.bbwexchange.com)

An online reference site for broadband wireless news, white papers, and many other resources.

Security, Privacy, and Antivirus Resources

You may have noticed that I like to stress security, and I'm going to stay in character here by recommending some good sites for security and privacy information, as well as throwing in a shameless plug for my own site.

Shields Up!! Gibson Research Corporation (www.grc.com)

InfoWorld columnist and programmer Steve Gibson created the Shields Up!! Internet security checkup. Shields Up!! helps you determine how vulnerable your computer is and tests your firewall software. Millions of people have taken advantage of this free tool and you should too.

Spybot Search & Destroy (www.safer-networking.org)

This site has useful software that can detect and remove spyware (software that tracks your surfing habits and reports your private information to advertisers) from your computer.

www.vmyths.com (www.vmyths.com)

This site exists solely for the "eradication of computer virus hysteria." Run by virus expert Rob Rosenberger, this site is committed to straight talk about virus threats, dispelling myths, and exposing hoaxes. If you want facts about computer viruses, visit this site and get them from people who don't answer to antivirus companies.

Security Focus (www.securityfocus.com)

Security Focus is one of the most comprehensive security sites on the Web. It maintains the Security Focus vulnerability database and the Bugtraq security mailing list. Check this site often to keep abreast of vulnerabilities that affect your systems.

Electronic Frontier Foundation (www.eff.org)

The EFF is a nonprofit, committed to protecting our right to "think, speak, and share our ideas, thoughts, and needs using new technologies, such as the Internet and the World Wide Web." Visit and support the EFF.

CERT (www.cert.org)

The Computer Emergency Response Team (CERT) is located at the Software Engineering Institute (SEI) at Carnegie Mellon University. CERT is a reporting house for security incidents and vulnerabilities, and it's a great place for you to get the facts about a new threat or reported incident.

Razorwire: The Security Portal in Plain English (www.rzrwire.com)

A security portal in plain English, this site translates security news from "geek to English," and attempts to provide the average person with security facts, devoid of hysteria and hyperbole. I run and edit this site and attempt to make it as useful for laymen as Security Focus is for IT professionals. Go here and sign up for the free security bulletin, stay informed, and amaze your friends.

Performance-Related Sites

There are a number of ways you can improve the performance of your computer, WLAN, and Internet connection. The following sites provide useful information about doing just that.

SpeedGuide (www.speedguide.net)

This is one of the leading broadband and performance sites on the Internet. It's a great resource for novice and advanced computer users alike.

Tweak3D (www.tweak3d.net)

Tweak3D provides tips for improving computer performance and stability. It has useful "how-to" guides to help novices install and maintain hardware.

Broadband Reports (www.broadbandreports.com)

An informational site about broadband Internet service for residential and small business customers, the site includes reviews and forums that visitors can participate in as part of the broadband user community.

PC Pitstop (www.pcpitstop.com)

At this site, you can have your computer's performance checked by online automated diagnostic tools. There's lots of great information and it's well worth a visit.

Groups and Associations

Many groups promote wireless in one form or another. Some are industry-related, while others formed around user groups or other independent organizations.

Wi-Fi Alliance (www.wi-fi.org)

The Wi-Fi Alliance is a membership organization that certifies product compliance to the 802.11b, 802.11g, and 802.11a wireless standards. Over 200 companies are members of this nonprofit organization. The Wi-Fi Alliance promotes the use of Wi-Fi (WLAN) use worldwide by encouraging manufacturers to comply with the 802.11x standards when designing their networking products. The Wi-Fi Alliance promotes 802.11x technology to home, SOHO, and enterprise consumers, tests networking products independently to ensure that they are compliant with the 802.11x standard, and tests interoperability among certified products.

Freenetworks.org (www.freenetworks.org)

Freenetworks.org is a voluntary cooperative association that promotes education, collaboration, and the creation of free digital networks. In their own words, they are "an affiliation between community wireless networking projects around the globe."

IEEE 802 LAN/MAN Standards Committee (www.ieee802.org)

The Institute of Electrical and Electronics Engineers (sometimes called I-triple-E by engineers) is an international nonprofit technical professional organization. The IEEE, through its members, is the leading authority in many technical areas, including computers, telecommunications, and power generation. With 37 societies and 4 technical councils, the IEEE seems to have a working group dedicated to just about everything that can be plugged into an outlet. This is the site of the IEEE committee that oversees the development of the networking standards used in Ethernet and Wi-Fi networking.

Miscellaneous Sites

Here are some useful sites for checking facts and finding useful information.

The AFU and Urban Legends Archive (www.urbanlegends.com)

Since 1991, this site has been the archive for the alt.folklore.urban USENET newsgroup and the premier site for urban myth and legend info. That crazy story you heard from someone at the office is probably a myth and, if so, it's on this site. Don't get taken in, check here first.

Urban Legends (http://urbanlegends.about.com)

This site is a good source of information about Urban Legends and myths. Check here before you spread "true" stories you heard from a-friend-of-a-friend.

Wardrive.net (www.wardrive.net)

A great Web site full of information and links to wireless security resources. This is the best place to start if you're serious about securing your WLAN.

CIAC Hoax Busters (http://hoaxbusters.ciac.org)

The U.S. Dept of Energy Computer Incident Advisory Capability (CIAC) maintains a site full of information about e-mail virus hoaxes. Hoaxes can cause many problems, especially when thousands of people believe and then forward them. Next time you get a virus warning, check here before you forward the e-mail.

Mobile Wireless Resources

This appendix is a collection of Web resources pertaining to mobile devices. It includes links to Web sites that offer software, including ring tones, for mobile devices and other fun diversions. The sites in the "Wireless Web Links" and "Fun Stuff" sections are accessible with any WAP-enabled device. This is not a comprehensive list; just a place for you to start. You'll be able to find plenty of other mobile friendly resources.

Useful Software and Resources

The following is a list of useful PDA Web sites that you can access from your desktop computer or a PDA with an HTML browser.

Handango (www.handango.com)

PDA software downloads, plus hardware and accessory sales.

PocketMatrix (www.pocketmatrix.com)

A comprehensive Pocket PC community site with reviews, downloads, articles, and more.

PDArcade (www.pdarcade.com)

A comprehensive game site that calls itself "your one-stop resource for PDA gaming." It provides news, reviews, and more.

PDA Buyer's Guide (www.pdabuyersguide.com)

Reviews and news about PDAs, software, and accessories.

5 Star PDA (http://5star.freeserve.com/PDA)

PDA software downloads, shareware, and demos.

PDA Street (www.pdastreet.com)

PDA software downloads, shareware, and demos.

PilotZone (www.pilotzone.com)

Download shareware and freeware (hosted by Tucows).

HandMark (www.handmark.com)

Purchase and download software for Palm, Pocket PC, and smart phones.

PocketGear (www.pocketgear.com)

The complete Pocket PC resource: software, news, and more.

PDATopSoft.com (www.pdatopsoft.com)

Resource for Palm OS, Pocket PC, Windows CE, EPOC, RIM, and smart phones.

pdaPointer (www.pdapointer.com/)

Software portal for all major PDA brands and operating systems.

PDAGeek (www.geek.com/pdageek/pdamain.htm)

PDA resource section of Geek.com.

PalmGear (www.palmgear.com)

Software for your Palm OS device.

Wireless Web Links

The following is a list of useful WAP sites that you can access from your WAP-enabled mobile phone or PDA.

Google (http://wap.google.com)

The WML portal for the Google search engine, which translates search results into WAP.

Mobone.com (http://wap.mobone.com/index.wml)

An expansive WAP search engine and wireless Web directory.

Raging Search (http://wml.raging.com)

AltaVista's WAP search page.

Yahoo! (http://wap.yahoo.com)

Personalized service that includes e-mail, calendar, contacts, news, finance, sports, and weather.

AOL Mobile (http://mobile.aol.com)

AOL users can access their services here.

Babelserver (http://babelserver.com)

WAP-enabled translation services.

Bolt (http://wap.bolt.com)

Teen-oriented portal with plenty of content as well as communication services.

ClickServices (www.clickservices.com)

Instant-messaging, e-mail, reminders, greeting, and so on.

InfoSpace.com (http://phone.infospace.com/phone.att/index_find.hdml)

Phone number and e-mail search with reverse lookups.

Lycos (http://wap.lycos.com)

Search portal that offers stocks, news, and so on.

M-Central (http://m-central.com)

The Wireless Intelligent Portal (WIP).

MSN Mobile (http://mobile.msn.com)

Site that includes Hotmail, yellow pages, travel, and news.

Breathe (http://wap.breathe.com)

News, lifestyle, and more.

go2online (www.go2online.com)

Location-based information services provider.

INetNow (www.inetnow.com)

Accesses a human Internet surfer who searches for requested information.

mopilot.com (http://mopilot.com/wml/index.wml)

Search engine, messaging, games, and news.

yourwap.com (www.yourwap.com/index.wml)

Set up a customized portal with contacts and e-mail.

Fun Stuff

The following sites offer ring tones, games, graphics, and other fun diversions.

Sony Music Mobile (www.sonymusicmobile.com)

Downloadable ring tones.

ToneTribe (www.tonetribe.com)

Ring tones, graphics, and screen savers.

CellularMagic (http://wap.cellularmagic.com)

Trivia games, casino games, and more.

Cosmic Infinity (www.cosmicinfinity.com/wap/cosmic.wml)

Crosswords, checkers, and more.

Cranium Crank (www.pktbo.com)

Jokes, word games, and more.

Distractions (http://my-eq.com)

Interactive trivia, riddles, and more.

Game On! by Indiqu (http://c7.indiqu.com/www/games/welcome/gomenu.po)

Gambling, arcade, board games, and more.

PocketBoxOffice (www.pktbo.com)

Humor, Dear Abby, games, movies, and fashion features.

Wap Boy (http://wap.com.ph/games)

Hangman, Minefield, and more.

Wirelessgames.com (www.wirelessgames.com/index.wml)

Games for single and multiple players.

X-Alien.net (http://x-alien.net)

Directory of wireless Web games sites.

nGame (http://wap.mviva.ngame.com)

Multiplayer games and simulations.

Yahoo! Games (http://mobile.yahoo.com/games)

Play puzzles as well as trivia, role-playing, and other games.

Manufacturers

Y ou have choices in shopping for wireless products. To get you started, I've assembled a quick list of companies that produce wireless equipment. I've included a link to each manufacturer's Web site as well as some general information about their product offerings.

Wi-Fi Networking Hardware

The following manufacturers produce wireless hardware targeted toward home and SOHO consumers.

3COM (www.3com.com)

Dr. Robert Metcalfe, one of the inventors of Ethernet, founded 3COM in 1979. The 3 "COMs" in the name are computer, communication, and compatibility. 3COM manufactures a wide array of networking products, including wireless.

Wireless Products: access points, adapters, antennas, Bluetooth adapters, bridges, and routers.

AmbiCom (www.ambicom.com)

Founded in 1997, AmbiCom produces a full line of wired and wireless products, specializing in solutions for mobile wireless, producing wireless adapters for laptops, PDAs, and printers, as well as GPS cards for the Pocket PC.

Wireless Products: access points, adapters, Bluetooth adapters, GPS cards, and routers.

Apple Computer (www.apple.com)

Apple should need no introduction. Founded in 1976 by Steve Wozniak and Steve Jobs, Apple has been one of the most innovative companies in the computer industry. In addition to its computers and software, Apple produces wireless products that work with both Mac OS and PC systems.

Wireless Products: AirPort Extreme wireless access point.

Belkin (www.belkin.com)

Founded in 1983, Belkin produces a full line of wired and wireless networking products.

Products: access points, adapters, antennas, Bluetooth adapters, and routers.

Buffalo Technology (USA) (www.buffalotech.com)

A subsidiary of Japan's Buffalo, Inc., Buffalo Technology (USA) produces wired and wireless networking products and computer memory.

Products: access points, adapters, antennas, bridges, repeaters, and routers.

D-Link Systems (www.dlink.com)

D-Link produces a full line of wired and wireless networking products. It also produces many other wireless products, including cameras.

Products: access points, adapters, antennas, Bluetooth adapters, bridges, cameras, repeaters, and routers.

Hawking Technology (www.hawkingtech.com)

Hawking Technology produces a full line of wired and wireless networking products.

Products: access points, adapters, antennas, Bluetooth adapters, print servers, and routers.

Linksys (www.linksys.com)

A division of Cisco Systems, Linksys produces a full line of consumer wired and wireless networking products.

Products: access points, adapters, antennas, cameras, game adapters, Bluetooth adapters, print servers, wireless media centers, and routers.

MiLAN Technology (www.milan.com)

MiLAN produces wired and wireless networking equipment.

Products: access points, adapters, and bridges

NETGEAR (www.netgear.com)

NETGEAR designs and manufactures wired and wireless networking equipment, focusing entirely on products for home and small office users.

Products: access points, adapters, antennas, bridges, print servers, and routers.

SanDISK (www.sandisk.com)

SanDISK produces flash data storage products and some Wi-Fi cards for the Pocket PC.

Products: CF card Wi-Fi adapters and flash storage.

SMC Networks (www.smc.com)

SMC produces a full line of consumer wired and wireless networking products.

Products: access points, adapters, bridges, and routers.

Startech.com (www.startech.com)

Startech.com manufactures a variety of computing and networking hardware, including wireless hardware.

Products: access points, Bluetooth adapters, adapters, bridges, and routers.

TRENDware International (www.trendnet.com/us.htm)

TRENDware manufactures networking products for home and small business users.

Products: access points, adapters, antennas, Bluetooth adapters, bridges, print servers, and routers.

U.S. Robotics (www.usr.com)

U.S. Robotics has been around for more than 30 years. Chances are you've connected to the Internet with a USR modem. Now USR also produces wireless networking equipment.

Products: access points, adapters, bridges, and routers.

Mobile Phones and PDAs

Here's a list of the major manufacturers of popular mobile phones and PDAs. Remember to check which devices your service provider supports before buying either.

Dell (www.dell.com)

One of the largest personal computer manufacturers, Dell also produces a line of handheld Pocket PCs.

HP (www.hp.com)

Hewlett-Packard manufactures the popular iPAQ series of Pocket PC handhelds.

palmOne (www.palmone.com)

After acquiring Handspring, Palm became palmOne. They manufacture Palm OS handhelds.

Motorola (www.motorola.com)

Motorola manufactures a line of mobile phones.

Samsung (www.samsung.com)

Samsung manufactures a line of consumer electronics, including mobile phones.

Sony Ericsson (www.sonyericsson.com)

Sony Ericsson manufactures a popular line of media-rich mobile phones.

Nokia (www.nokia.com)

Nokia is one of the world's leading manufacturers of mobile phones. Nokia also produces the N-Gage handset, which integrates video gaming with a mobile phone and music player.

Software

The following is a list of software developers whose products are of particular interest to wireless users. This list is far from exhaustive; further resources can be found on the Web (read Appendixes A and B for more suggestions).

BlueNomad (www.bluenomad.com)

Blue Nomad produces BackupBuddy for Palm OS handhelds.

ExpertCity (www.gotomypc.com)

ExpertCity produces GoToMyPC software that allows you to remotely access your computer from anywhere, even using a PDA.

Pro Softnet Corporation (www.ibackup.com)

Pro Softnet provides the IBackup service, which allows you to back up your device remotely over the Internet.

Internet Security Systems (http://blackice.iss.net)

ISS is the developer of BlackIce, a personal firewall for computers.

McAfee (www.mcafee.com)

McAfee is the developer of VirusScan, Personal Firewall Plus, and other security-related applications.

Omega One (www.omegaone.com)

Omega One produces the Journal Bar and several other applications for the Pocket PC.

Pumatech (www.pumatech.com, www.loudpc.com)

Pumatech is the developer of Intellisync and LoudPC, an application that allows you to access your PC remotely from a mobile device.

SilverWARE (www.silverware.com)

SilverWARE produces TravelTracker, travel organizer software for Palm OS handhelds.

Sprite Software (www.spritesofware.com)

Sprite Software is the developer of Pocket Backup Plus and other useful PDA applications.

Symantec (www.symantec.com)

Symantec is one of the largest producers of antivirus and firewall software. They produce Norton AntiVirus, Norton Personal Firewall, and other utilities.

ZoneLabs (www.zonelabs.com)

ZoneLabs is the developer of ZoneAlarm, one of the easiest-to-use and most effective personal firewalls available.

Miscellaneous

Here's a short list of producers of miscellaneous products useful to mobile users.

Garmin (www.garmin.com)

Garmin manufactures handheld GPS units. It also produces the IQue, the first Palm OS PDA with integrated GPS capability.

Kensington (www.kensington.com)

Kensington manufactures many computer peripherals, including mice. They also produce protective cases for PDAs and the Wi-Finder, a device that simplifies the location of wireless hotspots.

StuffBak (www.stuffbak.com)

StuffBak produces ID labels that facilitate the return of your property if it's lost. I recommend that you use StuffBak's identification labels on all your mobile devices. The service really works and it is easy to use.

1G   The analog mobile phone networks originally rolled out in the 1980s. 1G (first-generation) networks carry voice traffic only. Because analog networks broadcast calls in the clear, 1G networks are not secure and it is possible to intercept calls with a radio frequency scanner.

2G   A system that uses digital encoding to transmit voice over a wireless network. 2G (second-generation) networks offer superior call quality, and better security. Although 2G systems primarily support voice traffic, many 2G networks provide low-speed, circuit-switched data service as well.

2.5G (or 2G+)   A system that is an interim step toward 3G networks. 2.5G or 2G+ networks integrate technology that extends 2G networks to include packet-switched data service.

3G   A forthcoming technology that aims to bring enhanced services to mobile users worldwide. The general improvements in 3G (third-generation) over previous networks will be in bandwidth and speed. 3G networks will deliver real-time multimedia and high-speed data, as well as enhanced voice services and Internet connectivity.

802.11   The IEEE family of wireless LAN (WLAN) standards; includes 802.11a, 802.11b, and 802.11g.

802.11a   An 802.11 physical layer standard. 802.11a devices operate in the unregulated 5 GHz radio band and have a maximum connection speed of 54 Mbps. Because it operates on a different frequency, 802.11a is not compatible with 802.11b or 802.11g.

802.11b   An 802.11 physical layer standard. 802.11b devices operate in the unregulated 2.4 GHz radio band and have a maximum connection speed of 11 Mbps. 802.11b came on the scene in 1999 and has since risen to dominate the Wi-Fi marketplace.

802.11g   An 802.11 physical layer standard. 802.11g devices share the unregulated 2.4 GHz radio band with 802.11b devices and have a maximum connection speed of 54 Mbps, although in practice they rarely achieve over 30 Mbps.

802.11i   A new security supplement to the 802.11 MAC layer. 802.11i addresses security holes in the 802.11a, b, and g protocols; and improves encryption, key management, distribution, and user authentication.

802.11 IR   Developed around the same time as the original 802.11 standard, a system that sends data with ultrahigh frequency infrared light (beyond that which the human eye can see) and supports the same speeds as the original 802.11 specifications.

802.11x   A generic reference that journalists and authors use to refer to any and all 802.11 protocols.

802.15.1   The IEEE standard based upon Bluetooth. The IEEE licensed a portion of the Bluetooth specification when forming the 802.15.1 standard, creating one that is fully compatible with existing Bluetooth.

802.15.3   A wireless personal area network (WPAN) standard that operates in the same 2.4 GHz frequency as 802.11b (and coexists without incident). This standard supports speeds up to 55 Mbps and purportedly supports up to 245 wireless devices in an ad hoc fashion.

802.15.4   A low-data rate WPAN standard. It operates in the 868 MHz, 915 MHz, and 2.4 GHz bands. It's being developed for use in industrial controllers and monitoring equipment.

802.16a   The IEEE specification standard for wireless metropolitan area networks (WMAN) utilizing the 2–11 GHz frequency band at speeds up to 280 Mbps for a maximum distance of up to 30 miles.

access point (AP)   Standalone 802.11x transceivers that connect clients in a WLAN and act as hubs or routers, providing a point of connection between a wireless network and a wired LAN.

ad hoc mode   Devices in an ad hoc network that do not communicate through an access point but rather directly between one another. Bluetooth piconets are a good example of an ad hoc network.

Advanced Mobile Phone Service (AMPS)   A 1G (analog) technology that was originally tested in the late 1970s and later became a commercial service in the early 1980s. AMPS used a technology called frequency division multiple access (FDMA) and was the primary mobile phone service in North America prior to the arrival of 2G networks.

analog   A representation of an object. Analog phones convert sound waves from your voice to an analogous electrical signal.

antenna   A radio component that directs radio waves to and from a transceiver.

Asymmetric DSL (ADSL)   The most common type of DSL that shares phones lines with analog phone signals. ADSL is called asymmetric because the download speed is greater than the upload speed.

attenuation   Loss of signal power when transmitting. This happens naturally as the distance increases from transmitter to receiver and can be exacerbated by interference from obstacles in the signal path.

Basic Service Sets (BSS)   An access point associated with one or more wireless devices that communicate through it.

Bluetooth   A wireless personal area networking (WPAN) technology developed by the Bluetooth Special Interest Group (founded by Nokia, Ericsson, IBM, Intel, and Toshiba). It operates in the unlicensed 2.4 GHz band. Developers named Bluetooth for the Danish King Blatand, who unified Denmark and Norway in the 10th century. Bluetooth does not compete directly with 802.11x standards; its range is too short and its throughput too slow to fill 802.11x's shoes. Bluetooth is a complementary standard to 802.11x.

Cable Modem Termination System (CMTS)   A device that cable Internet service providers install at the head end of their networks. A CMTS interfaces with an Internet service provider (ISP) and encodes Internet data into an MPEG video signal carried in the cable company's broadcast stream. The CMTS also separates data received from customers' cable modems from the cable network and passes it on to an ISP.

cantenna   A homemade Wi-Fi antenna created from a can. One popular version is the Pringles cantenna.

CDMA2000   A 3G technology based on CDMA that was the first to be used commercially (in late 2000, hence the name). There are several versions or evolutions of CDMA2000, supporting speeds up to 307 Kbps or 2 Mbps (for data only). A number of CDMA-based networks already use CDMA2000.

Cellular Digital Packet Data (CDPD)   A technology developed as an add-on to 1G cellular networks. CDPD allows a 1G analog network to handle digital packet data, although at only 19 Kbps. CDPD modems are available for notebook computers and PDAs. CDPD service is available from several different wireless carriers in the U.S.

circuit switching   A type of dedicated network connection for communication between two points. The circuit is temporary and ends when the communication is complete. The phone system is an example of a circuit-switched network.

Code Division Multiple Access (CDMA)   A method of transmitting multiple digital signals in the same channel. This means that multiple calls can take place simultaneously on the same channel. Qualcomm developed CDMA and Qualcomm digital handsets remain the chief users of this 2G technology.

Denial of Service (DoS)   Any attack that prevents users from accessing a network device or service.

Dynamic Host Configuration Protocol (DHCP)   A protocol that assigns IP addresses to WLAN clients as they connect to the network. These dynamic addresses change each time the client connects to the WLAN, for instance after a reboot, or when you return home and reconnect your laptop to the network.

Electronic Serial Number (ESN)   One of the codes used to authenticate your phone with your carrier's cellular network. Manufacturers encode the ESN on a chip within the phone.

Enhanced Data Rates for Global Evolution (EDGE)   An enhancement to GSM networks that increases the data rate up to 384 kbps, while using the same frequencies. Using EDGE, mobile customers are able to simultaneously use different services, such as web browsing and making a phone call.

Enhanced Messaging Service (EMS)   An extension that expands the capabilities of SMS. EMS allows users to send and receive formatted text, ring tones, sound effects, animations, and icons. EMS is backward compatible with SMS so that if users send an EMS message to an SMS phone, it will be displayed as SMS with no advanced features.

Ethernet   The 802.3 standard for wired networks. Fast Ethernet is common in LANs and supports transmission speeds of up to 100 Mbps.

firewall   A traffic filter between internal and external networks. Firewalls are used to secure LANs and prevent unauthorized access. A firewall can be a stand-alone hardware device or a software application running on a client computer.

first-generation   See *1G*.

Frequency Division Multiple Access (FDMA)   A technology that divided the 800 MHz radio band used by AMPS into 30 kHz channels.

Fresnel zone   Pronounced "Fray-nel" and named after French physicist Augustin-Jean Fresnel. It refers to the pattern of RF radiation between a transmitter and receiver. Shaped like an elongated ellipse, the Fresnel zone between two antennas must be free of obstructions, particularly trees, or the signal will weaken dramatically

General Packet Radio Service (GPRS)   Provider of packet-switched data service to GSM networks. Because it uses packet switching like the Internet, GPRS makes many Internet applications available over a mobile device. Unlike a circuit-switched connection that requires a dedicated line, GPRS allows for "always-on" Internet connections.

Global Positioning System (GPS)   A network of 24 satellites used for navigation. GPS satellites circle the earth in a very precise orbit and transmit signals back. By calculating the time it takes to receive a signal from at least three satellites, GPS receivers triangulate the receiver's location anywhere on earth. If the GPS device receives a signal from at least four satellites, it can determine the user's altitude in addition to latitude and longitude.

Global System for Mobile Communications (GSM)   A 2G digital mobile phone system based upon Time Division Multiple Access (TDMA). First deployed commercially in Europe in the early 1990s, GSM has since become the de facto standard there. It is widely used in mobile phone networks worldwide and by some carriers in the U.S.

high-speed circuit-switched data (HSCSD)   An extension of GSM networks designed for its data transfer capabilities. HSCSD uses circuit switching. Unlike GPRS, it requires a dedicated time slot for data transfer

HomeRF   A defunct wireless home networking standard. HomeRF operated in the 2.4 GHz frequency.

hybrid fiber coaxial (HFC)   A network infrastructure that combines fiber-optic cables for delivery of data to neighborhood nodes where it is then distributed to individual homes over coaxial cables. A common example of an HFC network is cable television.

i-mode   A proprietary service developed by NTT DoCoMo in Japan for browsing Internet pages on mobile phones, as well as providing e-mail, games, and chat services. The i-mode service is one of the largest Internet service providers in Japan, with more users accessing the Internet from their phones than from desktop PCs.

infrastructure mode   One of two modes of WLAN operation, in which infrastructure mode clients communicate on the network through access points

Institute of Electrical and Electronics Engineers (IEEE)   An international non-profit technical professional organization (called I-triple-E). Through its members, the IEEE is the leading authority in many technical areas, including computers, telecommunications, and power generation. The IEEE produced the 802.11x family of standards, the principal standards used in WLAN environments.

Integrated Digital Enhanced Network (iDEN)   A technology developed by Motorola that allows a single phone to support voice, data, SMS, and digital push-to-talk radio. iDEN uses a proprietary version of TDMA and operates in the 800 MHz and 1.5 GHz bands.

Internet Connection Sharing (ICS)   Windows software that allows a computer to share its Internet connection with other computers on the same LAN. To use ICS a computer must have two network connections, one for the Internet and one for the local WLAN.

Internet Protocol (IP) addresses   An address that every computer needs to be attached to a TCP/IP network. An IP address can be permanent or dynamically assigned by a DHCP server.

Internet Service Provider (ISP)   A company that provides customers with access to the Internet through dial-up or broadband connections.

Local Area Network (LAN)   A network that serves computers in the same local area—for example, an office or building.

line-of-sight (LOS)   A wireless connection that requires a straight point-to-point, unobstructed path between sending and receiving antennas.

local number portability (LNP)   New rules governing the portability of telephone numbers between carriers. Because of LNP you can switch to a new cellular company in the same local area and keep your old phone number

MAC address   The unique serial number assigned to every network adapter (NIC) by its manufacturer.

Media Access Control (MAC) layer   The protocol that defines how network adapters access the physical transmission medium of the network in the case of WLAN radio frequencies.

MMS Center (MMSC)   The intermediary server through which MMS users send messages, rather than sending them in real time. The MMSC receives messages and holds them until the receiving phone retrieves them; this is also known as store-and-forward. See *Multimedia Messaging Service.*

Mobile Identification Number (MIN)   Your cell phone's area code and phone number. The MIN is one of the codes used to authenticate your phone on your carrier's network.

mobile instant messaging (MIM)   Instant messaging or chat moved onto a mobile platform. Like traditional chat programs, users can have an alias, manage contacts, and know when their "buddies" are online. MIM takes place in real time and users can interact as if they were using AOL Instant Messenger or MSN Messenger, for example.

mobile telephone switching office (MTSO)   The central facility that links cell towers in a particular area. Each MTSO authenticates and routes calls between transceivers in its service area and handles billing. The MTSO also connects to the conventional telephone network and routes calls between cell phones and POTS phones.

Multimedia Messaging Service (MMS)   An enhanced service for cell phones that transmits multimedia messages between mobile phones and uses the Wireless Application Protocol (WAP). Multimedia messages can consist of pictures, audio, video, and formatted text.

network address translation (NAT)   The process by which routers and ICS software share an Internet connection. NAT translates internal LAN IP addresses into one or more public Internet IP addresses, allowing several computers to share a common public IP address.

Network Interface Card (NIC)   An adapter that allows a computer to connect to the local Ethernet or Wi-Fi network.

network latency   The amount of time it takes for data to make a roundtrip across a network from one point to another. Also referred to as the roundtrip time.

network throughput   The actual amount of data that can be transferred across a network in a specific amount of time, as opposed to the potential throughput that is often advertised by manufacturers. For example, 802.11g devices have an advertised maximum throughput of 54 Mbps, when in practice the actual network throughput seldom exceeds 30 Mbps.

non-line-of-sight (NLOS)   A wireless connection that doesn't require a straight, obstruction-free signal path.

omnidirectional antenna   An antenna that broadcasts in all directions at once.

packet switching   The way that computers divide data into smaller, individually addressed packets. Because each of these data packets contains a destination address, they can be switched so that they follow different paths to reach their destination. A packet-switched network uses network bandwidth more efficiently because users can share bandwidth and send their packets at the same time. Routers direct each individually addressed packet to its proper destination.

Personal Communication Service (PCS)   The name given to the digital cellular service in the 1.8 to 2 GHz range that the Federal Communications Commission (FCC) auctioned off in 1994 to commercial licensees. PCS is a generic term used to describe digital services offered by several carriers; it is not a standard unto itself. PCS carriers use different standards including GSM and CDMA.

personal digital assistant (PDA)   A small, handheld computer that stores schedules, calendars, contact information, and other productivity enhancing applications. The best PDAs are as powerful as desktop computers from five to eight years ago.

piconet   An ad hoc network created when between two and seven Bluetooth devices connect.

Plain-Old-Telephone-Service (POTS)   The name given to the regular, wired phone system we all grew up with.

Power over Ethernet (PoE)   A method of delivering power as well as data over standard Ethernet cables. This is possible because Ethernet cable has pairs of wires (4/5 and 7/8) that aren't used in data transmission. PoE equipment takes advantage of this to supply power to PoE-compatible Ethernet equipment. PoE allows you to install Ethernet equipment without worrying about the location of power outlets.

radio frequency (RF)   Electromagnetic frequencies above audio but below the frequency of visible light.

radio frequency channel   A section of the radio frequency spectrum assigned for communication between two or more devices.

reversed polarity connectors   Coaxial plugs and jacks that have the center pin reversed, compared to standard polarity connectors of the same type.

RF interference   Radio frequency noise or competing transmissions in the same frequency band as a WLAN. RF interference can prevent normal operation of a wireless network.

roundtrip time (RTT)   A term used in reference to the latency in a network connection. The RTT is the amount of time it takes for data to travel across a network connection and for a reply to return.

router   A device that forwards packets of data between networks. A broadband router receives data addressed to your assigned IP address and delivers it to the appropriate computers on your WLAN. This allows several computers to share the same IP address and Internet connection. Some routers also include firewall options to protect your network from people attempting to access it from the Internet.

satellite broadband   Internet service that is provided over a satellite modem. Signals travel from the user to the ISP through a satellite in orbit. Some early satellite systems used a phone line for upstream page requests, reserving the satellite connection for downloading data.

scatternet   An ad hoc network created by two or more piconets.

second-generation   See 2G.

Service Set Identifier (SSID)   A name up to 32 characters in length used to identify a WLAN. The SSID is the network's name; this is useful for distinguishing WLANs operating in the same area.

Short Messaging Service (SMS)   A method of sending short text messages, usually fewer than 160 characters, from one mobile phone to another. SMS delivers messages over the handset's control channel, which is separate from the voice channel. This way you can receive a message during a voice conversation. Messages are stored at a message center and then forwarded when the addressee's phone is on and connected to the network.

smart phone   A cellular phone with integrated PDA functions. Smart phones run an operating system like Palm OS or Windows Mobile.

software access point (SAP)   A computer running software that duplicates the functionality of a standalone hardware access point.

SOHO (small office/home office)   A term used to describe the market for products intended for small businesses and individuals working from home.

spoofing   When one device sends a false address or authentication information to gain entry to a server or host. A cracker can configure his wireless NIC to spoof the MAC address of a legitimate user on a WLAN. Pretending to be that user, the cracker gains access to network computers and services.

Subscriber Identity Module (SIM)   A chip in all GSM phones that contains the user's account data and contacts.

TCP/IP   The primary suite of networking protocols for the Internet. TCP/IP is actually composed of many protocols but it's named for two of the most important ones: the Transmission Control Protocol (TCP) and the Internet Protocol (IP).

third-generation   See 3G.

Time Division Multiple Access (TDMA) A digital encoding technology that divides an allotted radio channel into time slots, each one handling one call. There are several technologies in the TDMA family, including GSM, GPRS, and IDEN. All of these use different frequencies and channel sizes.

transceiver A device that transmits and receives radio frequency waves; basically, two-way radio. A Wi-Fi access point or client adapter is an example of a WLAN transceiver.

Virtual Private Network (VPN) A method of using encryption to protect data and allow organizations to network across the public Internet as if they were connected to a private LAN. Data sent across a VPN connection stays private even though the network being used is public. In effect, a VPN creates an encrypted tunnel between two points on the Internet.

warchalking Related to wardriving, people who mark a wall or sidewalk with symbols to indicate the presence of an open Wi-Fi network and connection instructions. Warchalking is based on the graffiti that hobos used during the Great Depression to convey information to each other.

wardriving The act of driving around a geographic area, using a wireless notebook computer or PDA to locate Wi-Fi networks and unsecured access points.

Wi-Fi (Wireless Fidelity) The consumer-friendly name given to the 802.11 family of wireless protocols by the Wi-Fi Alliance. Wi-Fi is used when referring to any of the three physical layer protocols: 802.11a, 802.11b, and 802.11g.

Wi-Fi Alliance A membership organization founded in 1999 that certifies product compliance to the IEEE 802.11x wireless standards. The Wi-Fi Alliance promotes the use of Wi-Fi (WLAN) use worldwide by encouraging manufacturers to comply with the 802.11x standards when designing their networking products. If a network component carries the Wi-Fi certified logo, it operates with other Wi-Fi certified products that operate in the same frequency range.

Wi-Fi Protected Access (WPA) A new security protocol designed to give Wi-Fi better protection than WEP encryption. WPA is based on the 802.11i protocol.

Wired Equivalent Privacy (WEP) A security protocol designed to give WLANs protection equivalent to Ethernet. WEP failed, however, due to unforeseen design and implementation flaws

wireless adapter An NIC or adapter that enables a computer or PDA to communicate on a WLAN.

Wireless Application Protocol (WAP) A standard that allows users of mobile devices to access the Internet and view data on mobile devices. Comparable to HTTP on the Web, WAP is secure and most mobile networks and operating systems support it.

wireless bridge An access point with WDS functionality that can communicate with other access points as well as network clients.

Wireless Distribution System (WDS)   A standard that allows wireless-to-wireless bridging. WDS allows traffic to flow from one access point to another as if it were traveling from one Ethernet port to another Ethernet port on a wired network.

Wireless Local Area Network (WLAN)   A local area network that uses the unlicensed radio spectrum (2.4 GHz or 5 GHz) for communication rather than Ethernet cables, as a wired LAN does.

Wireless Markup Language (WML)   The markup, or tag-based, language used to describe Web pages for WAP devices. WML is based upon, and similar to, XML.

Wireless Metropolitan Area Network (WMAN)   A wireless network that serves a large geographic area like a city or town.

Wireless Personal Area Network (WPAN)   A short ranged, low-power wireless network that serves a single individual or small group. Bluetooth has emerged as the principal WPAN standard. An example of a WPAN is a computer and printer connected with Bluetooth adapters, or PDAs communicating with Bluetooth. A piconet is a form of WPAN.

wireless repeater   A device that repeats the signal from an access point, extending the signal range of a WLAN. Most access points can be configured to act as repeaters.

Wireless Service Provider (WSP)   A provider of wireless services, including Internet, cellular, Wi-Fi, and satellite communications.

wireless sniffer   A Wi-Fi application that captures and examines Wi-Fi network traffic. Sniffers can be used to locate, identify, and access WLANs. Sniffers are software tools used in wardriving.

Wireless User Group (WUG)   An organization of wireless technology users. Through regular meetings, WUG members share information and improve their knowledge of wireless technology.

wireless Web   The World Wide Web accessed from mobile wireless devices. The wireless Web is not distinct from the World Wide Web; it just represents an alternate route to the same information.

World Wide Web   A service available over the Internet, like e-mail or FTP. The Internet is the network that moves information; the Web is the content.

X10   A proprietary standard for home automation that can turn off lights, adjust the temperature, and control other devices.

Index

continued

continued